Guide to Danish Architecture I
1000-1960

Guide to Danish Architecture I
1000-1960

By Jørgen Sestoft and Jørgen Hegner Christiansen

Arkitektens Forlag

Guide to Danish Architecture I, 1000-1960
© Arkitektens Forlag, Copenhagen 1991.
Editors: Kim Dirckinck-Holmfeld, Jørgen Hegner
Christiansen and Jørgen Sestoft.
Authors: Jørgen Sestoft and Jørgen Hegner Christiansen.
Illustration editor: Jørgen Hegner Christiansen.
Lay-out: Kim Dirckinck-Holmfeld.
Production: Inge-Lise Winther.
Translation: Peter Avondoglio.
Secretary: Irene Mollerup.
Reproduction and printed by Bogtrykkeriet i Skive

Published with financial support by:
Denmark's National Bank's Jubilee Fund of 1968
Margot and Thorvald Dreyers Fund.

ISBN 87 7407 111 4

Preface

This guide is the first part of a two-book series on Danish architecture. It describes the period from around the year 1000 until 1960. It will be followed by Guide to Danish Architecture II, 1960-1991.

This guide consists of two sections, the first being a survey by architect Jørgen Sestoft, who is professor of architectural theory at the Royal Academy of Architecture in Copenhagen. He describes the development of Danish architecture from prehistoric time up until Industrialism's breakthrough in the building trade.

The second section, the guide, was written by architect Jørgen Hegner Christiansen who is a architectural historian.

The selection of buildings to be included was made by Jørgen Sestoft, Jørgen Hegner Christiansen and Kim Dirckinck-Holmfeld.

The guide is organized chronologically, but also treats the various building types thematically.

Unique works are treated independently, such as Amalienborg and Frederiksstaden.

The chronological order is occasionally interrupted if geographical proximity or other factors demand that several topics be dealt with collectively.

The main reason for establishing a turning point in 1960 is that production conditions for the building industry underwent a revolutionary development at this time. Another ground for dealing with works from before 1960, is that a greater certainty can be exercised in determining their relevance in the development of the Danish architectural tradition.

This guide contains approximately 850 illustrations, which have been readily made available by a number of institutions and architectural personalities.

Arkitektens Forlag directs special thanks to mag.art. Lisbet Balslev Jørgensen at the Library of the Royal Danish Academy of Fine Arts, the National Museum, as well as architects Tobias Faber and Hans Henrik Engqvist and Hans Erling Langkilde.

Publication of this work was made possible through the support of Denmark's National Bank's Jubilee Fund and from the Margot and Thorvald Dreyers Fund. The publishers owe both of these funds a great deal of thanks.

Kim Dirckinck-Holmfeld

Contents

Preface	5
An outline of Danish architecture	8
Author Jørgen Sestoft	
Prehistoric time	8
The Middle Ages	9
The Renaissance	14
The King builds	16
Towns of the seventeenth century	17
Absolute monarchy	18
The Baroque	19
Frederiksstaden (Frederiks City) and Eigtved	20
The Royal Academy of Fine Arts, and Classicism	22
The agricultural reforms	22
C. F. Hansen in Copenhagen	23
Liberalism and Historicism	25
Accelleration of urban growth	26
Industrialism	29
National romantic and The Arts and Crafts Movement	30
Neoclassicism	32
Housing	33
Functionalism	35
The funtional tradition	35
Scandinavian Empiricism	37
Japanese and American influences	38
Guide	40
Author: Jørgen Hegner Christiansen	

1- 4.	Viking fortifications. App. A.D. 1000	40
5- 9.	The early Middle Age churches, 1100-1130	42
10- 16.	Round churches, 1100-1250	44
17- 18.	Saint Bendts Church in Ringsted and Sorø Monastery Church, 1160-1241	46
19.	Roskilde Cathedral, 1170-1400	48
20- 22.	Central churches, 1170-1225	50
23.	Århus Cathedral, 1197-1479	52
24- 26.	Ribe Cathedral, Løgumkloster, Haderslev Cathedral, 1170-1420	54
27- 31.	Gothic churches, 1285-1521	56
32- 33.	Monasteries and monastery churches, 1410-1500	58
34- 39.	Church frescoes, 1100-1600	60
40- 42.	Hammershus, 1250-1400	62
43- 44.	Spøttrup and Dragsholm, 1250-1500	64
45- 47.	Gjorslev, Tjele and Østrupgård, 1400-1550	66
48- 49.	Hesselagergård and Rygård, 1530-38	68
50- 51.	Egeskov and Nyborg 1549-50	70
52- 54.	Borreby, Vallø and Gisselfeld 1547-86	72
55- 57.	Voergård, Rosenholm, Gammel Estrup 1500-70	74
58- 60.	Brick town houses, 1460-1579	76
61.	Kronborg Castle, 1410-1590	78
62.	Frederiksborg Castle, 1560-1630	80
63.	Rosenborg Castle, 1603-1634	82
64- 66.	Christian IV's expansion of Copenhagen 1599-1643	84
67- 68.	Round Tower and Trinitatis Church, Nyboder, 1631-56	86
69.	Gentry houses in Ribe, 1525-1650	88
70- 72.	Gentry houses in Køge, Kalundborg and Kolding 1527-1681	90
73- 77.	Gentry houses in Aalborg and Copenhagen, 1616-81	92
78.	The Old Town in Århus, 1597-1816	94
79- 81.	Open-air museums, 1500-1850	95
82- 85.	Fortress buildings under the absolute monarchy, 1662-1725	96
86- 87.	Charlottenborg and Nysø, 1671-83	98
88- 89.	Vor Frelsers Church and Reformert Church, 1682-96,	100
90.	Clausholm, 1693-1723	102
91.	Frederiksberg Palace, 1699-1738	104
92- 93.	»The Red Palace«, Slotsholmsgade 4 and The Opera House, Copenhagen, 1701-21	106
94.	Fredensborg Palace, 1719-76	108
95- 97.	Odense Palace, Viborg Town Hall and the palace in Roskilde, 1720-33	110
98-103.	Conflagration buildings, 1729-37	112
104-106.	Viennese Baroque and French Rococo, 1733-45	114
107.	Eremitagen, 1734-36	116
108-110.	Ledreborg, Lerchenborg and Valdemar's Manor, 1743-54	118
111-112.	Gammel Holtegård and Turebyholm, 1750-57	120
113.	Frederiksstaden, 1749-60	121
114.	Buildings at Holmen, the Royal Dockyards, 1742-72	126
115-117.	Buildings on Christianshavn, 1738-81	128
118-120.	Nicolas Henri Jardin, 1759-71	130
121-123.	French Classicism in the contryside, 1765-95	132
124.	Christiansfeld, 1772-1826	134

125-126.	Tønder and Møgeltønder, 1730-1830	135		Workers Assembly Building in Horsens 1918-26	202
127-130.	Ærøskøbing, Ebeltoft, Sønderho, Varde, 1645-1800	136	208-210.	Neoclassicistic schools, 1923-26	204
131.	Eighteenth century Dragør	138	211-212.	P. V. Jensen Klint and Kaare Klint, 1916-40	206
132.	Svaneke, 1770-1861	139	213.	Studiebyen, 1920-1924	208
133-137.	C. F. Harsdorff 1777-99	140	214-221.	Bakkehusene and Thorkild Henningsen, 1921-28	210
138-141.	Country estates, 1800-06	144			
142-144.	C. F. Hansen's Classicism, 1805-22	146	222-225.	Classicism's large housing blocks, 1919-29	212
145-146.	Christiansborg Palace Church, Hørsholm Church, 1803-28	150	226-227.	Vodroffsvej, 2 and Vestersøhus, 1929-39	216
147-148.	Late Classicism dies off, 1811-36	152	228-229.	Blidah Park and Storgården, 1932-35	218
149.	Thorvaldsen's Museum, 1839-48	154	230.	Bella Vista and Bellevue, 1934-37	220
150-153.	M. G. Bindesbøll, 1830-58	156	231-236.	Modernistic commercial buildings, 1930-37	222
154-155.	J. D. Herholdt and the University Library, 1857-61	158	237-239.	Municipal buildings, 1931-37	224
156-158.	Early Historicism, 1859-69	160	240-241.	Crematoriums, 1927-1937	226
159.	Historicistic church restorations, 1864-92	162	242.	Mogens Lassen on Sølystvej, 1935-38	228
160-162.	Building society houses in Copenhagen, 1865-1903	163	243-244.	Århus University and Nyborg public library, 1938-46	230
163-165.	Vilhelm Dahlerup, 1872-94	164	245.	Århus Town Hall, 1938-42	232
166.	Ny Carlsberg Brewery, Jesus Church, 1880-1901	166	246-247.	Søllerød and Lyngby Town Halls, 1938-42	234
167-169.	Ferdinand Meldahl, 1873-94	168	248-249.	The Broadcasting House and Gladsaxe Town Hall, 1937-1945	236
170-171.	The National Museum of Art, The Glyptoteket, 1889-1906	170			
172-175.	Nyrop and Neoromanticism, 1885-1913	172	250-251.	Bisparken and Grundtvig's School, 1937-42	238
176.	Copenhagen's Town Hall, 1892-1905	174	252-254.	The row houses and linked houses of the forties	240
177-180.	Ulrik Plesner and the Neo-baroque, 1896-1910	176	255-256.	Voldparken and Mother Help, 1949-56	242
181-183.	Copenhagen's Main Station. Saint Andreas Church, EliasChurch, 1898-1911	178	257-258.	Søndergårds Park and Søholm, 1946-1955	244
184-186.	Århus Theatre, Århus Custom house, the National Library, 1895-1902	180	259-262.	New school types, 1948-58	246
			263-264.	Bellahøj and Høje Søborg, 1949-56	248
187.	Skagen, 1891-1924	182	265-268.	Post war single-family houses, 1950-59	250
188.	Villas in the Ryvangen district, 1904-1920	184	269-270.	F. L. Smidth & Co. and Tårnby Town Hall, 1952-59	252
189-193.	Anton Rosen, 1906-17	188			
194-196.	The Museums of Neoclassicism, 1912-17	192	271-273.	Kingo Houses, Søllerød Park and Nærum Vænge, 1955-61	254
197-198.	Ivar Bentsen and Marius Pedersen, 1913-29	194	274-277.	Arne Jacobsen, 1953-60	256
			278.	Louisiana, 1958-90	258
199-200.	Gudhjem line railway stations and Hegels country estate, 1914-16	196	279-282.	School buildings, 1956-60	260
201-203.	Better Building Practicies, 1915-30	198			
204.	Tibirke Hills, 1916-	200			
206-207.	The Police headquarters, Saint Lucas Church, Århus, The				

Index of places   262

Index of names   266

Photos   270

Litterature   271

An outline of Danish Architecture

Cairn near Overbjerg in Hornsherred. Drawing, 1862, by J. Kornerup.

Prehistoric period

Since the introduction of agriculture in Denmark during the fifth century B.C., shelter in the form of buildings has been a necessity. The lot of the peasant was to protect his valuables - family, livestock and crops - from climate, vermin and hostile people. However the means were primitive and the quality of finish was poor. Abandoned and with no maintenance, these ancient buildings soon became a part of nature's cycle. The excavation of these settlements has revealed their character and scope. They were long houses with thatched roofs, supported by one or two rows of buried columns or posts. The roofs reached the ground or to low embankments or stone walls. All living activities took place in the same undifferentiated rooms.

In a way, it would be unreasonable to begin an outline of Denmark's architectural history with ancient peasant buildings. Not because they no longer exist, or were built in a primitive fashion, but because they had a primarily utilitarian character as all other implements and tools that served to maintain life's necessities. Most of these buildings were considered as a simple means of providing the primary necessities of life, up until a few hundered years ago when our cultural tradition developed an independent, secular concept of beauty and its nature. From Hedenold til then, man offered his greatest resources to building monuments that symbolized the collective consolidation of the fragile life in the defiant nature. The concept of architecture, the origin of which is Greek and thus a latecomer to the Danish language, grew out of buildings dedicated to worship and rituals. From this point of view, it is not the no longer existing settlements, but the still existing burial mounds that represent ancient architecture. The cairns and passage graves from around 2000 B.C. and the Bronze Age domed mounds from about 1500-500 B.C. are still distinctive landscape features in many areas. For those who built them, they represented a reminder of a responsibility, a demand to carry on what was started by those who had been there before.

Iron Age finds, from 500 B.C. to about A.D. 1000 have supplied enough knowledge about the existing, common building types, to enable the reconstruction of an Iron Age settlement near Lejre. These finds also indicate that there was a major setback around A.D. 300, when a significant number of the existing buildings were abandoned. After the year 500, a new period of growth commenced, during which the village pattern, which still exists in many areas, was established. There was a period of great prosperity during the Middle Ages, between 1100 and 1300, that came to an abrupt end with the plague epidemic, the Black Death in 1350.

An exceptional example, in both a Danish and an international context, are the three viking forts, Trelleborg near Slagelse, Fyrkat near Hobro and Aggersborg near Aggersund. They were founded around 1000, based on the same concept and presumably used only for a short time as a training and assembly camp for expeditions against England. These forts are characterized by meticulously organized, geometric principles of composition for the location of paths and buildings within the circular earthen embankments. They reveal a highly developed building method, which was rare at that time.

The Middle Ages
Two other events, the introduction of Christianity in the first century, and the founding of the first real city community at about the same time, were of lasting importance for the country. Seen individually or as a whole, they represent the beginnings of a division of labour in society with the trading of wares and services, and at the same time, a symbol of Denmark's increasing integration in the European culture. There are certain common characteristics in the old towns that can be registered by their location. They all sought positions near rivers or deep fjords for easy access to the sea as well as protection from coastal plundering: Roskilde, Odense, Ribe, Ålborg, Randers, Slesvig were typical examples. Together with inland towns like Ringsted, Slagelse and Viborg, these towns indicated the main features of a nationwide traffic pattern. From north to south through Jutland, and east to west, from Skåne in Sweden across the islands to West Jutland.

The next expansion of the nation's infrastructure took place around 1200, when it was decided to fortify the various ports with coastal forts and let the town communities develop in their sanctuary. Because of this, many of these towns have names ending in borg, which means fortress, such as Vordingborg, Tårnborg (Korsør), Nyborg, Fåborg and Kalundborg. Absalon's borg Havn (Copenhagen) is also in this group. After this dynamic period, the existing town pattern was established and the founding of new merchant towns stagnated during the centuries

Tveje Merløse Church.

that followed. Most towns grew pragmatically according to natural growth principles, though with a tendency to be influenced by the form of the market square and its location. However there are examples of towns established according to prepared plans, such as Køge, which was founded in 1288, and the expansion of Helsingør in 1426.

While it was the King's right to decree a town special privileges for trade and production, He and the rest of this feudal society were strongly dependent on the church and thereby the pope. The great, Middle Age hierarchal social order was an organism in which each part had its own fixed place and function, in a religious as well as a secular and political context. Regardless of the fact that the church, in the later phases of the Middle Ages, fell into businesslike speculation in fear of losing its position, it still gave the individual a standpoint and a universal interpretation that gave a meaning to life. The Christian church was, without comparison, the major architectural symbol for the hierarchal social order. It was the gathering place for all technical and artistic development, and housed other art forms like music and painting.

Church building brought Denmark a tangible contact with the international building culture, even though the country could not manage large scale projects and lacked sources of suitable natural stone materials. The earliest wooden churches were superseded by a wealth of small stone churches during the period of prosperity from 1100 to 1250. Not only were an impressive number of churches built, an estimated 2000, but more surprising and exceptional in an international context, is that over 1500 of them still exist and with their landmarklike towers represent an inalienable part of the Danish cultural landscape, despite modern competition from silos, chimneys and high-tension masts.

The building materials used in these village churches were the soft and easily formed tufa limestone or hard granite, employed as untreated

Sorø Church.

fieldstone or as square hewn blocks. The latter method, which was common in Jutland, was extremely time consuming. About the middle of the twelfth century, fired clay brick was introduced, probably from Lombardy. It was then possible to utilize the country's enormous store of well-suited clay for the production of brick. Brick in bond with lime mortar as a binder, gave an almost everlasting outer wall construction, a factor that has greatly influenced Danish building ever since. Some of the first examples of brick buildings were the monastery churches in Ringsted and Sorø, started about 1160, the same time as Valdemar the Great's Dannevirkevold fortification along the fortified southern border.

A fascinating feature of the Middle Age churches is the wealth of individual variation over given, determined themes. The most common type is the long church, which owes its origin to the west Roman basilica. Either as a simple village church hall with a separate chancel separated by an interior triumphal arch, or as a merchant town's more spacious and technically complicated triple bay church with a high nave and clear-story windows over the aisles. The long churches most clearly expressed the religious symbolism that was tied to the points of the compass and thus to the church's orientation - the chancel toward east and the tower toward west. East was the direction of paradise, the congregation should face the light, which the sun spread upon the earth. The sun set in the west down to the world of the devil. That direction portended the final days, the end of the world, the day of judgement. South was the direction of abundance and grace, while the shadows of the north were the land of the godless.

The more unusual church types, with various forms of central plans are rare, and therefore of great interest. This is true of the massive, multi-storey round churches on Bornholm and the somewhat enigmatic church in Kalundborg. Five towers were built here with considerable technical boldness, over a central, Greek cross plan.

In the history of architectural styles, the first great period of church building is called the Romanesque. This implies a relation to the highly developed building methods derived from the golden age of the Roman empire. These were adopted by the Christian church and spread throughout Europe as the religion grew. Among its notable features was the round arch employed as both a structural and decorative element. In connection with vaulting work, the round arch allowed a square building grid, which transferred the great side thrust to the outer walls thus limiting the size of the windows. However, this problem could be solved by using Gothic arches combined with exterior buttresses. The Gothic style was developed in France during the middle of the twelfth century and allowed an unprecedented, slender supporting structure, and thus, large window areas. Under Danish conditions, where the use of brick was an almost unavoidable necessity, the Gothic churches were taller and more slight than the Romanesque. However they never achieved the filigreelike grace that the use of natural stone allowed in the central European cathedrals.

This development can be discerned in the Danish cathedrals, despite the fact that the long building periods of that time, and subsequent renovations, often meant that different stylistic features from different periods could appear in the same building. An example of this can be seen at the cathedrals in Ribe, Roskilde, Haderslev and Århus, which were started as Romanesque, but finished off with somewhat Gothic features. At the Haderslev and Århus cathedrals, new and brightly lit nave areas were added around 1400. However the cathedrals in Viborg, and Lund, in Skåne Sweden, which at that time was part of the Kingdom of Denmark, are pure Romanesque. To a certain extent, both of these examples are reconstructions dating from the latter half of the

Århus Cathedral.

nineteenth century. Built during the Gothic age and generally preserved in their original state, are Saint Knud's in Odense, begun around 1300, and the cathedral in Maribo, which was built during the fifteenth century, as well as several large parish churches such as Saint Olai's in Helsingør, Saint Mikkel's in Slagelse, Saint Peder's in Næstved and Saint Nikolai's in Køge. The Gothic village churches are not as numerous, but during the Gothic period, many of the older churches were expanded with towers and stepped gables with blindings, as well as pointed groin vaults and windows.

Compared with the rich Middle Age legacy of churches, little remains of other building types. In most instances, this is due to the fact that their technical quality has not been able to withstand the centuries. In other cases, the building's original function ceased and it was demolished, either for the purpose of reusing the materials, or in order to create space for another building. Only the church was able to sustain a social significance that left its places of worship unchallenged, until they achieved status as historical monuments about a century ago. The Middle Age buildings in the town and countryside, which were built of half-timber, wattle-and-daub and with thatched roofs, have totally vanished. Many of those in the towns were destroyed by the numerous and extensive fires. Secular buildings of brick were rare during the Middle Ages but some still exist in a few cities such as Helsingør, Næstved and Randers.

The strategically situated castles and fortresses, which were meant to protect what was still a far from unified national state, from external and internal foes, are preserved only as rudiments or ruins. Examples of these are Kalø, Gurre and the immense Hammershus on Bornholm. They can also be found at Kalundborg, Nyborg, Korsør and Vordingborg. In the latter two instances, the refuge and defense towers have been preserved. For functional reasons, the fortresses were soundly built with respect for their practical use and the local topography. However they lacked the symbolic regularity of the sacred architecture. Related to the fortresses, were the feudal headquarters, built by either the clergy or the nobility. As late as a century after the Middle Ages, the possibility of political unrest and assault necessitated a design whereby survival could be ensured behind moats and protective ramparts. Their normal function as great agricultural manors afforded them even better possibilities of survival than the fortresses, even if such features were seldom part of their original design. Examples of these are Dragsholm, Gjorslev and Tjele. The compact and unapproachable Spøttrup in Salling and the more richly formed Rygård, on Funen, are original to a great degree and from the same period around 1500. In form and location they contribute to our notion of the rugged Jutland and the mild Funen.

The Renaissance
"Renaissance" signifies rebirth. It arose in the wealthy trading cities of

Ruins of the Hammershus Fortress on Bornholm.

Northern Italy during the early part of the fifteenth century as an artistic and philosophical orientation toward Antiquity through studies of sources and traces left behind. The classical idiom of architecture was rediscovered through surveys of ruins and studies of ancient texts, and it was given an undisputed authority. In terms of the Nordic region, it was more a discovery than rediscovery of the light of transfiguration, which the ancient culture of the Mediterranean area continued to emit throughout centuries of ignorance and barbarianism that characterized the Middle Ages.

Over a century passed before Danish architecture was influenced by the Renaissance and even then, it retained Gothic features like high gables and steep roofs. A long time elapsed before the Danish Renaissance obtained that closedness, regularity and equality, which were commanded by the ideals. Presumably, a well-bred Italian would have considered most of what we call Renaissance as being dilettantism. On the other hand, the Nordic version radiates a jaunty enthusiasm for the heterogeneous, variegated and magnificent with its Italian gables, spires and sandstone bands on red brick facades.

The Reformation of 1536 signified a break with the church's authority and its position of economical power. With this, the state, symbolized by the king, was strengthened. The royal Lutheran church took over the medieval houses of God, which for liturgical reasons, obtained new furnishings. Many of the splendid Renaissance altar pieces, pulpits, pews, galleries and organ facades have been preserved. The Catholic church's convents, on the other hand, had a sorry fate. They were closed, and with only a few prominent exceptions like the Carmelite cloister in Helsingør, they were demolished, while their functions as centres of education and research devolved to the state.

The latter half of the sixteenth century was marked by international political instability, not to mention great wars. At the same time, Denmark experienced an economic growth based on the export of grain and livestock, permitting the construction of a large number of private and state buildings. It was thus the manor estates that first felt the Renaissance. Hesselagergård, with its Venetian-inspired gables, Gisselfeld, Vallø, Egeskov and Voergård, are examples of transitional forms in between the military castle and the civil palace, where leisure elements, such as ornamental gardens and parks, were added.

The King builds
Without a doubt, the royal palaces were the most conspicuous of the state's buildings. The four-winged Kronborg Castle, built about 1580, was a veritable fortress that controlled the gateway to the Øresund strait. However, with its imposing appearance, it was just as much a demonstration of power. A more recent monument, of international standing, is the three-winged Frederiksborg Castle, which is exemplary of King Christian IV's first building initiatives and was soon followed by Rosenborg, the leisure castle situated outside Copenhagen's ramparts. The style was the Dutch Renaissance, which the king had commissioned through his Dutch building experts, but which later was

Plan of Birkholm estate. A detailed example of a Renaissance garden.

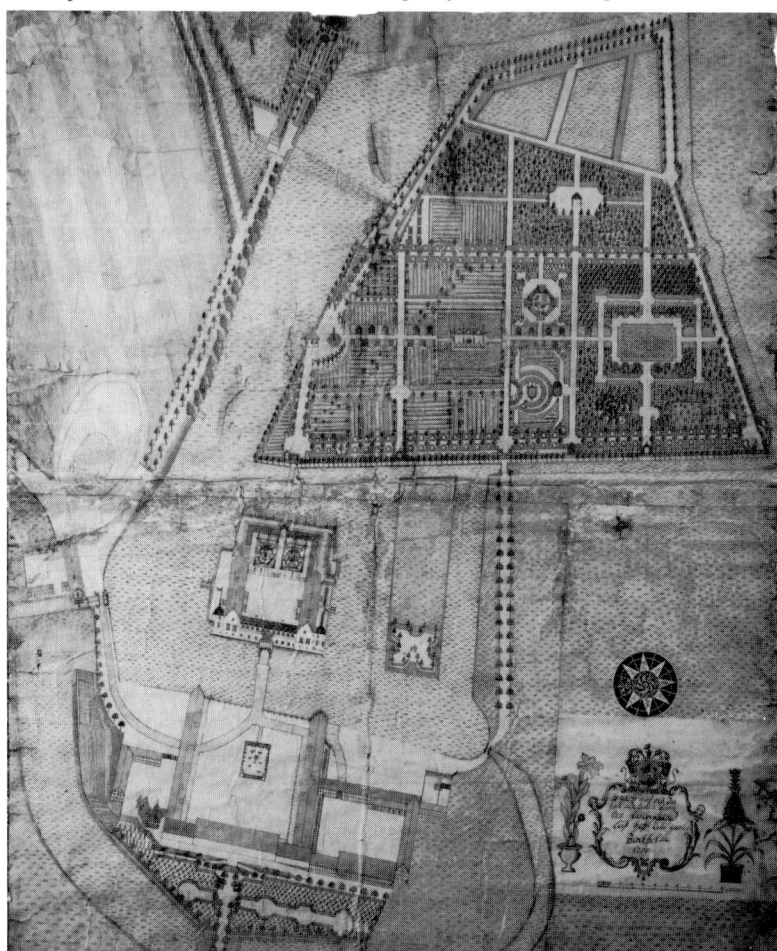

Kronborg Castle, Helsinore.

identified with the king himself and regarded as typically Danish. The tenor of the times dictated the strengthening of the national state and through a widespread self sufficiency, rendering it as independent of foreign countries as possible. Military forces and initiatives to encourage trade and industry were the means in the so-called mercantilistic policy, which made its debut at the close of the sixteenth century and continued until the beginning of the nineteenth century. The multifarious building activity of King Christian IV must be seen in this light. There are still a few rudiments of the enormous naval shipyard at Bremerholm-Gammelholm in Copenhagen dating back to his Father, Frederik II. Among these are the stately Renaissance gable from the original anchor smithy that subsequently became the south gable of Holmen's church. Christian IV continued with the construction of a new naval harbour with supply stores and armoury on Slotsholmen. He more than doubled the area of Copenhagen with the construction of a new fortification ring running from what is now Gothersgade to Kastellet. However this rampart was first completed during the reign of his successor, Frederik III. Nyboder was built on this new area to house naval troops and shipyard personnel. The form of this exceptional housing scheme dates back to the eighteenth century.
In the hope of attracting Baltic commerce to Copenhagen, Christian IV built the Stock Exchange on Slotsholmen, but his endeavour met with disappointment as the time was not ripe for this activity. In the shallow area opposite Slotsholmen, he established Christianshavn as an independent, fortified borough. Following the dramatic developments in artillery, which made a science out of fortification construction, city planning could not disregard defense planning. A number of new fortified cities, situated chiefly in the more remote areas of the kingdom, which today belong to foreign countries, were annexed by the initiative of the king, such as Glückstadt, Holstein, Kristiansstad, Skåne

and Kristiania in Norway. Christian IV's abortive participation in several wars after 1625 impoverished the country and resulted in a cessation of territory to Sweden.

Towns of the seventeenth century
It was especially the provincial towns that now faced what was to be a long period of stagnation. Up to this point, Copenhagen had been the nation's only city with a population of international scale. In 1672, Copenhagen with 42,000 adult inhabitants, was ten times as populous as the second and third largest towns, Ålborg and Helsingør. By 1787, Copenhagen, with 90,000 inhabitants was sixteen times larger than the next largest provincial town, which was then Odense. As a consequence of this, the contribution made to the Danish building heritage by these provincial towns, was of course relatively moderate, particularly when demolitions and town fires are taken into consideration. Nevertheless, entire streetscapes composed of three-storey, half-timber gentry houses can be seen in towns like Køge, Kalundborg and Ribe. Common housing types from around 1600-1800 from provincial towns are represented at the Århus "Old Town" open-air museum. Not many of the gentry were capable of coping with the more pretentious stone houses of the time and thus few are preserved. Among them are Borgmestergården on Amagertorv, and houses on Strandgade in Copenhagen as well as the unusually large and richly decorated Jens Bang's stone house in Ålborg from 1624.
The oldest preserved farms and farm buildings surrounding the various estates date from around 1600. The rural building methods were largely

Half-timber house from the Open-air Museum, »The old Town« in Århus.

17

reliant on half-timber with wattle-and-daub or brick nogging, but the building character of each region varied according to tradition and the kind and availability of local building materials. For example, there is much more solid timber in East Jutland's and in Funen's half-timber structures than in Zealand's. On the other hand, these common building methods were resistant to the changing signals in architecture, which primarily influenced the detailing, such as new profiles and decorative elements. Open-air museums with reconstructed rural buildings can be found in Lyngby, near Copenhagen, in Odense and at Hjerl Hede in Jutland.

Absolute monarchy
The hardships suffered by the nation during the reign of King Christian IV did not cease with his death in 1648. A war with Sweden ten years later threatened the integrity of the national state. However, Copenhagen was successful in holding the enemy at bay. This time, the terms of peace were the cessation of Skåne and Blekinge. The political result was the initiation of an absolute monarchy in 1660, brought about through an alliance between the Crown and Copenhagen's gentry, which broke the feudalist aristocracy's power monopoly. The new state was to be built up as a hierarchical, sophisticatedly constructed political machine that organized every area of society. The king was at the top of the pyramid as the symbol of the state with a hitherto unseen egotism and formalization. In the area of architecture, this centralization gave the state supervision over most of society's building activities, the administration of which was delegated to a general master builder, who managed both the practical and artistic matters on behalf of the king. The first general master builder was the Dutchman, Lambert van Haven, appointed to that post, as well as court painter, in 1671.
It was first during this period of the style-conscious and ambitious autocracy that the modern architectural culture, which was introduced by the Italian Renaissance, made a breakthrough in Denmark. In place of the picturesque and capricious Nordic Renaissance style, a more controlled and regular, formal and harmonious architecture arose, characterized by being finalized in the project phase, in a form where nothing could be added or subtracted. Thereafter the responsible party for the project, the architect in a modern respect, became identified with the work. Among the very first examples of this new architecture is the four-winged city palace, Charlottenborg, located at Kongens Nytorv and built during the 1670's for the king's half-brother, the vice-regent in Norway. The general master builder did the drawings for another of the monarchy's first major architectural works, namely Our Saviour's Church in Christianshavn, which was consecrated in 1696.

The Baroque
The style of the first architectural manifestations of the absolute mo-

Charlottenborg palace with the original characteristic Baroque garden. Painting by Coning.

narchy is referred to as the Baroque. This style had been developed in Rome during the preceding decades as a continuation of the Renaissance, with emphasis shifted from an additive to an integrated, unifying principle of composition. Even though the Baroque rarely attained that same perfection of tenseness in Protestant northern Europe that it had attained in its birthplace, Italy was still the source of inspiration, and journeys there for the purpose of studying its classic and modern monuments became a must for future master builders and architects. The bright Frederiksberg Slot, highly situated in an Italian fashion, is a direct result of Frederik IV's trips abroad, just as Fredensborg Slot has its Italian predecessors. Eventually, the use of stuccoed and white-washed facades fully supplanted the red brick facades, which with their Dutch heritage had characterized the early Baroque architecture. However the red building on Slotsholmen, built in 1720 as the headquarters for the monarchy's central administration, was again in red brick.

In 1728, Copenhagen was hit by the worst fire yet, leaving the medieval town, between Vestervold and Gothersgade, in ashes. This gave the state the opportunity of commissioning standard projects for three-storey gabled-attic houses, the so-called Conflagration Houses, which were employed in the rebuilding of the city. Many of them still exist but rarely in their original form. As a consequence of this reconstruction, a large number of craftsmen were imported from neighbouring countries. Many of them found permanent occupations, as Denmark was poised on the verge of an economic boom, which lasted until the nation's abortive participation in the Napoleonic wars in 1807.

In the palmy days of Danish overseas trade, which this long period of prosperity was called, international commerce and overseas shipping trade flourished, largely due to a successfully implemented foreign policy. However the distribution of wealth was both geographically and socially inequitable, as the population in the provincial towns and the countryside experienced very little improvement in standard of living. The centralization of the monarchy favoured Copenhagen, which was modernized and became a capital city of European calibre during the eighteenth century. It is both striking and consistent with the tenor of the times, that efforts were concentrated on buildings that had ceremonial functions, rather than those of practical necessity. The profits of the kingdom were primarily used for extravagant, yet at the same time, artistically worthwhile buildings in Copenhagen. The cultural and power elite were one in the same.

The most ambitious project by far from this period was the new residential palace, Christiansborg, situated on the site of the medieval castle that had once been of vital necessity for the city's existence. The architect of this Baroque palace was the general master builder, E. D. Häusser, assisted by two younger architects, Thurah and Eigtved, each of whom had the opportunity of making a major contribution to Danish Baroque architecture. This exorbitantly furnished palace was totally destroyed by fire in 1794, while the riding grounds south of the palace and the crown prince's palace that now houses the National Museum, have been preserved. Yet another major monument from about 1740 was lost, namely the palace in Hørsholm, which was demolished in the beginning of the nineteenth century.

Frederiksstaden and Eigtved

The three hundredth anniversary of the Oldenborg Dynasty was celebrated in 1749 with the laying out of a new city quarter, Frederiksstaden, which was placed on an open area, inside of Christian IV's fortification ring. One of the more pragmatic reasons for its establishment was the need by large-scale commerce for more space in the harbour area than was available in the inner city or Christianshavn. Frederiksstaden was designed and built primarily as an ideal baroque city plan with a perpendicular street grid, codes for the subdivision and heights of the buildings and last but not least, a central, octagonal square, bordered by four identical Amalienborg palaces. An immense domed church was planed on the scheme's transverse axis, and only partially built during chief architect Eigtved's lifetime. Its subsequent fate was a decisive factor for the superseding of classicism, by baroque in Denmark.

A number of large warehouses situated at the harbour attest to the source of wealth in those palmy days of Danish overseas trade with China, India, Africa, the West Indies and the North Atlantic countries. The oldest of these warehouses are primarily in Christianshavn whereas the more recent ones are located on the waterfront in Frederiksstad, where they are now being converted to hotels and housing. A well-preserved, and whole complex is the headquarters and warehouse facility

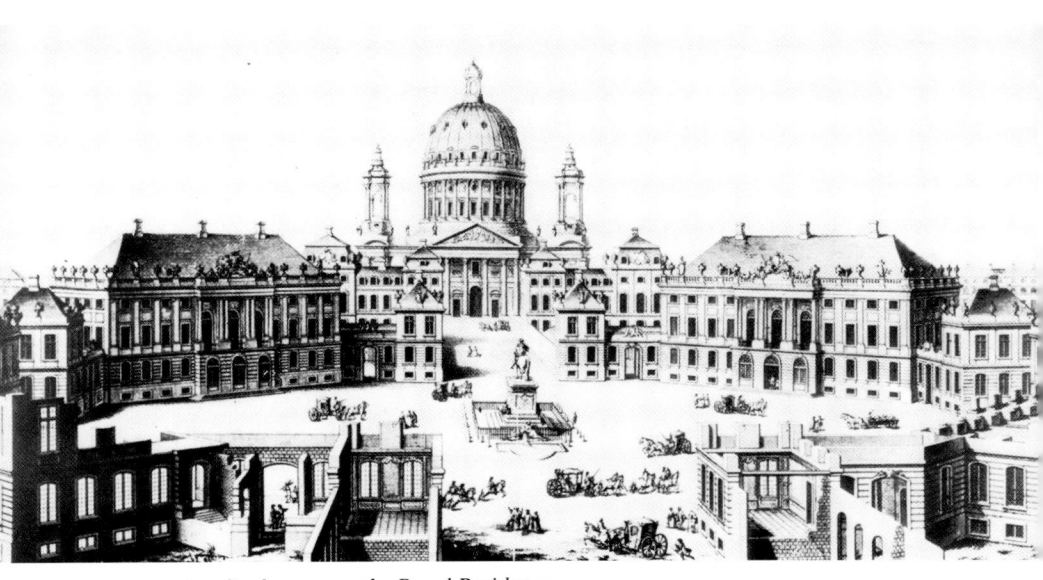

Amalienborg, now the Royal Residence.

of the Asiatisk Kompagni, built around 1740-1780, which today houses part of the Ministry of Foreign Affairs. The naval forces that secured the commercial routes left a beautiful area containing an arsenal and a shipbuilding yard on Holmen, north of Christianshavn. During this period, few new towns were established, but Frederiksværk, from 1760, was an exception. Its existence is due to the establishment of a cannon foundry and a gun powder mill near a source of water power. In the first half of the eighteenth century, the design of manor houses nurtured many architectural commissions. Defence considerations had been long since abandoned in favour of the pursuit of beauty. This was manifested in extravagant, formal compositions of farm buildings, manor houses and parks, just as the show of wealth and magnificence was replaced with considerations of comfort. There are numerous examples of this, one of the most prominent is Ledreborg on the Lerchenborg estate on Zealand.

The Royal Academy of Fine Arts, and classicism
In 1754, the Academy of Fine Arts was founded at Charlottenborg Palace in Copenhagen, where it still is located today. When its first

Amaliegade 1:750.

rector, the court master builder, Eigtved, died shortly after the academy opening, the occasion again arose to bring in expertise from abroad, this time from France. N. H. Jardin, an advocate of classicism, was brought to Denmark, and thus for the first time, Denmark was in tune with the newest currents from abroad. Jardin was commissioned to continue construction of the Frederiksstad domed church in the new spirit of the times, however work was stopped in 1770 and the church was not completed until a century later and according to a quite different project. In other ways, Jardin exerted a significant influence upon Danish architecture. For instance, he was the architect of the Ministry of Foreign Affairs' country manor, Bernstorff, located north of Copenhagen. The influence was also evident in his talented student, C. F. Harsdorff, who with his neighbouring building to Charlottenborg, provided an ideal for the appearance and furnishing of the gentry houses of the time. Traces of this influence can also be seen in the work of the master builders in the provinces. Harsdorff was also one of the first to show respect for historical architecture. As an example, his classicistic chapel for Frederik V, at Roskilde cathedral was in red brick in respect for the unity of the scheme. Facades of exposed brick were considered alien to classicism.

The agricultural reforms

With the agricultural reforms of 1788, a process started that eventually had widespread consequences for the cultural landscape. Following the decline of the village community and the manor estate enclosure movement, the tenant farms were moved out to their newly allotted properties. Often, the light, half-timber structures could be dismantled, moved and reassembled again. In this way, the basic building pattern was altered from the densely grouped village farms, to detached farms

The Pebringe farm, The Open-air Museum in Kongens Lyngby.

in the open fields, which ever since have been a characteristic feature of the Danish landscape. Here again, typical drawings of rational building types for the new agriculture structure were prepared by the state.

The awakening Romantic attitude brought a number of external similarities to the peasant's farms and the townsmen's country estates, but at the same time, they expressed contradictory tendencies. The peasants' buildings were still marked by necessity and adequacy, and available resources allowed only half-timber and thatched roofs. On the other hand, the same rustic, country idyll that the urban upper-class surrounded themselves with, reflected Rousseau's slogan "back to nature", which represented an escape from the artificial and over-civilized urban culture back to a presumably original state of innocence. At this point, the tradition- and the reality-bound stood opposed to the modern and self-reflective consciousness. The most important examples of the sublime, Romantic country estates are Liselund on Møn, and The Sparrow's Nest, Spurveskjul, near Furesøen. The era's evocative gardens belong to this same genre and were occasionally supplemented with hermit huts and caves and the pursuit of Denmark's own history and nature. The familiar, well-known landscape elements such as the cairns, farms, and medieval village churches became artistic themes that influenced the common perception of national identity, and thereby also architecture as well.

C. F. Hansen in Copenhagen
In 1795, the year following the Christiansborg fire, Copenhagen was ravaged by yet another conflagration. This time it started in the Orlogs Shipyard, near Holmen's church, and was first stopped at the western ramparts, Vestervold. Upon reconstruction, the inner city was strongly marked by simple, classicistic, gentry houses in the spirit of Harsdorff. After Harsdorff's death, C. F. Hansen, a native of Copenhagen, who had been the provincial master builder in Holstein, was summoned to supervise the reconstruction of the Christiansborg palace. This marked the beginning of an epoch in Danish architecture, dominated by one person, and presumably the first to place Denmark in the international history of architecture. His epoch was marked in many respects by external difficulties, but was also characterized by opportunity. Denmark had profited from the Napoleonic wars up until the English attack in 1807, when the long period of prosperity abruptly ended along with Copenhagen's position as an important centre of commerce. During the bombardment, another part of the city, which contained the Our Lady Cathedral, was also destroyed by fire. The state bankruptcy followed in 1813 and shortly afterward, the peace treaty, which involved the dissolution of the Danish united kingdom, which at that time included Norway.

In the meantime, C. F. Hansen was responsible for certain large and momentous assignments, which considering the unsettled times, had

Christiansborg Palace, C. F. Hansen's project. Most of it burned down in 1884.

to be solved with an exceptional sense of economy. These tasks included the reconstruction of Christiansborg and of Our Lady Cathedral, as well as the replacement of Copenhagen's burned-down and demolished town hall on Nytorv, which later became the Court House. With the palace and the cathedral, he was forced to reuse the remaining walls, which he did while satisfying his own architectural aims. He wanted "the noble simplicity", which he found in simple geometric blocks with smooth surfaces and few, but consciously employed details. He was thus able to place much more weight upon the effect of contrast between the forms themselves and upon their sharp delineation through light and shadow. Among the many classicistic tendencies present at the time, Hansen was considered to be Romanesque. Today, one could also find a relationship between him and the French, so-called revolution architects, Ledoux and Boullée. Through his position as Superintendent Director of Building, as the job of general master builder had been renamed, he had a firm grip on the public building works throughout the country. As Hansen grew old, it cannot be denied that his death came as a relief for the younger generation of architects. Among these younger architects, H. G. Bindesbøll distinguished himself in a special way. His first independent work, the Thorvaldsen's Museum, built 1839-1847, appeared as one of the most original monuments in Danish architecture, despite the fact that it too was based on one of Christianborg's burned down buildings. In contrast to C. F. Hansen, Bindesbøll cultivated the polychromatic and had a totally undogmatic attitude toward the architectural ideals. Prior to his relatively early death, he was able to demonstrate his many-sidedness in other, somewhat modest projects. Such as the exemplary workers' housing design, the Medical Associations housing scheme, the Royal Veterinary and Agricultural College in Copenhagen, and the mental hospital, Oringe, near Vordingborg.

Liberalism and historicism
By 1850, Copenhagen was still a fortress city lying behind the ramparts of King Christian IV. With 130,000 inhabitants, the city was greatly overpopulated and unhygienic, and the many gardens had been over-built with high-density back buildings. It is quite remarkable that in comparison with its size, Copenhagen has never before or since, housed so many illustrious persons known far beyond Denmark's borders. The sculptor Thorvaldsen and the architect C. F. Hansen died in the middle of the 1840's, but the physicist H. C. Ørsted, the philosopher Søren Kierkegaard, the father of modern general education N. F. S. Grundtvig and the storyteller and poet H. C. Andersen could still be met on the street.

In many respects, the halfway point of the century marked a turning point and a farewell to the old social order. The monarchical autocracy was replaced by a democratic constitution in 1849 and freedom of trade according to liberalistic principles was introduced in 1857. The first railroad, from Copenhagen to Roskilde, opened in 1847 and soon after, the railway net was rapidly expanded, electric telegraphy was introduced in 1854, and Copenhagen was outfitted with gas in 1857 and with pressurized water in 1859. The old, and militarily useless, ramparts were demolished in 1852 and in consequence, the highly crowded city was allowed to spread out into Nørrebro, Vesterbro, Østerbro and Amagerbro. Previous to this, in 1844, the Tivoli amusement park - still today one of the city's main attractions - had been laid out on the embankment terrain. In 1847, J. C. Jacobsen founded his new lager brewery, Carlsberg, adjacent to the railway west of the city, as one of the few large-scale enterprises. Jacobsen's construction of a personal residence on the brewery grounds was a remnant from the disappearing patriarchal period. The separation of home and work place was to become the common norm.

Modern times reached Copenhagen within a short span of years, but not especially early in comparison with other European capitals. The great Cholera epidemic of 1853 was a harsh admonition of the city's inadequate sanitation facilities. This led in 1863 to the construction of the Municipal Hospital, which was extremely modern for its time. The hospital's aesthetically severe architecture accentuated a current tendency to choose an architectural style according to the particular character of the project. The somewhat government approved architecture that C. F. Hansen had advocated, disappeared with him and the absolute monarchy. It was succeeded, for the next half century, by a kind of architectural liberalism, in which historical references were employed as an association-forming accompaniment to the building's function or interplay with the surroundings. The period was given the name, "eclecticism", an allusion to the selection of a style that was appropriate for the particular project. Succeeding generations came to regard this way of working as superficial plagiarism and poor artistic ethics. However this particular historical view of the period has since

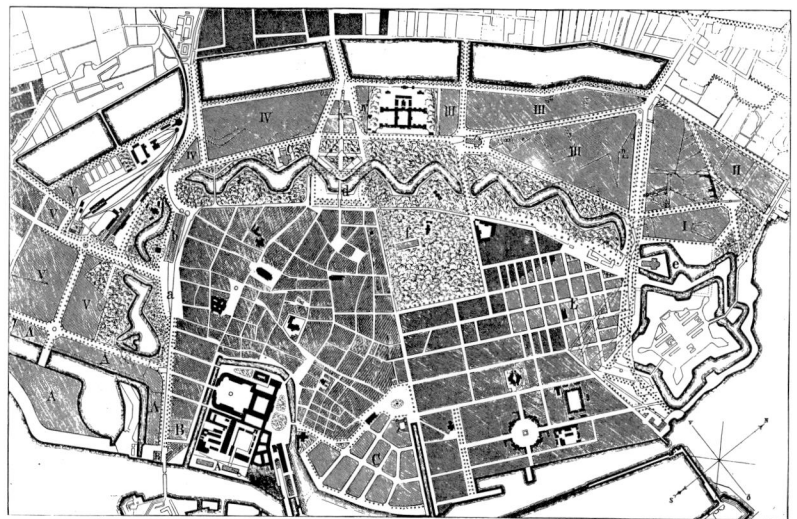
Architect F. Meldahl's proposal for the conversion of the old ramparts in Copenhagen.

been modified.
Symptomatic of these altered architectural and technical attitudes, was the University Library located at Frue Plads and built in 1861 by J. D. Herholdt, a work that introduced the immense cast-iron construction method to Denmark. The richly detailed red brick facades are a liberal paraphrasing of the medieval themes, which emphasized the display of the inherent value of materials and structure as architectural elements. Through its faultless consistency, the University Library stands as a manifesto for the Nordic-Italian tendency, that free historicism, which characterized a great deal of Danish architecture in the last century.
While Copenhagen's position as a commercial centre faltered during the first decades of the nineteenth century, a growth in prosperity started about 1830, in the provincial towns and countryside, based on a propitious export of grain. The orderly Copenhagen classicism left its mark on a large number of gentry houses, in many instances, replacing the old and more picturesque half-timber buildings. A vigorous construction of town halls, schools, customs houses and harbour storehouses was further proof that the new times had arrived in the provinces. This process was further accelerated by the expansion of the railway network, and the railway station was added as a new building type that possessed its own typical architectural symbolism. From the intersection of the railway with old country villages or roads, a new type of town emerged, the junction, which as a local business and service centre, was often in bitter competition with neighbouring provincial towns.

Accelleration of urban growth
Throughout the nineteenth century, some of the larger provincial towns experienced a relatively more accelerated growth than that of Copenhagen. At the midpoint of the century, Odense was still the nation's second largest city and was outfitted with gas and pressurized water installations before Copenhagen. In 1830, Århus, with a population of over six thousand, was the fifth largest city, after Odense, Ålborg and Helsingør. By the turn of the century, its population had grown to over 50.000 and from then on, Århus was the nation's undisputed second largest city.

By the middle of the nineteenth century, a significant growth and modernization of the brick industry had occurred. This not only satisfied the needs of urban construction, but also agriculture's requirements for buildings and irrigation drainpipes. New farmhouses and buildings were built as rational and comfortable brick structures. Unlike earlier, and the later Romantics, the new breed of independent farmers held no great enthusiasm for the country idyll with its half-timber walls, thatched roofs and bumpy cobblestones. Prosperity in the agricultural industry also led to the construction of the last generation of manor estates. Here, where Spartan considerations of prudence were not forced upon the economy, the architectural ideals of the time could come into their own. The manors attested to the fact that the building's owners preferred an identification with the opulent, spire-embellished magnificence of Christian IV's time than with the gracious perfection of style found in the eighteenth century estate buildings, when allusions to historical prototypes were so characteristic. There are numerous examples, Frijsenborg, built in Jutland by Ferdinand Meldahl in 1865 is one of the most ostentatious of these country manors. However, agriculture's prosperity ended in the 1870's, when the steam-powered shipping trade began to inundate the European market with cheaper overseas grain.

Copenhagen's expansion in the latter half of the nineteenth century occurred primarily in the new neighbourhoods that grew up in the old rampart areas, where there was a hectic activity with property speculation and privately financed building of multi-storey, high-density tenement housing. The population of the city, which had been 130,000 when the ramparts were removed, grew to 400,000 by the turn of the century. The source of growth was primarily from the countryside, whose surplus of population sought their livelihood as workers in the new urban industries.

Copenhagen underwent great changes during the century, not only in population and size, but also in character. The old residential city behind the ramparts and moats, with its commercial bourgeoisie, official functionaries, military personnel and peasant population, was superseded by a new type of city, characterized by industrialism's monotonous factory quarters and tenement houses as well as the modern metropolis' conspicuous display of a wide range of institutions and establishments. Theaters, hotels and shops with mirrored windowpanes brought the first real city ambiance to Copenhagen. For better or worse, posterity has preserved a mild and conciliatory picture of pre-industrial Copenhagen, however the social contrasts had hardly become greater, but were honed instead.

As was true in other great cities throughout Europe, Paris was Copenhagen's ideal of the modern metropolis. This can be seen in the architecture as well as in certain tendencies in planned urban building, which clashed with liberalism's goal of "laissez-faire" and its aversion to any restriction of private privileges. The newly established financial and industrial upper class leaned toward the French-inspired beaux-arts style of architecture, so named after the famous school in Paris. This style was based upon certain rules of form and composition and was thus, essentially different from the contemporary Nordic-Italian trend that was orientated primarily to materials and construction. Among the chief works in the beaux-arts style are: The Royal Theater, built in 1874 by Vilh. Dahlerup; the neighbouring Magasin du Nord department store; the housing on Søtorvet, and last but not least, Meldahl's project for the completion of the main church in Frederikstad, the Marble Church and its surroundings. Private patronage characteristically played an important role here. For example the completion of the Marble Church was paid for by the banking and industrial magnate, C. F. Tietgen, the reconstruction of Frederiksborg Castle after the fire, was

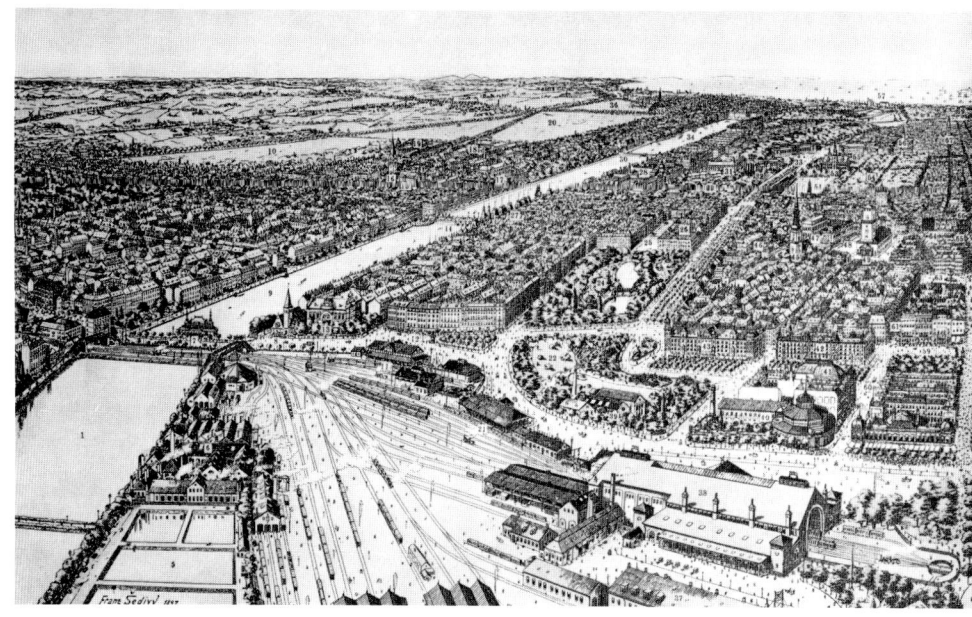

paid for by brewer J. C. Jacobsen, and the Ny Carlsberg Glyptotek was financed by his son, brewer Carl Jacobsen.

Christiansborg Palace, the seat of the government, which was rebuilt by C. F. Hansen following the conflagration of 1794, suffered a fire again in 1884 that left only the palace church undamaged. At this time, the contemporary attitude toward C. F. Hansen's architecture was basically unfavorable and his great simplicity was considered to be pure penury. A reconstruction, which should have been the most obvious move, was thus not even discussed, and for political reasons, twenty years past before any decision was made concerning the future of the palace.

Industrialism

A period of industrial growth began in the 1890's and lasted until the First World War. Electricity had gained acceptance, and reinforced concrete was being used as a building material. One of the first projects where they were employed together was the large-scale construction of the free port area in Copenhagen, which also included a public park and the city's quay of honor, Langelinie. Industry's increasing self awareness was reflected in the imposing factories they built, some as an early form of corporate architecture and others as individualistic extremes, such as the Ny Carlsberg brewery, built in 1900. Another market for the display of individualism was the increasing activity in

Palm House in the Botanical Gardens, Copenhagen.

villa construction in the suburbs of the larger cities. The villa located out in the green areas of nature represented the ideal framework for respectable family life. Its past was the city-dweller's old country house culture and its future was to be as the most prevalent housing form in Denmark. Architecturally, the spectrum was great, varying from Nordic Viking style to Swiss-type houses and Italian tower villas. The restoration of the medieval churches was a very special chapter, running through the later decades of the nineteenth century. One aspect was that funds were available for more than just necessary repairs, another aspect was the style-historical pedantry of the times, which manifested itself in an aversion toward the various additions and alterations made on the churches throughout the course of the previous centuries. In many instances this led to drastic restorations to what was ostensibly believed to be the original form. A textbook example of this is the cathedral in Viborg, which after restoration, looked more like a copy than a restoration of a Romanesque cathedral.

The restoration of the churches was a sign of a lively interest, and a beginning appreciation for the national building heritage, not only in terms of architectural monuments, but also the anonymous style of building that was determined by a particular time and place. Under such circumstances, the Nordic-Italian trend in architecture became Danish Romantic. The chief work in this style was the Copenhagen Town Hall, completed in 1905 as the result of a 1889 design competition won by Martin Nyrop. This building, with its multiplicity of architectural references and symbols, its informality and complexity, was meant to be the home of liberal democracy. It was to connect history with the present, and the city with the countryside. It was made in a popular style and yet did not oblige the old establishment's culture nor the new rich bourgeoisie.

By the turn of the century, Copenhagen was no longer alone in setting the architectural standards of the nation. Hack Kampmann's activity in Århus - The Customs House Building, the Theater and the National Library - introduced a new epoch wherein the larger provincial towns began to obtain their own individual architectural profiles.

National Romantic and The Arts and Crafts Movement

There was a latent background in Denmark for a popular architecture that sought its roots in the domestic tradition. This was largely the result of activity in the folk high schools and the strengthening of that widespread civic self-awareness, which the rural co-operative movement was also an expression of. Following the crisis in the grain trade that occurred during the 1870's, the farmers mobilized their energy to redirect their production toward more refined animal export goods. This changeover not only brought an increase in employment, but also an extensive construction of farms, dairies, slaughterhouses and buildings for companion industries of various kinds. Increasing emphasis was placed on building types that combined economy and practical sense with an architectural dignity, rather than individual whims. Gradually, the junction cities became targets for the transplantation of pretentious, foreign architecture to provincial settings. This was supported by certain Copenhagen architects who, beyond idealistic motives, presumably entertained expectations of a future market in the smaller cities and in the countryside. At the National Exhibition held in Århus in 1909, the Academic Architect's Association displayed a full scale model of a junction city, meant to typify how an exemplary

Junction town at the National Exhibition in Århus in 1909.

Brøndums Hotel, Anchersvej, Skagen. Architect: Ulrik Plesner.

and up-to-date style of building ought to be. Endeavors to define "the Danish house" as a concept and type had extensive implications upon the construction of smaller buildings, including single-family houses, and led to the establishment of the National Association for Better Building, in 1915. This organization's efforts in disseminating information among building owners and craftsmen yielded results that can be seen throughout the country, even today.

A certain introspectiveness among architecture's leading figures, concentrated as they were around the cultivation of national identity and traditional deep-rootedness, hampered the assimilation of new impulses from abroad at the beginning of the twentieth century. Thus the sensitive and sophisticated Jugendstil or art nouveau, although present in the nation's handicraft, is only modestly represented in Danish architecture. "The Arts and Crafts Movement" was the title given to that transitional form that lay between National Romantic and Jugend. Its conceptual basis was in debt to the English, William Morris movement. In the residential villa quarter known as Ryvangen, which the municipality of Copenhagen laid out around the turn of the century in order to counteract the flight of prosperous taxpayers to the suburbs, there are numerous large single-family houses, clearly influenced by the English country house tradition.

An important architect, with a distinctly international orientation, was Anton Rosen, whose buildings in Copenhagen, built in 1906-1910 were dramatically different from the ordinary Danish pursuit of tradition. This is obvious in the use of modern frame construction, large areas of glass and ornamentation in the spirit of art nouveau.

Faaborg Museum. Architect: Carl Petersen.

Neoclassicism

The so-called spire case in 1910 had started as a mere trifle but eventually had a great significance for Danish architecture. It all started when the patron, brewer Carl Jacobsen, offered to donate a spire to C. F. Hansen's classicist cathedral in Copenhagen. The offer split the architects into two camps, with many of the older architects approving, while many of the younger, under the leadership of Carl Petersen, maintained that a spire would destroy the unity of the church, and compromise C. F. Hansen as an architect. The opposition was up against the National Romantic generation's predilection for overloading architecture with quaint details and popular symbolism. In contrast to this, from the outset, new classicism followed architecture's fundamental and universally valid qualities - an abstraction toward the Doric, the original, which was realized in C. F. Hansen's architecture. Thus at that point, Danish neoclassicism was not so much an eclectic selection of earlier architectural devices as it was a search to analyze and reformulate the essential tendencies, which have always characterized architecture everywhere. Such traits were the relation between space and mass, the penetration of surface, form's delineation in light and the mutual proportional relationship between elements.

In 1915, Carl Petersen produced the first, prototypic example, namely the museum in Fåborg. In spite of its modest size, it possesses a monumental format in the spirit of C. F. Hansen. Thorvaldsen's Museum was undoubtedly the source of inspiration for the colourful interiors and the mosaic floors. There were very close ties between the first and the second phases of Danish classicism and in some cases, 1920 can

Housing project, »Ved Classens Have«, Copenhagen. Architects: Carl Petersen, Ole Falkentorp, Peter Nielsen and Povl Baumann.

be difficult to distinguish from 1820.

Housing

Neoclassicism was, in the words of its practitioners, a restricted art, whose results depended on self-discipline and sublimation. Paradoxically enough, its period of development occurred during the First World War and immediately after, when society was shaken by chaotic economic and social conditions. The intimate, classicist villas and country houses could be built with the profits from the war business, while the housing shortage increased due to the coinciding of the population influx to the cities and the stagnation in the construction of new flats. This situation brought the public authorities, for the first time, into the role as a major builder or guarantor for housing. This subsidized housing included many smaller buildings, which democratized the ideal of the garden house. However the most conspicuous were the cooperative housing societies' huge, five-storey urban blocks with endless rows of windows. These immense blocks, which lie in a ring around Copenhagen's old rampart districts, are permeated with gardens and lawns as opposed to the back buildings and narrow courts of the old tenement houses. Despite their Spartan standard, the new buildings were an undeniable step toward the humanization of the rental flat. Architecturally, the huge blocks were marked more by neoclassicism's ethic and discipline than by its style. During the 1920's, the endeavours toward the universal and typical, which had characterized neoclassicism from its beginning, led to an almost timeless, matter-of-fact and simple architecture as the classicistic references

Housing project, Bella Vista in Klampenborg. Architect: Arne Jacobsen.

slowly disappeared. This deep-rootedness in familiar qualities had presumably hampered the influence of the radical, international modernism, which gained a relatively late footing in Denmark.

The architects' entrance into the great housing construction boom of the twenties had a great significance. At the same time, and as part of this work, an interest in urban planning, as a humanistic and architectural discipline, began to propagate. However the legislation was still too flimsy to bring about any important results.

With respect to scale and degree of detailing, the major neo-classicistic work was the Main Police Station in Copenhagen, built by Hack Kampmann, with Aage Rafn as the chief architect. Outwardly austere and unapproachable, and inwardly spatially dramatic and refined, it suffered the indignity of being created too late in time. Upon its completion in 1925, it was harshly criticized as being formalistic, by many, including the renowned cultural commentator and lighting designer, Poul Henningsen. In his periodical, "Kritisk Revy" [Critical Review], with a quick-witted combination of satire and common sense, he struck a note for open-mindedness in life style and the conception of art, for an audience that was both inquisitive and easily offended.

Funktionalism

The goal for that culturally radical modernism, which began to be accepted, was to assist in the establishment of a democratic, classless mass culture that was free of the anachronistic heirlooms from the wardrobe of the bourgeoisie. Rational planning of cities and housing in a new and active relationship to nature ought to vouch for the results. It was now a question of functionalism, commonly abbreviated to "funkis".

The intentions were never realized, aside from the PH-lamp, which eventually became the common man's property. Instead, functionalism

Århus University. Architects: Kay Fisker, Poul Stegmann and C. F. Møller.

branched off into three different, mutually related movements. The first of these, literal functionalism, prioritized simple, physical utilitarian values and technical rationality over aesthetic values. The second branch was, on the other hand, conspicuously style conscious, even at the expense of function. Here we find the Danish version of the international modernism that Le Corbusier and the Bauhaus had described. Arne Jacobsen introduced it with sophistication and artistry, in the Bellavista scheme located in Klampenborg, built in the first half of the 1930's. The third functionalist tendency allied itself with the Danish tradition for matter-of-fact building, determined by experience with proven types, materials and construction methods. In an undogmatic fashion it continued the stripped neoclassicism of the 1920's with traces of Bindesbøll's architecture from the 1850's.

The functional tradition
"The functional tradition", as the latter tendency came to be called by its most illustrious figure, Kay Fisker, was, however, not as pragmatic as it might sound. That which was familiar was cleansed and cultivated with a critical aesthetic sense. This movement had a long and stabilizing influence upon Danish architecture, emanating from its major work, Århus University, the first phase of which was built in 1933.
During the international crisis of the 1930's, Denmark was characterized by a social-liberalistic policy in which the public authority gained influence on several areas of society, while expanding its institutions for health care, culture and education. The modern architecture, adapted to a Danish context, was at its best in projects in this area, such as Copenhagen's schools of the period and in the subsidized

Airport terminal in Kastrup, 1937. Architect: Vilhelm Lauritzen.

housing, which realized clear improvements in standard that often resulted in outstanding solutions. The multi-storey block form, which had characterized the housing boom of the 1920's, was now superseded by an open form of building with parallel blocks situated in parklike surroundings, though rarely as schematically planned as in Germany where the form originated. Modern residential furnishings such as bathrooms, central heating and garbage chutes became common features of the housing projects of the time. Balconies became wide-spread and brought new facade types, with the partially built-in balcony-bay version being the most popular. The Bispebjerg suburb of Copenhagen is dominated by this type of housing, which was also very prevalent in the larger provincial towns.

To some degree, functionalism altered its character during the 1930's. Whereas it had started in Central Europe as a radical, frontier program, the crisis, political reaction and lack of inspiration throughout the rest of Europe, made it a common Nordic gathering point for the social-liberalistic ideals in architecture and social planning. The isolationism that grew with the approach of World War II advanced the process of Nordic identification, while modern architecture was given a high official status. In this connection, Denmark's contribution was an elegant, almost exclusive building style with ostensible, ceremonial functions, such as the Broadcasting House in Copenhagen and the Kastrup Airport by Vilhelm Lauritzen, as well as the town halls in Århus and Søllerød, by Arne Jacobsen and his associates.

The Second World War precipitated a severe decline in the building industry, which was due to a general lack of materials as well as a limited supply of various specific materials. The lack of cement and steel during the war years was evident in the way buildings were planned and constructed. This was supported by a tendency to emphasize the domestic tradition to make an aesthetic virtue out of necessity. This does not imply an interruption in development, as the trend continued within the framework of functionalist tradition and could still be traced many years after the war.

Scandinavian Empiricism
The period from 1945 up until 1960, where this outline ends, was marked by several, occasionally opposing tendencies. Denmark had a huge production backlog after the war, but not the drastic rebuilding problems that were present in many other places throughout Europe. This is one of the reasons for the particularly high quality in Danish architecture and design during the post-war years, which attracted attention from abroad, under the term of "Scandinavian Empiricism". There were two branches of 1950's functionalism, which to an equal extent, aimed at meeting the practical challenges of the times. However, their points of departure were essentially different. The first concentrated on small scale housing, based on a familiar and well-established practice. An architecturally successful example of this is Søndergårdsparken in Bagsværd. The second was the ambitious attempt to take up functionalism through rationalization, large-scale operation and non-traditional building methods. This endeavor was manifested in the first great high-rise housing on Bellahøj in suburban Copenhagen, where the first phase was built in 1951.

During the post-war period, the younger architects were particularly receptive to foreign influences. At first their interest was directed toward the "warmer" attitude to materials and the adroit treatment of form and space that was characteristic of Frank Lloyd Wright and Alvar Aalto's architecture. Shortly after, impulses from Mies van der Rohe and the American system architecture began to enter the scene, its constructive clarity and precision of detail met with a certain degree of sympathy among Danish architects. There seems to be a synthesis of these two tendencies inherent in traditional Japanese architecture, wherein rich and varied spatial relationships could occur within a fixed

Rødovre Town hall. Architect: Arne Jacobsen.

modular construction system, in a combination of freedom and restraint, which to a great extent, became characteristic for the best of Danish architecture during the nineteen-fifties.

Japanese and american influences

The purest prototypic examples can be found in the single-family houses designed by Jørn Utzon, Halldor Gunnlögsson and Erik Christian Sørensen, among others. However the philosophy behind this endeavor became normative for projects on a larger scale, such as the beautifully designed art museum, Louisiana, which Bo and Wohlert started building in 1958, as well as many of the schools and low-rise institutional buildings, built after 1960. Arne Jacobsen cultivated the crystalline and de-materialized curtain-wall architecture with skillful finesse in projects such as Rødovre's town hall and the SAS Royal Hotel. His rendition of what constituted the familiar types of the time was unsurpassed, and in the course of the 1950's Jacobsen won significant recognition abroad in the fields of architecture and design, as forerunner for many different projects executed beyond the nation's borders.

Another event that contributed to an international awareness of Danish architecture, was Jørn Utzon's 1957 winning competition proposal for the Sydney Opera House. His projects in Denmark were modest in scope, but aroused attention by functioning as directives for architectural development. Prior to his trip to Sydney, where he was to direct the construction of the opera house, he built the courtyard house scheme known as the Kingo houses, in Helsingør, and the Terrace scheme in Fredensborg, with which he anticipated the coming low-dense ideals in housing.

Danish architecture earned a favorable reputation during the 1950's. Impulses from abroad inspired a wider variation than in the preceding decade. At the same time, the new trends could be absorbed in the local tradition for homogeneity. New materials and new methods opened up possibilities instead of setting limits, because generally speaking, building construction was still characterized by the versatility and high quality of Danish craftsmanship. Toward the end of the decade, an economic upswing began, though almost imperceptible at the time, in retrospective, it can be considered a turning point. The great productivity increase in the building industry based on prefabrication and montage methods, together with the rapid expansion of mass automobile transport, were factors that greatly influenced housing forms and the cultural landscape. The urban area was radically increased by extensively utilized zones for a variety of functions. The immense montage projects, which contained up to two thousand flats were, like the motorway environments, extremely conspicuous. The square kilometres of tract housing were more subdued, but no less monotonous. The environmental debate and the critique of functionalism were close at hand.

1-4. Viking fortification, ca A.D. 1000

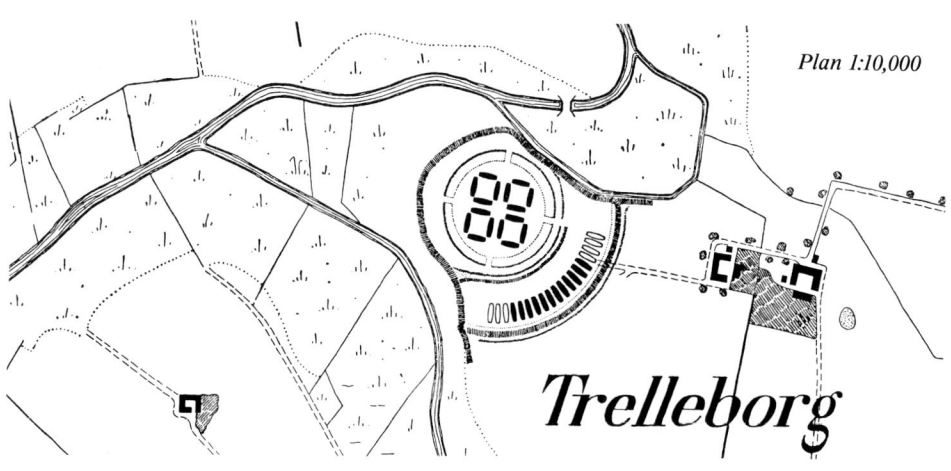

1. *The Viking fort Trelleborg, ca A.D. 1000. Between Slagelse and Korsør.*

Plan 1:10,000

Trelleborg

On a little neck of land, between the confluence of two streams, near the Storebælt strait lies a grass covered fortification called Trelleborg. Excavations have established that it is a series of fortified barracks from the close of the viking period, ca A.D. 1000. The scheme is based on strict geometric principles, the main element being a massive, precisely formed circular embankment with an inner diametre of 137 metres. The front was reinforced with timber and palisades. Toward the four compass points, the embankment was interrupted by narrow, covered portals that appeared almost as tunnels. Toward east there is a moat, the other three sides being protected by water ways. The portals are connected by crooked paths that divide the interior space of the fort in four parts. In each of these were four long houses around a closed court, 16 buildings in all. In a bailey, east of the ring embankment, lie 15 more buildings of the same type, radially oriented from the main fort. A reconstruction of these buildings with their curved longitudinal walls, narrow ends and shingled roofs supported by side purlins has been erected next to the main entrance. The interior was divided up in a centre hall with a fireplace in the middle of the floor and a smaller room at each end. Recent research has revealed that certain details, such as the exterior gallery, are not correct. The scheme was built by the Danish king, possibly Svend Tveskæg, but as this type of complex is unknown in other countries, the question of origin is still unanswered.

Three other Danish examples are known at this time: Fyrkat near Hobro, Aggersborg near Aggersund, and Nonnebakken below the Middle Age quarter of Odense.

Reconstructions at the Archaeological Experimental Centre at Lejre give a good impression of how the common living units were, from the Iron Age around 500 B.C. up until A.D. 1000.

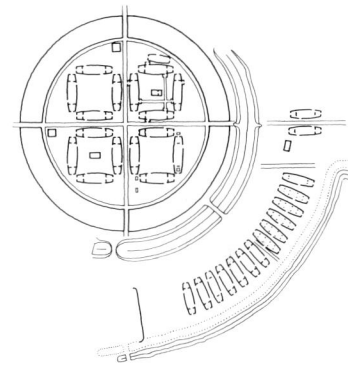

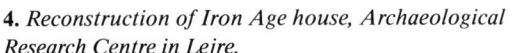

1. *Trelleborg, 1:6000. building site on the bailey 1:750.*

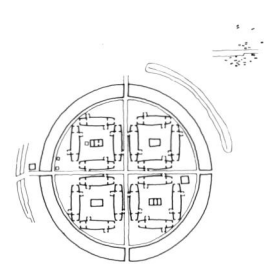

2. *Fyrkat near Hobro. Ca A.D. 1000. Plan 1:6000.*

4. *Reconstruction of Iron Age house, Archaeological Research Centre in Lejre.*

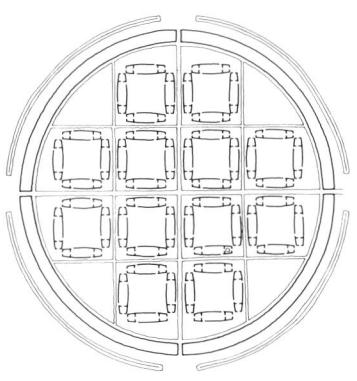

3. *Aggersborg near Aggersund. Ca A.D. 1000. Plan 1:6000.*

5-9. The early Middle Age churches, 1100-1130

5. Hover Church. Ca A.D. 1100. Plan and elevation 1:750.

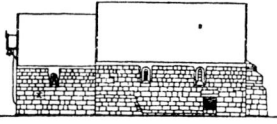

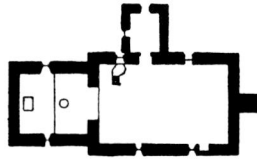

Right: **6.** *Mårup Øde Church near Lønstrup.*

Hover Church near Ringkøbing is a good example of a twelfth century parish church in it simplest possible form: A church hall consisting of a rectangular nave and a smaller square or rectangular chancel. The first wooden churches were also built in this way and Hover is a stone version of this type. The material is granite blocks on a mitered base. The blocks are meticulously hewn with a pick hammer to the same height though with varying widths. Most of the high, narrow windows have been preserved, and the double splayed windows gather and spread light in a remarkably effective way. The only alterations are the porch from the early sixteenth century, a bricked-up north door, and a shored-up buttress on the west wall.

Another example of an early granite church is Mårup Øde church in Lønstrup between Hirtshals and Løkken.

Venge Church, north of Skanderborg, is also built of tufa stone during the twelfth century, but the plan is somewhat more complex. The chancel has an apse and the nave has side chapels toward north and south, both in two storeys and each with its own apse. The existing tower over the south chapel is a later addition. The original tower was situated at the west end, where remnants of the base can still be seen in the wall thickness. Its form was due to the fact that the church originally belonged to the Venge Benedictine monastery.

Vestervig near Hurup in Thy was the bishop's residence until the 1130's and the large granite block church is from this period. The chancel, apse, nave and aisles are original, and were first restored during this century. A large transept with sacristies and small chapels no longer exists. The west tower is from the late Middle Ages.

Tveje Merløse Church, south of Holbæk was built around 1120-30 from a combination of granite boulders and limestone. The west end is terminated by a tower with twin spires, which is connected to the main nave by arched openings on the ground floor as well as on the upper level that houses a private tribune. The builder was presumably nobleman Asser Rig of the famous Hvide family, and the model, the old limestone church in Roskilde.

7. *Venge Church.*

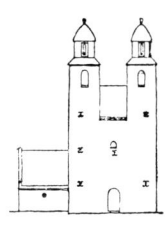

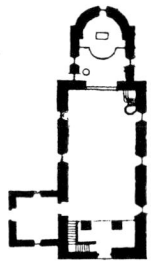

9. *Tveje Merløse Church. Plan and elevation 1:750.*

Left: **8.** *Vestervig Church.*

43

10-16. Round churches, 1100-1250.

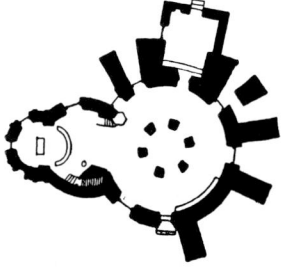
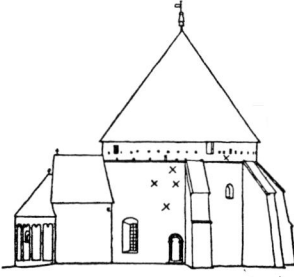

10. Østerlars Church, ca 1200. Plan and elevation 1:750.

13. Nykirke, (new church) Bornholm. Not shown.

Right: **14.** Horne Church, Fyn. Early twelfth century. Plan and elevation 1:750.

15. Bjernede Church near Sorø. See page 162.

Østerlars Church on Bornholm, built around 1200, is the largest Danish example of a Middle Age central church, though special in that it was built as a defence tower with the church room on the ground floor, an escape and storage room on the middle level and a defence level on top with an open gallery. This was covered by a roof during the seventeenth century, but the original spouts that drained rainwater from the gallery are still visible on the outer wall. The various levels are roofed by a circular barrel vault, which is supported by an enormous, hollow centre pillar. This construction was not substantial enough as is evident by the seven heavy buttresses, which were built in order to strengthen the outer wall. The original form of the roof is not certain, but the eaves must have been behind the parapets and the centre pillar could have continued up as a small roof tower.

There are three other similar round churches from the same period, Nylars, Nykirke and Ols Church. The concept was primarily the same, but they were smaller and have massive centre pillars. Together they comprise a unique chapter in Danish Middle Age architecture.

There are three more round churches in Denmark: Horne round church on Funen from the first half of the 12th century, Bjernede Kirke near Sorø from the later half of the 12th century, and Thorsager Kirke, north of Kalø Vig on Djursland, built in the beginning of the 13th century. They differ however from the Bornholm churches in that the vaults are supported by four central columns.

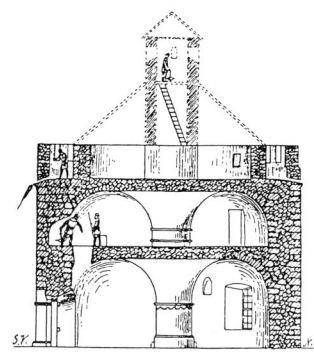

11. *Nylars Church. Section in reconstruction of original form, by Hugo F. Frölén.*

12. *Ols Church. Interior and plan 1:750.*

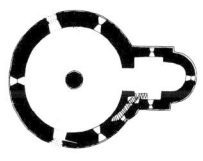

16. *Thorsager Church, Djursland.*

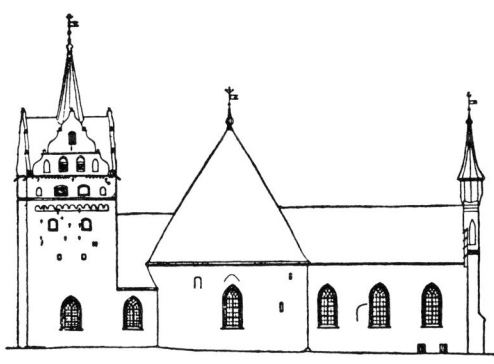

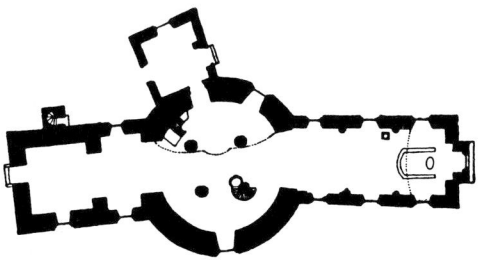

17, 18. Saint Bendts Church in Ringsted and Sorø Monastery Church, 1160-1241.

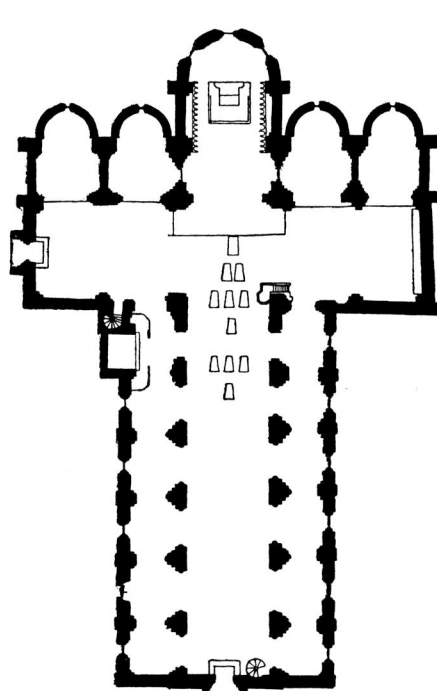

17. *St. Bendts Church, Torvet in Ringsted. Plan and elevation 1:750.*

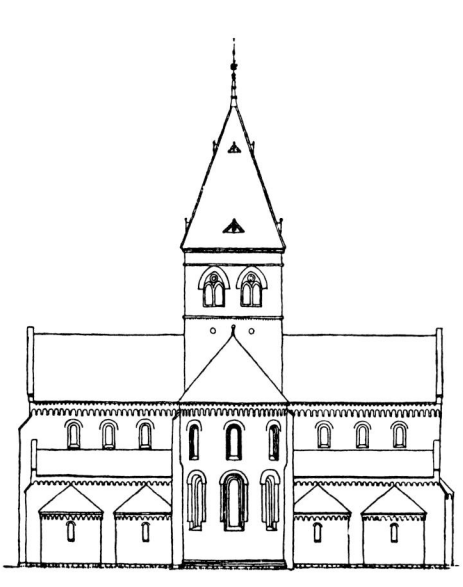

The introduction of brick to Denmark as a building material had an enormous influence on the building culture as one was no longer dependent on local sources of natural stone. One of the first large churches built in this new material was Saint Bendts Church in Ringsted. It was started in the 1160's as part of a large four-winged Benedictine Monastery, with King Valdemar the Great as the builder. He also employed brick in the construction of Dannevirke the great defence wall, the oldest recorded use of brick, that was to protect the country from enemies in the south. The plan of the church was a Latin cross with five apses on the east end that terminate the chancel and the four transept chapels. Many features, both in style and method of construction, can be traced back to northern Italy. Most likely, both the building supervisor and brick makers were recruited from Lombardy. The exterior length of the church is 66 metres, almost half of which is the chancel and transept. The aisles, east chapels and apses were originally vaulted and the main nave after a fire in 1241. The tower over the intersection of the nave and transept was added during the 16th century. After several centuries of disrepair, a rather heavy handed restoration was carried out between 1900 and 1909 by architect H.B. Storck. His proposal was forwarded already in 1877, and is perhaps the first Danish proposal for a historical restoration.

Sorø Church was built about the same time and was completed shortly after 1200, as part of a Cistercian monastery founded by bishop Absalon in 1162. The plan here was also based on a Latin cross, but the eastern end of the chancel and the four transept chapels have straight walls. The church was laid out on a square grid, with the square nave bay corresponding to two square aisle bays. This principle was soon supplanted by the so-called through system with rectangular bays, as can be seen at Saint Bendts Church, and was later used in almost all multiple-nave churches. Originally the main nave had a flat wooden ceiling, but after a fire in 1247 it was vaulted as the rest of the church. It is evident here that brick was a new material, and an increased confidence in its use can be seen as the building work proceeds from east to west.

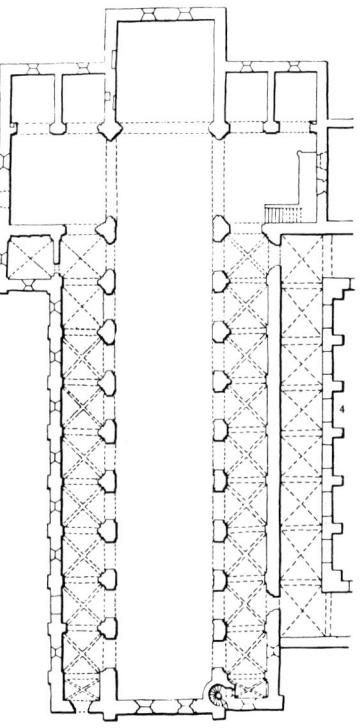

18. *Sorø abbey church. Plan 1:750.*

19. Roskilde Cathedral, 1170-1400.

19. *Roskilde Cathedral, Stændertorvet in Roskilde.*

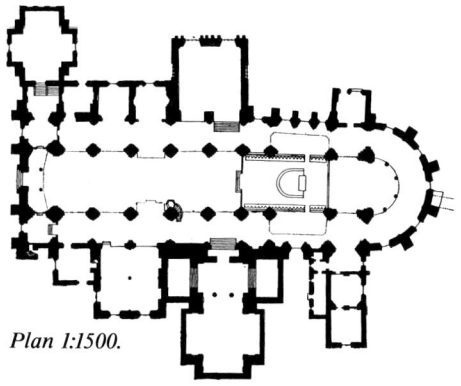

Plan 1:1500.

Left: *Frederik V's Burial chapel at Roskilde Cathedral, C.F. Harsdorff 1774-1825.*

Frederik IX's Chapel. Architects Vilhelm Wohlert, Inger and Johannes Exner 1985-86. In the background, on the right, Christian IX's Chapel.

Denmark's most distinguished brick building was started about 1170 by bishop Absalon, as a replacement for a smaller, three-aisle limestone church. The impressive plan included a long, three-aisled nave with three-aisled, protruding transepts as well as an apse and an ambulatory on the east end. Only the apse and the crossing were built according to this plan, as Absalon's successor, Peder Sunesøn, just home from France, altered the building program under influence of the new, Gothic style. The ambulatory was given larger windows, the transepts were abandoned and the main nave completed according to gothic principles, with vaulted bays. The bays toward west and the tower were presumably not completed until about 1400.

Aside from its clear relationship to the oldest Danish brick churches, Roskilde Cathedral represents a transitional form, more akin to early French Gothic although the building materials are quite different.

Christian IV's Chapel, 1642.

During the course of time, a number of additions have been spread along the walls of the church. The first was the so-called Absalon arch, which connects the chancel with the bishop's residence. After this came several small chapels and the distinguished, late Gothic, Oluf Mortensen's porch on the north side of the chancel. Later came the ring of royal sepulchre chapels with Christian IV's Chapel from 1642 being the most distinguished example. The same king also enhanced the church in other ways, such as the characteristic, slender, tower spires. A unique building work can be found in Frederik V's sepulchre chapel on the south side, started by C.F. Harsdorff in 1774. It is not only one of his major works, but also one of the most significant during the classicistic period. Later additions were Christian IX's Chapel built in 1917-24 by Andreas Clemmensen, and finally, somewhat apart from the church, Frederik IX's Chapel, built in 1985-86 with Vilhelm Wohlert and Inger and Johannes Exner as architects.

Oluf Mortensen's porch.

20-22. Central churches, 1170-1225.

20. *Our Lady Church,
Torvet/Adelgade,
Kalundborg.*

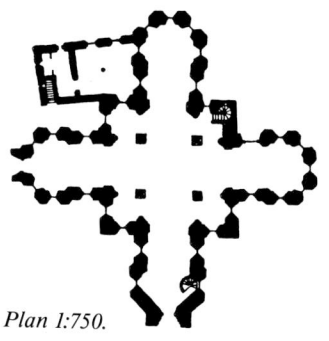

Plan 1:750.

Our Lady Church in Kalundborg, with its distinctive profile, is one of the most unusual buildings in Danish architectural history. One must seek far from Denmark to find anything like it. As opposed to the traditional, longitudinally oriented churches, it is a central building with a Greek cross plan and towers over the square nave and the ends of the transept. Recent research has revealed what one intuitively feels: That the plan, dimensions, and numeral symbolics form a synthesis, which has biblical implications from the account of holy Jerusalem in the Revelations. According to tradition, the church was founded by Esbern Snare in 1170. All indications imply that only the central, square Maria tower was planned from the beginning, while the four octagonal transept towers were conceived during the construction period.

Another central church is the octagonal church in Store Heddinge, the only one remaining in Denmark, and presumably built during the end of Valdemar the Great's reign, about 1180. Later renovations and restorations have altered its appearance. Originally eight, massive interior columns supported a high, towerlike central section, and the high, two-storey square chancel is preserved up to the roof cornice. There is a clear relationship to a number of European court chapels, which all were derived from Karl the Great's sepulchre chapel in Aachen. The church originally was neighbour to a no longer existing manor estate.

Another unique example is Ledøje Church, built around 1225, of large medieval bricks with interior siding of granite slabs. The nave and chancel have square plans and are unusual in that they are two-storeys high and connected by an opening in the nave, supported by four granite columns with beautifully carved capitals and bases in Belgian marble. The church is no doubt built by a nobleman whose manor lay directly west of the tower, and who used the upper floor as his private chapel. A restoration by architect H.B. Storck 1887-88 was responsible for the present appearance, which is primarily based on a re-creation and free reconstruction. This applies to most of the upper floor.

22. *Ledøje Church, interior and plan 1:750.*

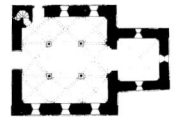

Below: **21.** *Store Heddinge Church.*

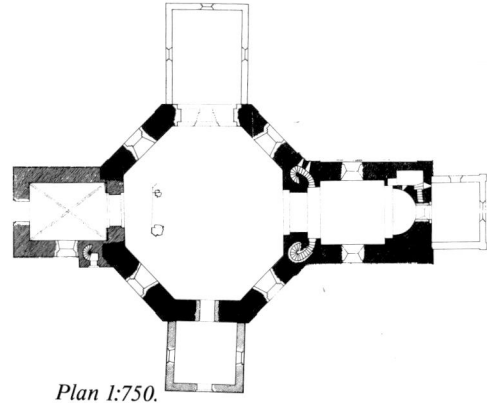

Plan 1:750.

23. Århus Cathedral, 1197-1479.

Århus Cathedral, started in 1197 by bishop Peder Vognsen, is Denmark's longest church. The oldest parts, toward east, are related to the old brick churches in Sorø, Ringsted and Roskilde. The original plan was a three-aisled basilica, with dominant transepts and a long nave, presumably terminated by an apse. On each of the transepts' east sides were three continuous chapels, the centre one with an apse, the two nearest the chancel were probably topped by towers. The main nave was considerably higher than the aisles, which originally must have had lean-to roofs, but later, perhaps inspired by a similar arrangement at Roskilde Cathedral, they were given pointed gables to appear as small chapels, each with its own pitched roof. At the west end, two towers were started, which protruded in front of the nave's west facade, however they were never completed. In the beginning of the 1400's, a renovation was started that radically altered the church's appearance. To the west, instead of the twin tower facade, a hugh tower flanked by sepulchre chapels was built. It was originally topped by a high, octagonal pyramidal spire. The nave and transept were increased in height and roofed with a vault. Most important of all, the chancel was enlarged to three aisles, with four bays along the chancel gallery, where the raised, high chancel is cut off from the gallery with a brick counter. Two slender, cylindrical stair towers were inserted in the corners, between the centre nave's three-sided east end and the aisles. Each bay in the aisles is marked on the facade by buttresses, independent gables and transverse pitched roofs. The thirteen, tall windows fill the space with light, and clearly convey the new interpretation of church architecture. The contrast to the Romanesque transept's east chapels is striking. The enthusiastic builder, bishop Jens Iversen Lange granted a new altarpiece to the new, high nave. This magnificent work was presented in 1479 by the Lubeck master, Bernt Notke.

23. *Århus Cathedral, the chancel. Bispetorvet/Store Torv, Århus.*

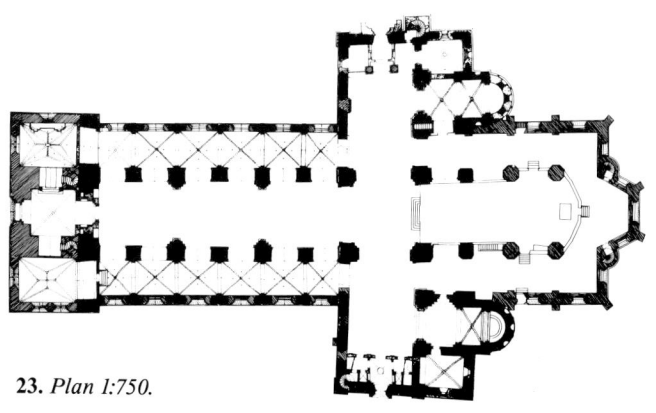

23. *Plan 1:750.*

24-26. Ribe Cathedral, Løgumkloster, Haderslev Cathedral, 1170-1420.

24. *Ribe Cathedral, Torvet.*
Plan and elevation 1:750.

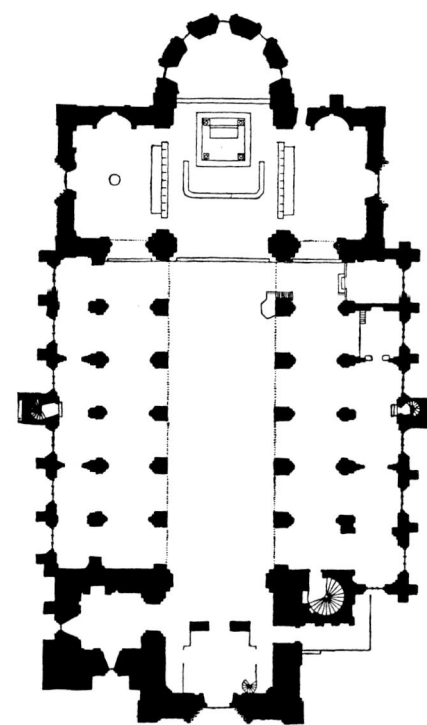

Ribe occupies an exceptional position among Denmark's medieval cities, due to its significant sea trade connections to England, Germany and Flanders. This had a great influence on the city's cathedral, whose inspiration comes from the lower Rhine area, as do the major building materials, volcanic tufa and trachyte, which are supplemented with local granite. This can be seen in the church's oldest parts toward east, which were presumably finished at the end of the 1170's. The other stage, the nave and the west front, consist mainly of brownish-red sandstone from Weser. Ribe has the most well-preserved, original character of all the Danish Romanesque cathedrals: the transept and apse without a connecting chancel, the tripartite nave with its triforium above the aisles, and to the west, a tower complex that seems to have been planned with a square central tower, flanked by stair towers. However, the present church room was built between 1225 and 1250 and included the vaulting of the nave and transepts. The dome over the crossing is unique in Nordic countries and was also added at this time. The almost two metre wide centre opening has unfortunately been blinded, but presumably admitted daylight from a roof lantern. The triple towers on the west front were never realized. Instead the large, brick "city's tower" or "Tocsin tower" was built between 1283 and 1333. The church used the lower floors for chapels and the city used the upper levels for the tocsin, archives and watchman's quarters. A tight row of chapels and porches were built along the outer walls, however during the late Middle Ages, they were joined as a sort of outer aisles. Centuries of disrepair were finally brought to an end with architect H.C. Amberg's restoration in 1882-1904. Although somewhat heavy-handed, he displayed a respect for the church's architectural history.

26. *Haderslev Cathedral, Torvet, Haderslev. The chancel. Plan 1:1000.*

Løgumkloster Church was built between 1225 and 1325 as the north wing of a large Cistercian monastery complex, very similar to the monastery in Sorø. The east end, with its windows framed by pilasters and arches, is a good example of the transition from Romanesque to Gothic forms, while the three, richly edged windows on the west end are pure Gothic. Besides the church, only a small portion of the monastery's east wing remains.

The cathedral in Haderslev was started in the middle of the thirteenth century as a large single-aisle cruciform church with chancel, transept with small chapels on the east side, and long nave, similar to Løgumkloster. Only the transept remains, due to the period of Gothic influence during which it was heightened and the nave widened to three aisles of almost the same height, all under one roof. In the beginning of the fifteenth century, the old chancel was replaced by a new three-aisle, three bay long chancel, that with its three, almost 16 metre high windows, fills the room with an impressive light. Of the few existing examples in Denmark, Haderslev is the oldest of these so-called "hall-churches", which are quite common in south Slesvig and along the German Baltic coast.

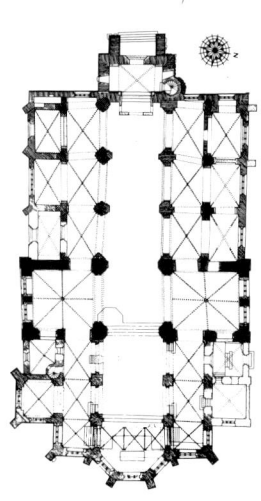

25. *Løgumkloster Church, Løgumkloster. Southern transept.*

27-31. Gothic churches, 1285-1521.

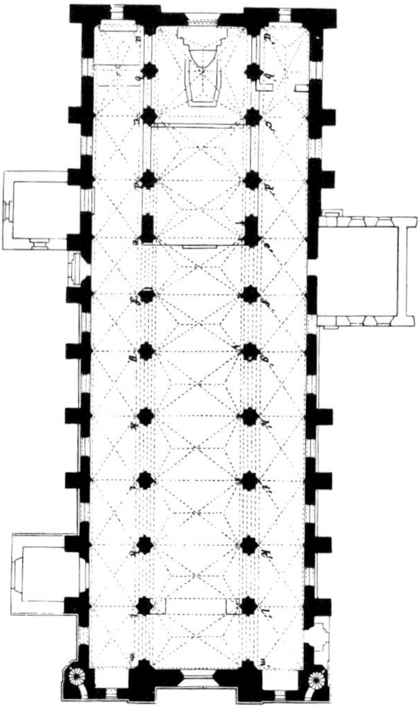

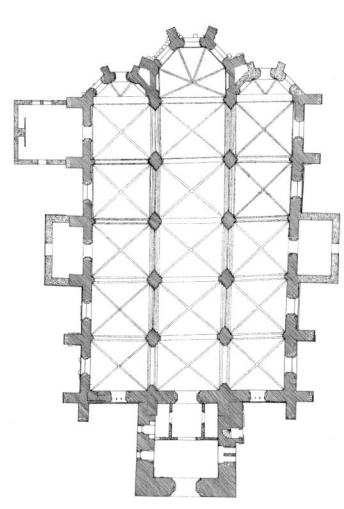

27. St. Knuds Church, St. Knuds Plads, Odense. Plan 1:750.

29. St. Mikkels Church, Slagelse. Plan 1:750.

The Gothic architectural ideals had their first major breakthrough in Denmark at St. Knuds brick cathedral in Odense. It was started by Bishop Gisico (1285-1301) as a replacement for an older limestone church, but was not completed until the end of the fifteenth century. The rectangular, three-aisle plan is simple and offers a striking contrast between the spartan exterior and the richly articulated interior. The mixture of pointed arches around the windows on the east and west ends are the most distinctive exterior motif, and reflect the narrow proportions of the nave, which are somewhat hidden by the partially completed tower from 1560. The interior is characterized by harmony and slender proportions, with a consequent use of pointed arches in all the structural elements, from arcades and triforium openings to the clerestory. All elements are richly profiled, and the height of the nave is emphasized by continuous vertical elements from which the stellar rib vaults emanate. The chancel is accentuated by a raised floor in the nave in the three eastern bays, above a crypt, an unusual feature in a gothic church, and probably a remnant from the older church.

28. *St. Olai Church, Helsingør.*

St. Olai Church, Helsingør's cathedral is an example of how an old, modest, town church was altered to a basilican cathedral. The original church was built about 1200-1250, and part of the north wall as well as the tower and trinity chapel have been preserved. The addition involved the east and south end, around the existing building, which was still in use. Work was started about 1475, but it was not until 1521 that a temporary consecration took place. The three-aisle plan can be compared to Køge, while the slender arcade bays of the chancel walls are unique.

St. Mikkel's church in Slagelse was started in the first decades of the fourteenth century and completed at the end of the same century. It has an interesting, short, broad plan with three aisles of approximately the same width with polygonal ends toward east. If the original plans had called for a hall church, something must have gone wrong during the construction phase. The nave is higher than the aisles and instead of windows, the upper nave walls were penetrated by triforiums which are now blinded, but originally opened to the aisle ceilings. The nave thus appears heavy and dark, only lit from the east by five slender, almost eight metre high windows in the chancel. The plan seems to imply that work was completed by a builder who was not familiar with the German Gothic traditions.

30. *St. Peders Church, Næstved.*

Many other provincial town churches were given grand extensions and additions, such as St. Peders Church in Næstved, which in 1375 was equipped with one of the most beautiful choir arrangements of the Gothic period, with strong influences from north Germany. St. Nicolai in Køge was rebuilt in 1375-1400 as a rather large, three-aisle, vaulted, long church with a straight east wall.

31. *St. Nicolai Church, Køge.*

32-33. Monasteries and monastery churches, 1410-1500.

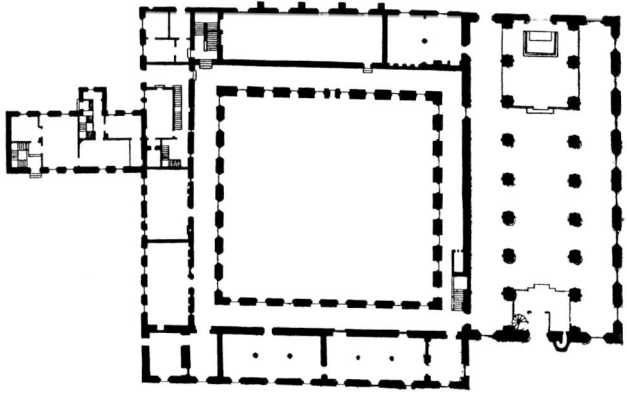

32. *Carmelite monastery and St. Maria Church, Helsingør.*

Chapter hall.

Plan 1:1500.

With the building of Krogen castle and the establishment of a toll for the use of Øresund strait in the 1420's, Helsingør also became an important religious centre. As early as 1430, the Carmelite monks, known as the white friars, established a church and a monastery here. The church was destroyed by fire twenty years later, and was rebuilt, together with the monastery wings, in the period up to the end of the century. The church is quite different from Denmark's other late Middle Age churches in that it has an unusual architectural simplicity. The plan consists of a long building divided up in eight vaulted bays, with a nave and two lower aisles gathered under one large tile roof crowned by a small ridge turret. The interior is lit primarily by the large windows in the end wall. The monastery lies in the other three wings surrounding the tranquil friar court. Here numerous beautiful rooms have been preserved, many covered by column-borne vaults, as the elegant capital hall. A somewhat heavy-handed restoration by H.B. Storck in 1900-1907 almost recreated the originally scheme. Despite this, it is still Denmark's most well-preserved monastery.

Another well-preserved monastery church is Maribo Cathedral, built as a church for the Bridgettine monastery in 1410-1470. The large, bright, ca 60 metre long hall church is divided in eight bays. The three, almost equally high aisles, are covered by loin and stellar rib vaults under a large roof. According to the precepts of the monastery, the chancel was located toward west above the crypt. Another unusual feature is the low arcade supported galleries along the aisle walls and east end, which separated the nuns from the monks and the congregation. Bridgettine monasteries housed both nuns and monks, strictly separated from each other, in buildings north and south of the church. Nothing above ground level remains of these monastery buildings.

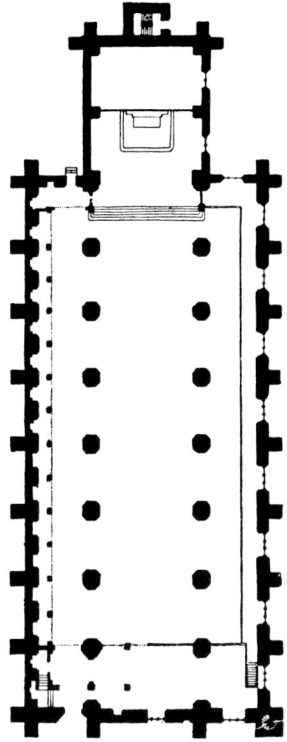

33. *Maribo Cathedral. Plan 1:750.*

33. *Maribo Cathedral, Klostergade, Maribo.*

34-39. Church frescos, 1100-1600.

The Danish church frescos represent a national art treasure of immeasurable value. Not that they are a special Danish phenomenon, but for various reasons, more of them are preserved than in most other countries. As with the architecture they complement, they represent an international art form whose ideals and motifs evoked a response in more or less local interpretations. These frescos appeared already in the very first stone churches, and as far as history reveals, most Middle Age churches were decorated with some form of imagery on the walls and vaulting. The earliest, from about 1100-1250, were done in the so-called Romanesque style, strongly inspired by Italian Byzantine mosaic art originating in the fifth and sixth centuries as in Ravenna. The paintings were often stiff and regular, with the enthroned God or Christ surrounded by evangelist symbols as the primary motif, often on a blue or green background and framed by meticulously painted ornaments. During the early Gothic transitional period, about 1250-1350, these figures became freer and more alive, almost always drawn on a white background with quick, light lines and not nearly as naturalistic as previously. The devil and fable animals began to appear. Only a few paintings from this period are preserved, as during the main Gothic period from 1350-1400, the church ceilings were given vaults. Because of this, new artistic possibilities arose and the curved, triangular severies were decorated with carefully drawn figures in bright clear colours on a white ground, while the ribs were decorated with profuse geometric patterns, also in bright colours. However more than half of the preserved frescos are from the late Gothic period, about 1400-1525. A characteristic trait for this period was the increasing throng of ornamentation and living creatures, which almost completely cover the painted surface in a so-called horror vacui effect. The choice of colours was limited to red, black, grey and an occasional green. Everyday episodes were often depicted in these holy pictures to indicate that they could also have taken place in ancient times. Besides the evangelist writings, the saints and their martyrologies are often depicted, sometimes as a whole series of pictures. After the reformation in 1536, the catholic saints disappeared in favor of old testament subjects and the jewish prophets, but otherwise, fresco painting continued throughout the Renaissance until about 1600. However the illustrated area densened and many details were hidden away like a puzzle picture. Throughout the seventeenth century, a change in attitude resulted in most of the Danish church interiors being whitewashed by the beginning of the nineteenth century.

37. Sulsted Church, north of Nørresundby, frescoes 1548.

38. Birkerød Church, Birkerød. High Gothic frescos. (1350-1400).

39. Viby Church near Kerteminde. Paintings ca 1625-50.

Opposite page, top: **34.** *Kjeldby Church, Møn. Frescoes from 1275, 1325 and 1480. Bottom left: 35. Hvorslev between Langå and Bjerringbro. Ca 1175; bottom right: 36. Østofte Church near Maribo. High Gothic frescos, ca 1400.*

40-42. Hammershus 1250-1400.

40. *Hammershus Castle ruins, near Hammerknuden, Bornholm.*

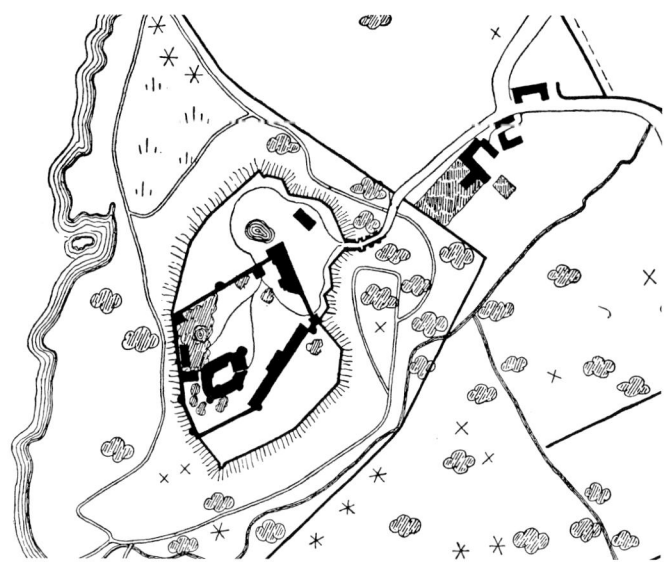

Plan 1:7.500.

High on a cliff top, about 74 metres over the sea, lies Hammershus, one of the largest Middle Age castle ruins in Northern Europe. The complex was presumably built in the 1250's by the archbishop of Lund, Sweden, Jacob Erlandsen, who occupied most of the island of Bornholm. Steep cliffs facing the sea and deep ravines toward north and south made the castle almost impregnable from this direction. The only approach was from the land side and during the late Middle Ages, a still preserved but heavily restored castle bridge was built, the only one remaining in Denmark. Along a paved castle road, through the barbican one is lead to the inner bailey and the keep, with its irregular rhomboid form and massive tower: the complex's oldest part. This tower served as a gate tower and residence, while the other rooms, like the chapel, kitchen, crew's quarters, etc. were distributed along the inner side of the ring wall on two levels. The inner bailey was surrounded by the enceinte, up against which, in the northeast corner, are the remains of the five storey storage building that housed the tariff products demanded from the island's peasants. Hammershus' military importance faded with the building of the Christiansø fortification in 1684.

Well-preserved remains of other fourteenth century castles can be found in Korsør, where the 23 metre high, red medieval brick tower keep was originally part of a no longer existing castle complex. Also in Vordingborg, where the round, seven-storey high Gåse tower is the only remaining part of the once so important Vordingborg Castle. In both cases, the existing roofs were added in the last century, they originally had parapet walls and flat roofs.

42. Gåsetårn fortress tower in Vordingborg.

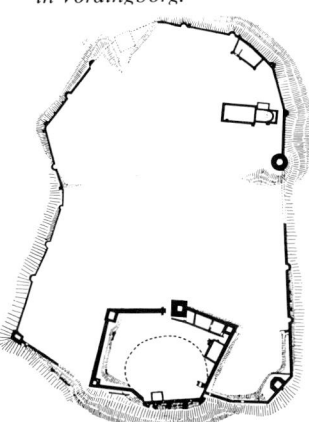

Right: **42.** *Vordingborg castle, plan 1:5000.*
41. *Tower keep in Korsør.*

43-44. Spøttrup and Dragsholm, 1250-1500.

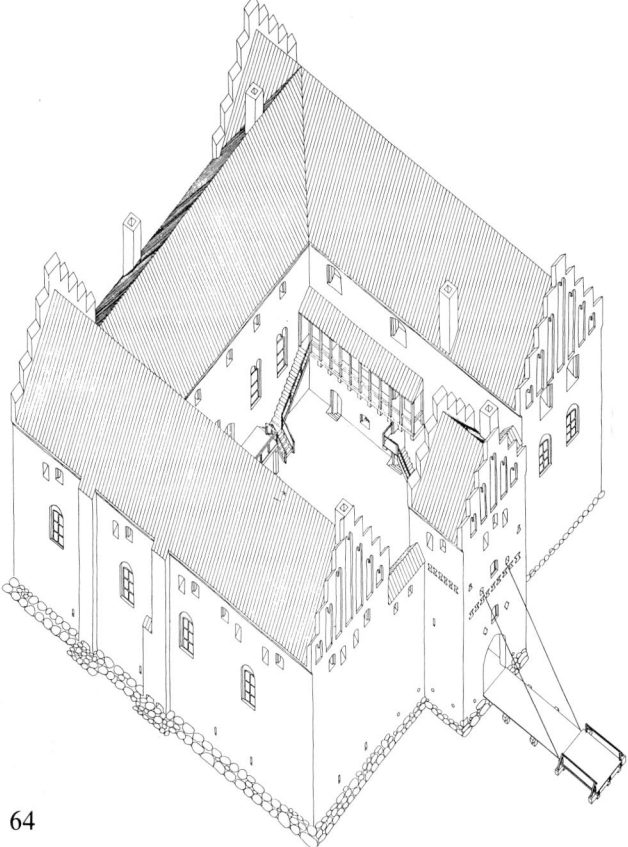

43. *Spøttrup castle near Rødding in Salling.*

Left: Reconstruction of Spøttrup app. 1500 by Mogens Vedsø. 1:600. From: »Bygningsarkæologiske studier 1986«.

Right: **44.** *Dragsholm castle, Sejrøbugten northeast of Kalundborg.*

One of the best examples of a Middle Age castle, protected by embankments and moats with a drawbridge as the only access, is Spøttrup, on Limfjord, south of Mors. The oldest part of the castle, the south wing, was built by the Viborg bishopric about 1450. The outer walls facing the moat were up to 1.75 metres thick. The east and north wings were added shortly after and the complex was completed by a gate house between two barrier walls to the west. All the wings had rib vaulted ground floors (only preserved in the east wing). In addition to the residence level there were galleries on the upper level with loopholes and machicolations. Access to the various levels was by exterior stairs and galleries. A modern convenience was the nine buttresslike toilet outlets, that mark the facades facing the moat. The western part of the north wing was set on fire under an attack during Grevens Fejde in 1534, and was later totally razed. Since then, this wing has been almost seven metres shorter than the north wing, and like the rest of the complex, subjected to numerous rebuilding efforts. A heavy-handed restoration between 1938-1941, by architects Mogens Clemmensen and Arne Nystrøm gave Spøttrup its present appearance as a Renaissance building that has been partially restored to its Middle Age appearance.

Even older than Spøttrup, is the Roskilde bishopric's castle, Dragsholm near Sejrø bay, northeast of Kalundborg. It consisted originally of two stone buildings to the south and east, connected in a right angle, and built sometime between 1200 and 1250. The south wing was the most important, with a large grand hall and a more utilitarian ground floor. Rebuilding work during the late Middle Ages resulted in a four-wing complex. The present baroque castle is the result of an extensive rebuilding during the 1690's.

45-47. Gjorslev, Tjele and Østrupgård, 1400-1550.

Top: **45.** *Gjorslev, manor estate, Stevns. Bottom:* **47.** *Østrupgård, Fyn.*

The wealthy, dynamic Roskilde bishop, Peder Jensen Lodehat, was also Queen Margrethe's chancellor and builder of the noteworthy Gjorslev castle. It is built of limestone and brick at the beginning of the 1400's. The four-winged plan is a Latin cross, with the long arm toward south. Above the crossing is a high, square tower, and the central space on the ground floor is roofed by a beautiful stellar ribbed vault. A great deal of the original building has been preserved, including the pillar hall in the north wing. But the narrow, spiral staircase in the tower wall became antiquated and a grand stairway in the east wing was built by the Dutch building master, Evert Janssen in 1665-67. By that time, the northern side wing in the inner bailey was built (rebuilt in 1713), and the southern wing followed in 1843, designed by architect G.F. Hetsch. Several of his beautiful interiors are also preserved.

The Tjele manor estate is an example of a smaller manor from the beginning of the sixteenth century. This somewhat irregular complex consisted of a two-storey stone building with a vaulted cellar to the south, an east wing, built later, with a kitchen and pantry, and along the north wall, a high two storey stone building as well as a large square tower to the east. Today the appearance of the complex is dominated by rebuilding work carried out after 1800.

Østrupgård on Funen is from the same period, with a heavy, two-storey building of field stone surrounded by one-story, half-timber-framed wings. However, the present scheme is of a much more recent date.

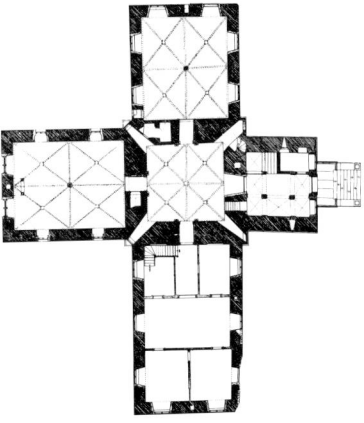

Above: **45.** *Plan of Gjorslev, 1:750.*

46. *Tjele, manor estate near Viborg.*

48-49. Hesselagergård and Rygård, 1530-1538.

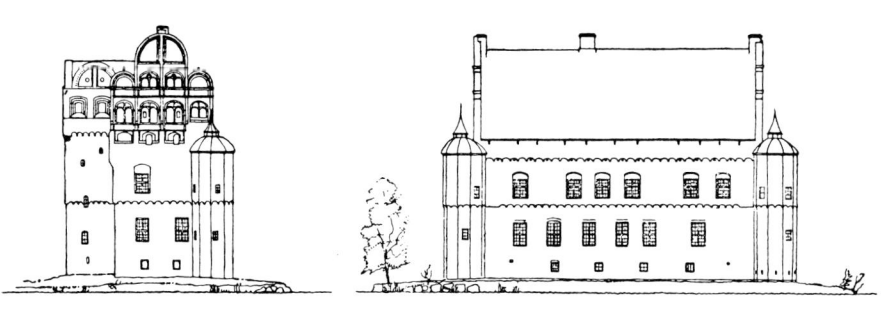

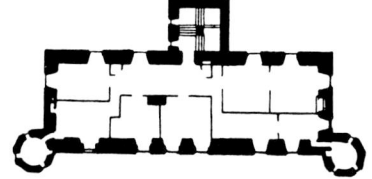

48. *Hesselagergård, manor estate, Hesselager on Fyn.*

Plan and elevations 1:750.

The end of the reformation in 1536 saw the end of the church's power, and the nobility began to dominate the political and economical scene. The period of agricultural prosperity led to a large number of manor estates being built, and in 1538, one of the kingdom's richest men, chancellor Johan Friis, built one of the most distinguished, Hesselagergård on Funen. What began as a Middle Age long house, was altered during construction to a Renaissance building, where the new architectural ideals were realized, though primarily in the detailing and decoration. The defence measures of the past were still quite pertinent, with moats and a drawbridge. Their was nothing very innovative about the plan which consisted of a vaulted cellar under the living quarters with a grand hall above, and a gallery on top with protruding hoarding on the long sides.

Hesselagergård was given corner towers at the northern end and a large square tower in the middle of the south facade with a wide, brick stairway that connected all the floors, and richly embellished gables, that with their tripartite, arched tops seem to have a clear Italian inspiration, most probably San Zaccaria church in Venice. A thorough restoration was carried out in 1904-05 by architect Helge Boysen Møller. This was followed by interior improvements in 1951 by architect Hans Henrik Engqvist.

On Funen, one can also find Rygård, a small four-winged complex on a low islet, which is now connected with the mainland. It was built about 1530 for the knighted Johan Urne, with the north wing being the oldest part. The interior of this wing was quite similar to Hesselagergård. All the gables are stepped and have high bricked blindings, which can also be seen on many of the church towers that were added to the Romanesque village churches during the same period.

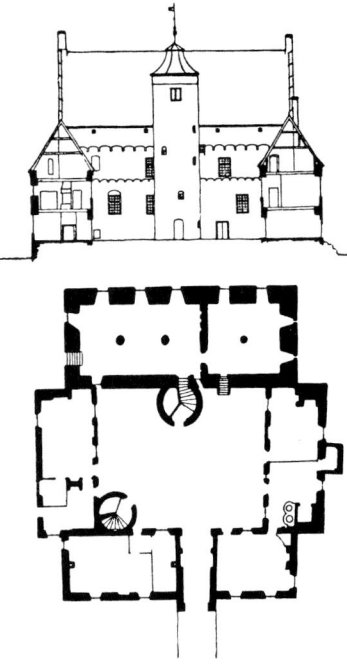

49. *Rygård on Fyn.*
Plan and section 1:750.

49. *Rygård on Fyn.*

50-51. Egeskov and Nyborg castles, 1549-50.

50. *Egeskov on Fyn.*

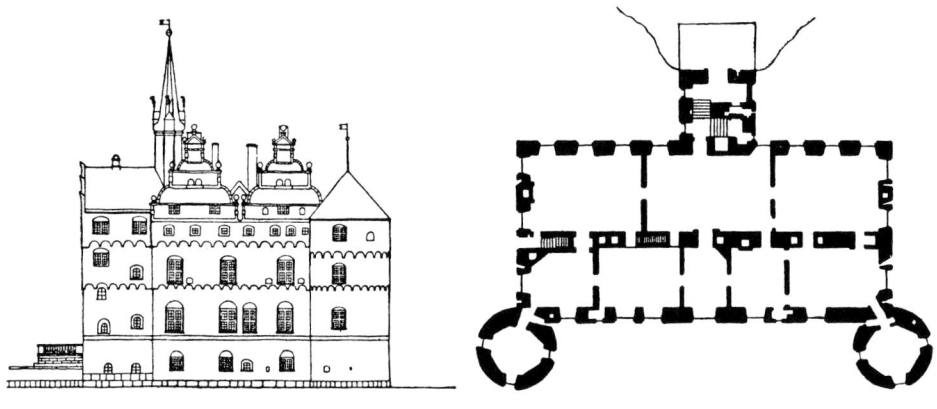

50. *Plan and elevation of the original south facade, 1:750.*

A similar architecture as the castles at Hesselagergård, Nakkebølle and Borreby can be seen in the Funen castle, Egeskov, built in 1550 for the Lord High, Frands Brockenhuus. It is still surrounded by water, and was built on piles and solid granite boulder foundations. The placement of the round corner towers and the square stair tower on the west side, as well as the protruding corbelled bands that mark each level are all common features of these castles. But where the others are comparatively small, Egeskov is built with double wings, side by side. This is evident in the double gable toward north and south, and the two parallel series of rooms, which allowed a much more differentiated plan than usual. The vertical division of functions from basement to the gallery was as earlier, but otherwise the castle was exceptionally well-equipped with fireplaces in all living areas and toilet drains from all rooms. The fortifications at Egeskov were also noteworthy, with a drawbridge in the stair tower and machicolations for the dispersal of solids and liquids down on attackers, as well as numerous embrasures. A very heavy-handed restoration was carried out in 1883-84 by the Swedish architect, Helgo Zettervall. Later restorations and renovations were supervised by architects H. Lønborg Jensen (1927-28) and Peter Koch (about 1962). The garden is laid out in a French style with magnificent trimmed hedges and is believed to be from the 1730's.

Frands Brockenhuus was the lord lieutenant at Nyborg Castle and its location on the Store Bælt strait required constant defence measures. The oldest part is from just after 1200, and still exists in the preserved north wing, which Christian III remodelled as a living quarters in 1549. A heavy state of disrepair ended with architect Mogens Clemmensen's extensive restoration in 1917-23, based on meticulous archaeological surveys.

51. *Nyborg castle, Slotsgade, Nyborg.*
Plan 1:1800. Reconstruction. Not correct.

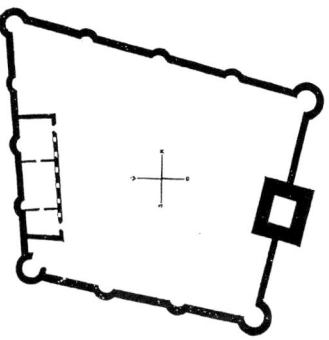

50. *The garden at Egeskov.*

52-54. Borreby, Vallø, Gisselfeld, 1547-1586.

52. *Borreby near Skælskør.*

Right: 53. *Vallø Stifts Adelige Jomfrukloster, Vallø.*

The influential and extremely wealthy chancellor, Johan Friis, who built Hesselagergård, also built the manor estate and castle, Borreby near Skelskør, which according to a sandstone plaque on the south side of the stair tower, was built in 1556. The building is somewhat larger, but the scheme is basically the same: A long building with a stair tower on the south side and corner towers on the north side, which in this case is square. Another square tower was added on this side, unusually asymmetric as is the stair tower to the south, which is strange as Renaissance architectural ideals cultivated order and symmetry. There is however a certain degree of order in the placement of the windows above each other, all topped by a flat, moulded elliptical arch, and the well-known corbel bands between the levels. The defence loft protrudes in a very pronounced fashion and is equipped with embrasures and machicolations. The corbel bands here are of hewn stone. The facade details were the subject of a great deal of attention, with moulded bands and white stuccoed closures over the windows and under all the corbel bands. In addition to this, a square, brick house from Johan Friis' time has been preserved, with stepped gables in the courtyard, the so-called "Tinghus". Both the main building and the courtyard lie on an islet, surrounded by a moat. Borreby was restored for the first time in 1884 by professor Mejborg, but the worst disfigurations were somewhat righted in 1924 by architect Mogens Clemmensen.

Gisselfeld, near Rønnede was built over a long period from 1547 to 1575, by seneschal, Peder Oxe. The 2-storey entrance wing was built first, followed by the two parallel wings at right angles to this, all gables elegantly decorated with blindings. The main building was rebuilt during the 1870's by J.D. Herholdt, and later restored by Martin Borch (completed in 1915).

Vallø, south of Køge has a long and complicated building history that goes back to the late Middle Ages, however the south wing with its portal, and the two large towers as well as part of the west wing were built in 1586 by Mette Rosenkrantz, wife of Peder Oxe. Later additions and increases in height respected the original style, until architect Lauritz de Thurah in 1735-38 built the east wing, "The white monastery". The entire castle burned in 1893 and was later rebuilt as close to the original as possible by architect Hans J. Holm.

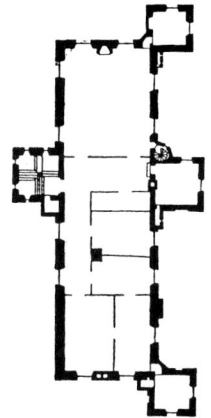

52. *Plan of Borreby, 1:750.*

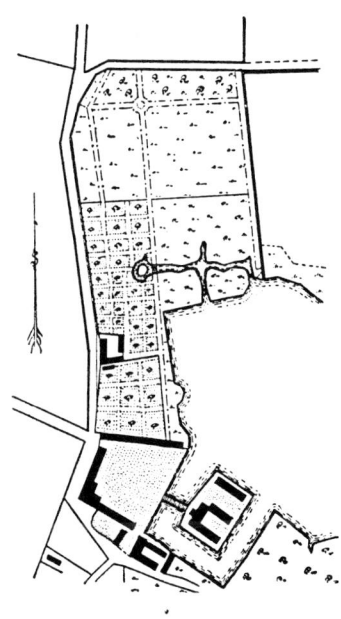

54. *Gisselfeld, manor estate near Rønnede. Site plan ca 1800. Ca 1:5500.*

55-57. Voergård, Rosenholm, Gammel Estrup, 1500-1580.

55. *Voergård, Vendsyssel.*
Left: The portal.

Voergård in Vendsyssel, between Dronninglund and Sæby, was built as a single-winged manor about 1520 by the notorious bishop Stygge Krumpen, on a castle motte surround by a moat. The concept was not unusual, with two storeys over a vaulted cellar, topped by a gallery with embrasures. Later renovation left little remaining of the original building, and today the castle is dominated by the east wing, which was added in 1586-91 by the wealthy widow, Ingeborg Skeel. This wing has two octagonal corner towers toward east and two stair towers facing the courtyard on the west, as well as unusually refined sandstone ornamentation around the portal and the window pilasters. The identity of the master builder is uncertain but the Dutchman, Philip Brandin has been mentioned. The north and east wings have been restored several times, most recently in 1955-60.

56. Rosenholm, manor estate.

Rosenholm, which lies between Århus and Randers, appears today as a closed, four-winged Renaissance scheme. However, the main wing originally stood by itself, built by Jørgen Rosenkrantz during the 1560's, with two storeys over a cellar and two round corner towers facing the moat. The middle section of the courtyard facade was originally planned with open, pilaster ornamented arcades. The formal, symmetrical entrance wing lying opposite, with its towerlike pavilions at the ends, was built about 1580, and the lower side wings shortly after. This was the first time the pavilion motif was used in Denmark, inspired no doubt by the French Renaissance castles.

56. Rosenholm. Plan 1:1500.

Nearby, east of Randers, lies the old Gammel Estrup manor estate, which was built about 1500 as a four-winged scheme, surrounded by water. The late Middle Age buildings were subject to a major renovation in the beginning of the seventeenth century, at which time a new south wing was added, the west wing was increased in height, and a new portal was added as well as corner towers and a stair tower. The present north wing was built in 1749. Today Gammel Estrup serves as a manor estate museum.

57. Gammel Estrup, manor estate.

58-60. Brick town houses, 1460-1579.

58. Helsingør. Stengade 72-76.

58. Helsingør. Stengade 66, Oxernes Gård.

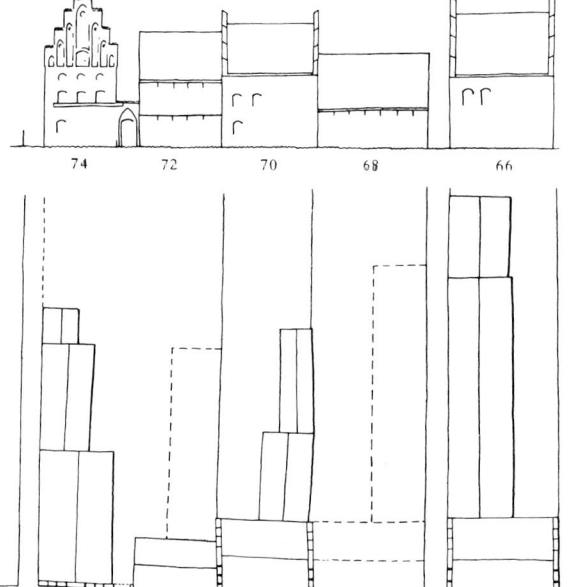

58. Helsingør. Reconstruction of houses on Stengade Nos. 66-74 before 1550. 1:750.

The oldest towns in Denmark consisted of free-standing, half-timber single family dwellings. After the introduction of fired brick, the wealthier citizens began building town houses in brick, as they were more fire-resistant, and were often tax exempt for the first ten years. This was true in Helsingør, where the income from the Øresund strait toll was the basis for numerous gabled houses in brick, built during the period around 1500. Some good examples of these can be found on Stengade, where No. 66, Oxernes Gård was built in 1459 and later rebuilt and renovated several times. Nos. 72-76 were built in 1551, 1500 and 1579. No. 74 has a refined stepped gable with pointed arches and circular blinds, similar to the gable on Oxernes Gård, as well as a limestone band between the first and second floors that bears an excerpt from the Bible in Gothic script. No. 76 also has a Gothic, stepped gable, but the sandstone window mullions and the triangular pediments have an air of Dutch Renaissance about them, which was also true in Frederik II's renovation of Kronborg from the same period. To the rear of the front buildings are typical Middle Age courtyard surroundings, where the narrow deep lots are built with side buildings, end to end, running down toward the harbour. Nos. 72-74 were extensively restored in 1932-36 by architect Volmar Drosted.

In 1484, south of St. Peders church in Næstved, Mayor Mogens Tuesen built a brick wing with seven connected dwellings, separated by half-timber walls, each with three bays and a cellar. Because of the sloping site, the cellars appear as ground level storeys toward south. At present the buildings are used by Næstved Museum for exhibitions.

The House of the Holy Spirit in Randers is about the same age and is presumably a remanent from the local Holy Spirit monastery, built prior to 1500 in red brick on a granite foundation. Both storeys and the basement have flat beamed ceilings, while the windows and doors have flat arches. The gables are stepped. The interior still has the remains of the original wall decorations. A restoration in 1894-97 by architect Hack Kampmann is a talented one, but has a number of romanticizing elements.

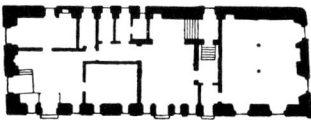

60. *Randers. Helligåndshuset. Plan and elevation 1:750.*

59. *Næstved. Dwellings near St. Peders Church. Plan and elevation 1:750.*

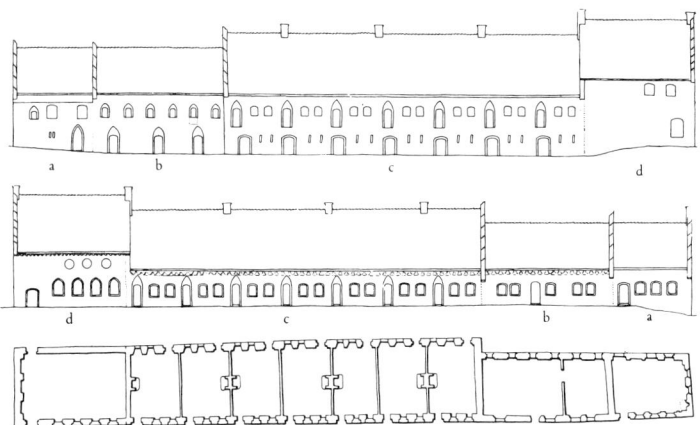

61. Kronborg, 1410-1590.

61. *Kronborg Castle, Helsingør. Below: Great hall.*

The introduction of Øresund strait toll was brought about by Erik of Pommern, who saw it as a effective means of filling the king's private treasury. Therefore, about 1410 he built the Krogen castle, north of Helsingør, on a point at the narrowest part of the strait, opposite the older Kärnan castle. The plan was an enormous square, about 80 x 80 metres, and the ring wall was as much as three metres thick. In each corner of the courtyard, against the wall, four buildings were built, of which the two-storey palace with a vaulted cellar in the southwest corner, was the most elegant. On the lower level was a large hall, which has been partly preserved. It had six stellar ribbed vaults and was lit by six high windows facing the courtyard. In the northeast corner, just inside the gate, lived the king in a three-storey building, of which his study with wooden columns and fresco remains can still be seen. In 1574, Frederik II, summoned the authoritative Flemish master builder, Hans van Paeschen, to lead an extensive rebuilding, not only to improve the fortifications but also to create a magnificent new castle. The north, south and west wings were totally altered and the bastions were rebuilt including the still existing Mørkeport gate. Disagreements led to the replacement of the building supervisor in 1577 by another Flemish master builder, Antonius van Opbergen, who with the help of the artists and craftsmen that accompanied him, managed to complete the castle within the following ten years. It was given the name, Kronborg. During the building period, decisions were made to cover the facades with Scanian sandstone, from what is now south Sweden. It was a excellent choice, both in terms of color and character and made a handsome accompaniment to the green copper roofing. The horizontal band on the facade and the heavy cornice frieze accent the horizontal effect, which is balanced by the four different corner towers and the bell tower. The rich sculptural work helps to complete the picture of one of Denmark's best preserved examples of Dutch Renaissance. The castle was heavily damaged during a fire in 1629, but was faithfully rebuilt. It suffered even more during the period from 1785 until about 1900 when it was used as barracks. This required an extensive interior restoration between 1924-29, which was carried out by architect J. Magdahl Nielsen.

Rusticated east wing facade facing the court-yard.

North wing.

Mørkeport.

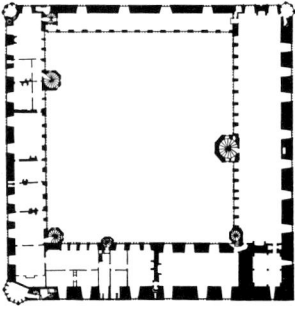

Plan 1:2000.

62. Frederiksborg Castle, 1560-1630.

Frederiksborg Castle in Hillerød had its beginnings as a Middle Age manor estate, Hillerødsholm, which Frederik II obtained in 1560. The previous owner, Herluf Trolle, was in the process of erecting several new buildings, which the king continued work with. However his son, Christian IV, had much greater plans and started from scratch with a magnificent castle that was to outshine anything ever built in the Nordic countries. This extensive complex is built on three islets on the west side of the castle lake, and the main entrance is still, as earlier, over a bridge from the main street to the southernmost islet. Over this bridge runs a road with stables and servant's housing on both sides, built during Frederik II's reign. The road ends in a S-shaped bridge, with access to a large gate tower on the middle islet. Here start Christian IV's buildings, and through the gate one comes in to the outer courtyard, built in 1613-23, which, together with the castle, is arranged on the basis of a regular, symmetric plan. The sides are marked by parallel, two-storey wings with stair towers. In the centre of the court lies the elegant Neptune fountain, a copy of the original. On the northernmost islet, lies the three-winged main castle with an inner palace courtyard, which opens to the outer court, separated only by a low terrace and a bridge over the canal. The building of this part of the scheme was started in 1602, and first completed during the 1620's, with Hans Steenwinckel the Younger as the final architect. Before this, in 1613, a sculpture decorated gate house was built by the edge of the lake, connected with the castle's north wing by a two-storey secret passage, supported by arches across the moat. This building, which served as an audience chamber, is built of grey sandstone like the passageway, as opposed to the rest of the castle, which is of red brick with sandstone decorations. The interior of Frederiksborg Castle was magnificently furnished, but unfortunately everything except the palace church was lost in a ferocious fire in 1859. Between 1860 and 1875 the castle was rebuilt by architect Ferdinand Meldahl on the basis of old surveys. It was established as a national history museum under the endowment of brewer J.C. Jacobsen.

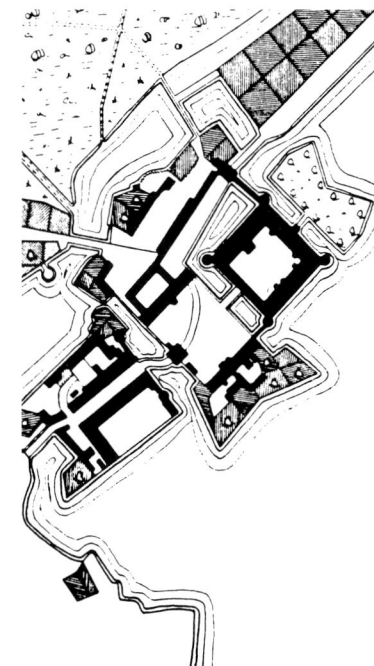

62. *Hillerød, Slotsgade Frederiksborg castle. Site plan 1809. Ca 1:6000.*

Opposite page: Chapel interior.

Frederiksborg castle, left in photo, Gate tower, right: Audience hall.

63. Rosenborg Castle, 1606-1634.

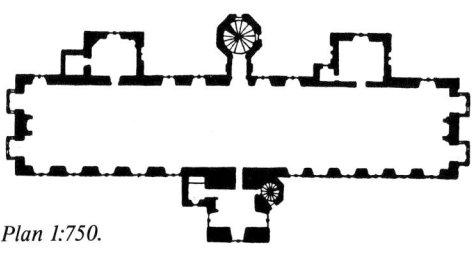

63. *Copenhagen. Rosenborg castle, Øster Voldgade 4A, Copenhagen.*

Plan 1:750.

In 1606, Christian IV purchased several properties outside the Copenhagen's North Rampart and began laying out the Kongens Have park, a breathing hole to counterbalance the old, somewhat closed in, Copenhagen Castle. At the same time, the erection of a small pleasure palace was started in the park. It was two storeys high and about half as long as the existing Rosenborg Castle. In 1613-15, it was expanded to its present length, and a 50 metre high tower was added to the west side several years later. The east side was outfitted with two smaller towers, of which the southernmost was a rebuilding. It wasn't until 1633-34, that the east facade was completed with a free-standing, octagonal stair tower, connected to the main building by a short gallery with sandstone ornamentation, possibly with Hans Steenwinckel the Younger as architect. Despite the fact that no final plan existed when building work started, the result is a fine, coherent building, whose architect is unknown. However the king, himself had a great influence on the design and its relationship to the somewhat older Frederiksborg Castle is quite evident, even in the detailing. The king and queen's privy chambers were on the ground floor, and the plan is still basically the same, with the king's rooms, almost untouched at the north end. The first floor was later totally rebuilt. The entire second floor houses a magnificent great hall, with the original fireplaces and an elegant stucco ceiling from 1706-07. An extensive restoration, after 1866, was carried out by architect Ferdinand Meldahl, where most of the weathered sandstone ornamentation was replaced. Since the 1830's, the slot has served as a museum for the Danish throne's historical collection.

The Marbled Room, 1660's.

Great hall with king Chr. V's gobelins. old photo.

64-66. Christian IV's expansion of Copenhagen, 1599-1643.

64. *Copenhagen. Børsen. Christiansborg Palace Square.*

65. *Copenhagen. Provision Yard. drawing by J. D. Herholdt, 1850's.*

Trade expansion was one of Christian IV's most active interests. A result of this, is the Stock Exchange building on Christiansborg Palace Square, built in 1619-20 on one of the king's embankments that extended out to Knippelsbro bridge, built at the same time. Also here, the king took active part in the building work, even though he had commissioned the architect brothers, Lorenz and Hans van Steenwinckel the Younger. The Stock Exchange was built as a trading hall with shops and offices on the upper floor, with access from the ends. There were warehouses on the lower level. The canal facade's dormers and the famous dragon spire were added in 1624-25, while the east end was not completed until 1640. In 1857, the building was converted to a modern exchange by architect H.C. Stilling, and somewhat later, the yellow, red-burnished brick facade was sided with a thin, dark red brick tile. The weathered sandstone ornamentation was renewed in 1902-06.

As early as 1599-1605, Christian IV had enriched the Slotsholm area with an imposing arsenal complex surrounding a square harbour basin, where warships could sail in to load provisions, weapons and ammunition. The Provision Yard near the northeast dock and the Tøjhus (armoury) by the southwest dock, still exist, the later serving as a weapons museum. The filled up harbour basin, now serves as a garden for the Royal Library, built by Hans J. Holm in 1898-1906, as a closing wing facing the harbour.

Across from the Stock Exchange, on the shipyard island, Holmen, lay an anchor smithy, built by Frederik II. In 1619, Christian IV converted it to a navy seamen's church, though he preserved the fine Renaissance gable facing the canal. Later it was enlarged to a cruciform plan in 1641-43. The long chapel along the canal was built in 1705-08 by architect J.C. Ernst. Holmens Church is the only church that was spared by the great Copenhagen fires and thus has its original interior.

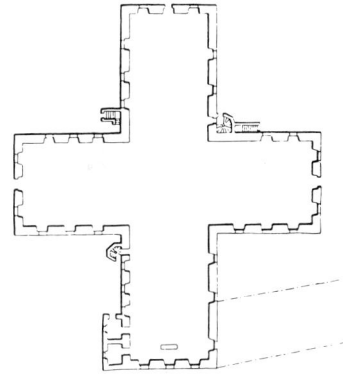

66. *Copenhagen. Holmens Church. Plan ca 1:1100.*

66. *Copenhagen. Holmens Church.*

67-68. Round Tower and Trinitatis Church, Nyboder, 1631-1656.

67. Trinitatis Church. Interior.

67. Round Tower seen from Købmagergade.

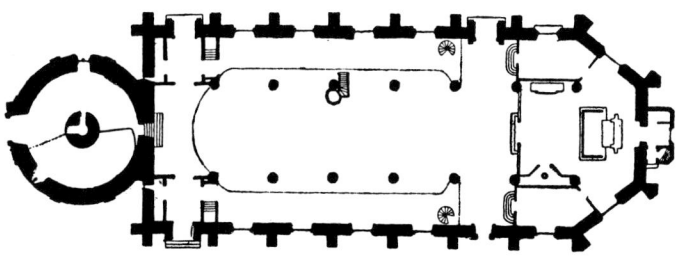

67. Copenhagen. Round Tower and Trinitatis Church, Købmagergade. Plan 1:750.

Above: Attic over Trinitatis Church, now used for exhibitions.
Left: Access is from the Round Tower's spiral ramp.

This building is one of the most unusual of all Christian IV's many enterprises, and it combines three quite different functions: a church, the library in the church attic, and an astronomical observatory in the tower, all associated with the University. The tower was built in 1637-42, while the church was not completed until 1656. Architecturally speaking, the building is heavier and less decorated than the king's earlier works. The most characteristic features are the alternate courses of red and yellow brick, the tower's massive cylindrical form and the uniformly placed double windows. The architect is believed to have been Hans van Steenwinckel the Younger, although the king had an important part in the decision making. An especially outstanding feature is the tower's spiral ramp, which gives access to both the church attic and the observatory. It was an original idea, even though a similar ramp at the Varberg fortress in Sweden may have served as an inspiration. The tower was used as an observatory until 1861, and has been recently rebuilt again for that purpose. The church's buttresses, pointed arches, high windows and three-sided chancel indicate clear Gothic roots. The bright, spacious interior has three aisles. However the furnishings are from the period just after the great Copenhagen fire of 1728, in which both the church and the University library in the attic were destroyed.

Architect Lauritz de Thurah (1706-59) is buried in the nave.

The Nyboder quarter was built as staff quarters for navy personnel and their families in the years after 1631. It was later rebuilt and has been drastically altered on several occasions, thus only one block remains in a somewhat original form, Skt. Paulsgade 20-40.

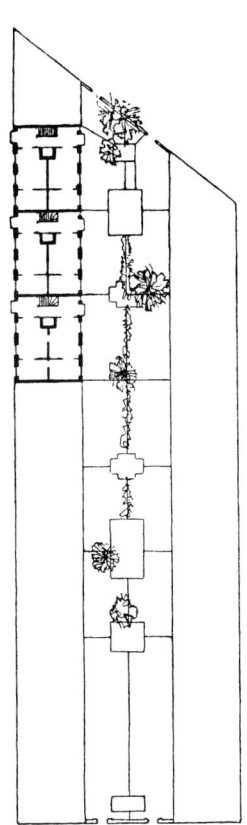

68. *Nyboder. Plan of houses on Hjertensfrydsgade, 1:750.*

68. *Nyboder, the oldest part, St. Poulsgade 20-40.*

69. Gentry houses in Ribe, 1525-1650.

69. *Aerial view of Medieval Ribe.*

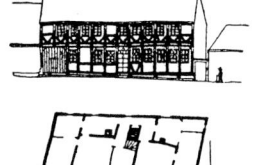

Kapellangården, Præstegade 15, plan and elevation 1:750.

Quedens house, Storegade 10. City museum (Bymuseet). (Bymuseet).

Ribe is one of Denmark's oldest towns. As early as 860, Ansgar was given permission to build a church here. Today, the town is mostly characterized by works from the sixteenth and seventeenth century. Many of the old buildings were built just after the last great town fire in 1580. However a few are older, such as the brick buildings, Tårnborg on Puggårdsgade 3-5, and Puggård on Puggårdsgade 22, as well as the Town Hall, which was created by connecting two old brick tenement buildings in 1528. There are more preserved half-timber buildings in Ribe than in any other town in Denmark, and the ancient town pattern with deep, closely built gable houses, separated only by small courts and eave-drip spaces, can still be found many places behind the later modernized front buildings. Good examples of houses with bracketed, overhanging storeys can be found at Nederdammen 28, from about 1650, Fiskergade 5/Skomagerslippe, from about 1550, and Sønderportsgade 37, built about 1650. Other buildings have lost their gables under rebuilding, but retained the gable house structure. This is true of Quedens Gård, Overdammen (Storegade) 10, from 1583, which is now the town museum, Grønnegade 12 built between 1525 and 1550, Sønderportsgade 17/Puggårdsgade from about 1600 and the fine gable-house court behind Mellemdammen 16 and 18, from the last half of the sixteenth century. The long houses are also represented, such as the richly ornamented Sønderportsgade 21, Kapellangården Præstegade 15, as well as a number of dwellings on the same street, Nos. 20-26 and 19-27, from about 1630, with No. 19 and 27 as the best preserved. In addition to this, Ribe has a conspicuous number of classicistic brick gentry houses from the turn of the nineteenth century, some of which are older, rebuilt Renaissance buildings.

Sønderportsgade 21.

Storegade (Mellemdammen) 18.

Grønnegade 12. Ribe's oldest half-timber house.

Sønderportsgade 37.

70-72. Gentry houses in Køge, Kalundborg and Kolding, 1527-1681.

Left: **70.** *Køge. Smedegården, Store Kirkestræde 13; right:* **70.** *Køge. Store Kirkestræde 20.*

Left: **70.** *Køge. Nørregade 31. Detail; right:* **70.** *Køge. Nørregade 4, Køge Museum.*

70. *Køge. Garvergården, Vestergade 7. Detail.*

71. *Kalundborg. Adelgade 17-19.*

90

Køge was laid out about 1200 on the basis of a clear and simple plan with Pomeranian origins, and by the Middle Ages it was already established as an enterprising town. It can boast of Denmark's oldest, dated half-timber building, the little house at Store Kirkestræde 20 from 1527. However Smedegården on Store Kirkestræde 13 from the last half of the 1500's, with the only preserved and functioning porch stone in Denmark is also extraordinary. Besides this, there are several well-preserved Renaissance buildings from the early 1600's, such as Nørregade 4 from 1610-19, which now houses Køge Museum, Nørregade 31 built between 1612 and 1615, Brogade 16 from 1636, the elegantly decorated Garvergården on Vestergade 7 from about 1600, as well as the more recent Vestergade 16 from 1644.

Kalundborg not only has a number of late Middle Age brick buildings, but also many half-timber houses from the seventeenth century. Other noteworthy buildings are the two connected houses on Adelgade 17-19 from the early 1600's, also the connected houses on Lindegade 1-3 from 1681, and the Adelgade wing of Lindegården, from the same period, now used as Kalundborg Museum.

As late as 120 years ago, Kolding had a huge number of sixteenth and seventeenth century half-timber buildings, which no longer exist. However one can still enjoy the unusually opulent gable facade on the chemist Reimingk's Gård at Akseltorv 2 from 1595, which is perhaps Denmark's most elegant, and the gable building at Helligkorsgade 18, built in 1589.

72. *Kolding. Helligkorsgade 18.*

72. *Kolding. Apoteker Reimingks Gård, Akseltorv 2.*

73-77. Gentry houses in Aalborg and Copenhagen, 1616-1681.

73. *Aalborg. Jens Bangs Stenhus, Østerågade 9.*

Right: 76. *Copenhagen. Amagertorv 6.*

74. *Aalborg. Aalborg manor.*

Up until the last century, Aalborg was Denmark's second largest city and a fine example of a well-preserved provincial town as they appeared during the sixteenth and seventeenth centuries. Street modifications and extensive building demolition have radically altered the city, yet there are still a number of older buildings worth mentioning. The grandiose, richly decorated brick house, Jens Bangs Stenhus on Østergade 9 from 1623-24, which was extensively restored in 1917-19 is a good example as is Østergade 25 from 1616, where only the facade is brick, and the neighbouring, three-storey building, No. 23 (about 1600), which is one of Denmark's largest half-timber buildings. Aalborg manor, the only lord lieutenant's manor left in Denmark has retained its fine half-timber construction facing the courtyard, which is primarily due to rebuilding work during the time of Christian IV.

In 1616, Mayor Mathias Hansen built his large, magnificent house at Amagertorv 6 in Copenhagen. With its festive, sweeping gables and rich sandstone ornaments, it was one of the leading examples of a Dutch Renaissance inspired gentry house, which by happenstance is one of the few remaining. On Strandgade 30-32, in the Christianshavn quarter, a major part of the two identical, brick buildings built between 1624 and 1636 has been preserved. The sweeping gables were removed long ago, and an extra storey has been added to No. 32. No. 28 is all that remains of three identical gable houses from 1626, and No. 14 was built with a sweeping gable in about 1650. Magstræde 17-19 is also one of the rare examples of the gentry houses from the period around 1640. The little blue gable dormer house at Nyhavn 9, built in 1681 has also retained its original appearance.

75. *Copenhagen. Strandgade 28 (right) and 30.*

75. *Copenhagen. Strandgade 14.*

Below: 77. *Copenhagen. Nyhavn 9.*

78. The Old Town in Århus, 1597-1816.

78. *The Old Town in Århus. Left: The old Borgmestergård.*

78. *The Old Town in Århus. Prospect by the canal.*

As opposed to other open-air museums, the Old Town in Århus is Denmark's only building museum for town houses. It's origins were based on the Gamle Borgmestergård from 1597, which was acquired for the National exhibition in Århus in 1909. It was originally located on the corner of Lille Torv and Immervad and its relocation to the exhibition area saved it from demolition. Here it became the basis for a historical exhibition. With support from public and private funds it was moved in 1913 to the Jyske Horticultural Society's Garden on Viborgvej. It was here in the years that followed that the town museum developed. The purpose was not only to be a collection of market town houses, but also to illustrate the market town concept. The museum's architect, S.F. Kühnel, in collaboration with Hugo Matthiessen from the National Museum, worked out a historical building plan for the area and the future complex. In addition, emphasis was placed on exhibiting homes from the different social levels and demonstrating the framework of the old, traditional trades such as printing works, dyeworks, hatmaking, tobacco factory, cobbler, miller, etc. There are now more than 50 buildings at The Old Town, most of them from market towns in Jutland, however one of the most recent is Helsingør's old theatre building from 1816. The market town milieu is very realistic and new additions are still being made.

79-81. Open-air museums 1500-1850.

By Kongevejen in Lyngby, on an area next to the old Agricultural Museum, part of Lyngby's Agricultural School, an open-air museum was opened in 1901. The purpose of this museum, which is a section of the National Museum, is to illustrate country life in the old days. This is primarily accomplished by disassembling and relocating old buildings from various areas of Denmark, also from regions that are no longer part of the kingdom of Denmark. The buildings are equipped with furnishings and household utensils, to give a realistic impression of the housing and living conditions in the various geographic areas and at the different social levels that prevailed in the old Danish farming society. Today, the 35 hectare museum park has about 50 different buildings, the oldest are from the middle of the seventeenth century, and the most recent from the middle of the last century. The placement of the buildings and their immediate surroundings attempt to reflect the original, typical regional conditions. In the course of a few hours, one can visit buildings as diverse as a grass-roofed farm from the Faroe Islands, a twin farm from Skåne Sweden with oak plank facades, a salt meadow farm from South Slesvig and a four winged farm from Bornholm. One is advised to go in depth with a few buildings at a time instead of trying to see them all in a superficial manner.

Similar to this yet more modest are the Funen Landsby open-air museum on the southern edge of Odense, and the Hjerl Hede museum near Flyndersø between Vinderup and Skive in Jutland.

79. *Open-air museum. Farm house from Ejdersted in south-west Slesvig. Ca 1653.*

81. *Hjerl Hede. Søgården from Vinkel near Viborg. First half of sixteenth century.*

82-85. Fortress buildings under the absolute monarchy, 1662-1725.

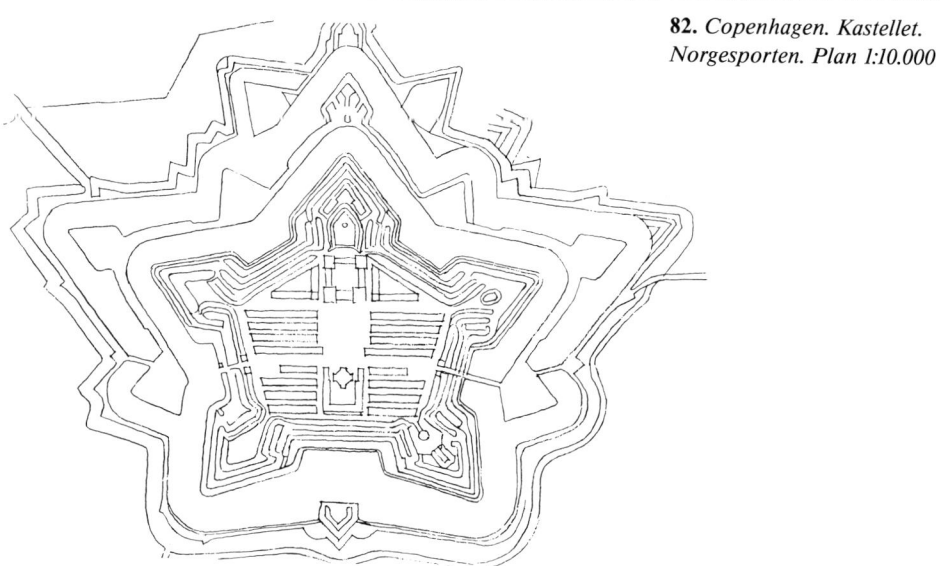

82. Copenhagen. Kastellet. Norgesporten. Plan 1:10.000

Christian IV's expansion of Copenhagen was fortified with embankments and moats, but as the art of war developed, the need arose for better defensive measures. Therefore, Frederik III invited the Dutch fortification engineer, Henrik Rüse to Denmark, where he in 1662-63 designed and built the Kastel complex based on the latest fortification principles. It was an enormous, and still partially preserved, fortress bastion system with double moats and gun batteries that covered every conceivable attack angle. Within the inner embankments, the area was laid out as a camp with main axes in the direction of the compass points. The east/west axis is accentuated by the commandant residence and the church. The north/south axis is marked by two gates, The Norway Gate to the north and the Zealand Gate to the south. The church was built first in 1703-04 and recently restored in 1985-87 by the Defence Departments Building Service. The commandant residence was not built until 1725, however some of the barracks are original.

Numerous other fortifications were established or enlarged during this period. The Christiansø fortification on the three small rock islands, Ertholmene, about 20 kilometres northeast of Bornholm was established in 1684, and the Fladstrand fortification near Frederikshavn from 1686, both with gun towers and powder magazines, were built by engineer officer Anton Coucheron. The round, granite Kastel in Rønne is also from about 1688.

84. *Frederikshavn. The Fladstrand fortification.*

85. *Rønne. Kastellet.*

83. *Ertholmene. The Christiansø fortification.*

86-87. Charlottenborg and Nysø, 1671-1683.

86. Copenhagen.
Charlottenborg.
Cupola room.

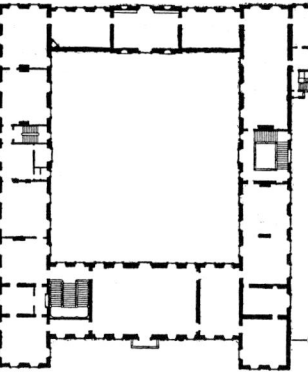

Plan 1:1500.

Facade facing Kgs. Nytorv.

Christian IV's expansion of Copenhagen left a large open area where the easternmost part of the old Østervold embankment had been. Christian V wanted this area laid out as a monumental square for the glorification of the absolute monarchy, with an equestrian statue in the centre surrounded by elegant, stately palaces. The largest of these was Charlottenborg, built in 1672-83 by the king's half brother, Ulrik Frederik Gyldenløve, who was governor of Norway and one of Denmark's most powerful men. Again Dutch master builders were approached to assure the latest architectural trends, and thus Charlottenborg became the oldest major monument in the Danish baroque style. The architect is unknown though the builder was Evert Janssen, and Gyldenløve had visited Holland several years before construction. The original plan was an H-shaped scheme with four, square, cupola roofed corner towers, however during the building period, the plans were enlarged to a three-winged building in which the main facade's corner towers appear as exposed extended pavilions. The palace was completed in 1677 and in 1683 a low, fourth wing was built closing the courtyard off from the gardens to the rear. In the centre of this wing is an open portal topped by a large domed hall, where a magnificent stucco ceiling suggests that architect Lambert van Haven may have been involved. The palace interior was grand but not especially practical. Since 1754, Charlottenborg has been the home of the Royal Danish Academy of Fine Arts. A close relation to this palace can be found at the Nysø manor estate near Præstø, built in 1671-73, also by an unknown architect. The formal interior and exterior symmetry and the small dark red brick, "Dutch clinker", are common characteristics of both palaces.

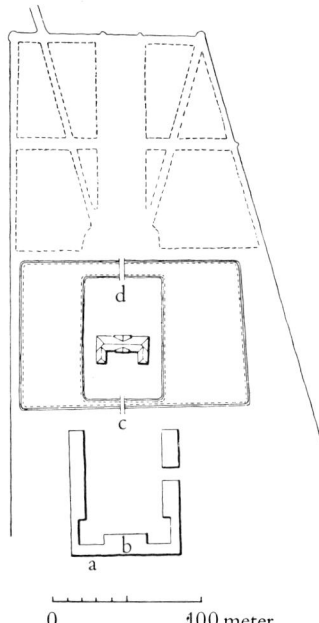

87. *Nysø. Site plan.*

87. *Nysø.*

88-89. Vor Frelsers Church and Reformert Church, 1682-1696.

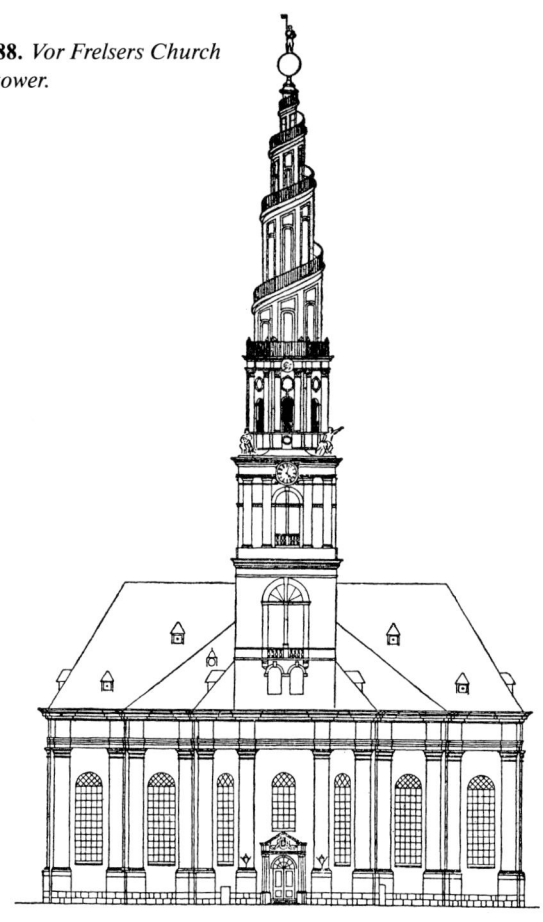

88. *Vor Frelsers Church tower.*

Above: **88.** *Vor Frelsers Church. Elevation facing St. Annæ Gade. 1:750; below plan 1:750.*

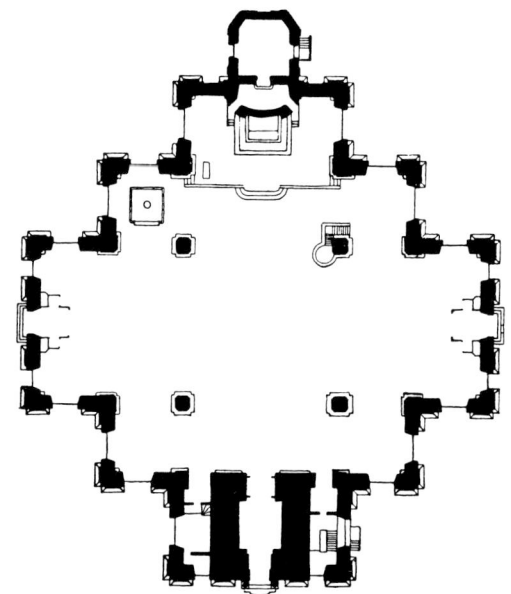

Since its establishment, the Christianshavn quarter of Copenhagen lacked a church. This problem was finally solved with the building of Vor Frelsers Church in 1682-96. Architect Lambert van Haven demonstrated the knowledge and ability he had acquired during his study trips to Rome, France and Holland. This first Danish baroque church is dominated by tall, round arched windows and large, red-brown brick wall areas marked by pilasters, tied together by huge cornices, which in a Roman fashion crank around the corners along the entire facade. The Greek cross plan is based on a square module that is one fourth of the square formed by the four centre columns. The symmetry of the plan and elevation is disrupted only by the tower, whose transept is slightly deeper than the rest of the building. The most beautiful, and architecturally speaking, most exceptional feature, is the helical spire added in 1749-50 by architect Lauritz de Thurah, who admitted being inspired by Borromini's little tower on San Ivo della Sapienza in Rome. Christian V's marriage to Charlotte Amalie of Hessen-Kassel, and the resulting religious freedom for German, Dutch and French Calvinists led to the building of the Reformert church on Gothersgade in Copenhagen in 1688-89, presumably with the Dutch stone mason, Henrik Brockam as architect. The rectangular building is decorated with Ionic pilasters and oval blindings under the high, round arched windows. The interior is organized as a hall church, with galleries along three sides and a pulpit above the alter on the long side opposite the entrance.

88. *Copenhagen. Vor Frelsers Church, Christianshavn.*

89. *Copenhagen. Reformert Church on Gothersgade.*

90. Clausholm, 1693-1723.

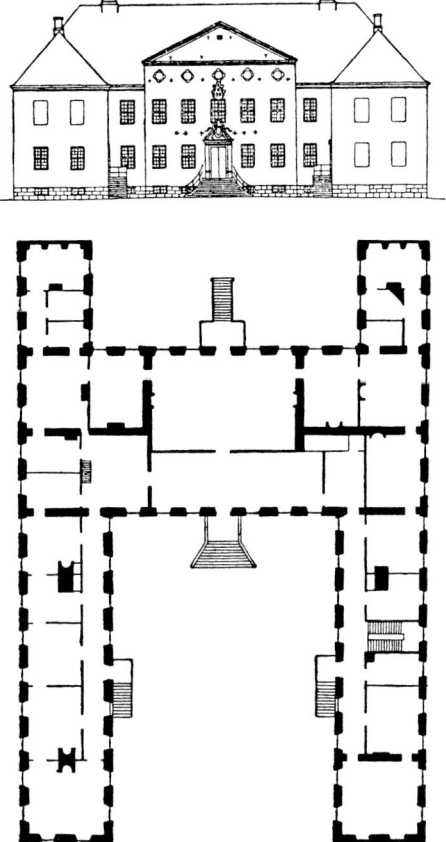

90. *Clausholm near Randers.*

Plan and elevation 1:750.

The early baroque requirements for more imposing settings, with high bright spaces, wide straight stairways and enough room for the growing staff of servants, can be perceived in the new Clausholm, which Chancellor Conrad Reventlow commissioned in 1693-99, near Randers. The architect was Ernst Brandenburger, a master builder who had displayed his individual talents earlier by building Stensballegård near Horsens. Clausholm is a three-winged, symmetrical scheme with two identical storeys over a vaulted cellar. The exterior is simple and massive, animated only by a wide triangular gable over four bays facing the courtyard, with small round windows and entrance portal, the latter designed by one of the architectural greats of the time, the Swede Nicodemus Tessin the Younger. The interior, on the other hand, was magnificently furnished with elegant stuccowork on the walls and ceiling, which still can be seen, especially in the grand dining hall. Above this lies the great hall, whose high vaulted ceiling originally extended to the roof and admitted light from the round, gable attic windows, as there was also a gable attic facing the garden. However in 1769, this was replaced by a flat ceiling. The innovative feature at Clausholm was the mutually connected corridors toward the courtyard, from which there was direct access to almost all the rooms so that it was no longer necessary to pass through one room to get to another. The short south wings were added in 1722-23 at the same time that the facades were stuccoed.

View from dining room toward the fountain complex, planned by C.Th. Sørensen 1974-76. The Bowl fountains were designed by Jens Chr. Varming from Roman prototypes. Below: Clausholm's dining hall.

91. Frederiksberg Slot, 1699-1738.

91. *Frederiksberg castle.*

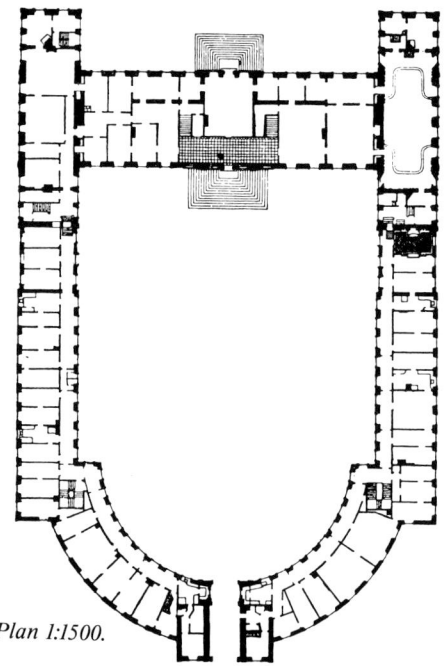

Plan 1:1500.

Frederik IV, while still crown prince, made his first journey to Italy where he greatly admired the Italian villas, which were common in the Roman suburbs. This inspired him, on arrival home, to build Frederiksberg Palace, placed in the open countryside surroundings near Valby hill, in the middle of an extensive park area. The first palace was built in 1699-1703 under the supervision of master builder Ernst Brandenburger, and was a single-winged scheme with slightly protruding side pavilions. By the time it was completed it proved to be insufficient in size and in 1708-09 was rebuilt and expanded by architect J.C. Ernst. Two transverse wings were added at the ends so the plan became H-shaped. The facades were white painted stucco with painted sandstone ornamentation. The width was emphasized by horizontal lines in the form of cornices, bands and closely spaced window pediments. The palace church, located in the east transverse wing, was returned to its former splendour by a restoration in 1928-32, and many other rooms in the palace with superb stucco ceilings from the time of Frederik IV are still preserved. The north and south facades were originally identical, but were radically altered in 1733-38 with the addition of two, lower side wings to the south, which ran forward to an existing gate house, creating the existing closed palace court. The architect was Lauritz de Thurah who also designed the humorous pancake kitchen for the princesses in the east side wing. In 1770-71, architect C.F. Harsdorff built the royal dining hall and the elegant marble bath in the basement. The gate house facing Roskildevej is the result of a rebuilding in 1829 by architect Jørgen Hansen Koch.

The marble bath.

The pancake kitchen.

Garden facade.

Chapel.

92-93. Slotsholmsgade 4 and the Opera House, Copenhagen, 1701-21.

The building on Slotsholmsgade 4, popularly known as the "Red Palace" was built by Frederik IV between 1715 and 1720 under the supervision of master builder, Johan Conrad Ernst. The three-winged scheme still functions as a ministerial building, and the main facade, facing the old Stock Exchange, is dominated by long rows of windows and a slightly extended center portion topped by an enormous, semicircular pediment with a large relief depicting the king's bust surrounded by symbols of war and peace. The interior houses many well-preserved baroque rooms with stuccoed and painted ceilings.

As a replacement for the wooden opera house in the Amalienborg Gardens, which burned together with Sophie Amalienborg in 1689, a new brick building was erected in 1701-02, on the corner of Fredericiagade and Bredgade by Frederik IV. This opera house was of impressive size for its time and strongly influenced by Dutch baroque, with its continuous pilasters, although the patterned brickwork was clearly Italian. The architect may have been W.F. von Platen. Already in 1718-21, Johan Conrad Ernst converted the building to a naval academy, which later required the establishment of a mezzanine level in 1769. This was carried out by architect C.F. Harsdorff. In 1918, the building was occupied by the East High Court and the maritime and commercial court. In 1902-03 an L-shaped addition was added facing Bredgade by architect Martin Borch.

93. *Copenhagen. The opera house on Fredericiagade, now High-court.*

Left above: **92.** *Copenhagen. The red palace. Slotsholmsgade 4; below: The finance Ministry's meeting hall.*

93. *Copenhagen. High-court. Martin Borch's addition on Bredgade. 1902-03.*

94. Fredensborg Palace, 1719-1769.

94. *Fredensborg Palace, seen from the access drive's two pavilions. Below: Jardin's marble garden.*

Another building inspired by Frederik IV's journeys to Italy was Fredensborg Palace, built in a forest, east of Esrom Lake on the site of an early royal hunting lodge, and where Christian V had carved out a star-formed system of hunting paths, which still exist. At the junction of these paths, a pleasure palace was built in 1719-22, in the form of a smooth stuccoed, square, two storey pavilion with a hall in the centre, crowned by a high, four-sided cupola, topped with a lantern. Toward north and south respectively, lay a conservatory and a Guard hall. Toward the east and west were living quarters. To the south of the building is a octagonal courtyard, originally surrounded by one-storey wings, and to the east is the riding grounds with the long stable wing. West of the palace, the "Red Wing" was built as housing for the servants. The architect was J.C. Krieger, who was considered the leading garden artist of the time and a specialist in gazebos, and leisure buildings. He also designed the palace church, built in 1725-26, with two flanking marshal buildings, strongly influenced by Dutch baroque. Renovations and additions during the fifty years that followed, by some of the country's leading architects, gave the palace its present appearance. As early as 1741, Thurah increased the height of the main building's top storey, and in the 1750's four, two-storey corner pavilions were added by Eigtved. After Eigtved's death in 1754, Thurah connected the two west wings with a new wing and built the four, tall minaretlike chimneys at the corners of the cupola. Finally in 1774-76, C.F. Harsdorff raised the wings around the courtyard an extra storey, rebuilt the two pavilions at the entrance, and altered the main facade according to classicistic ideals. The different building periods are also reflected in many of the well-preserved interiors, of which the cupola hall and the church go back to the time of Frederik IV. N.H Jardin redid the park in 1759-69, adding the marble garden west of the palace and some of the marble sculptures by sculptor Johs. Wiedewelt.

The Cupola hall.

Below left:
Site plan 1809.
Ca 1:6000.

Chapel.

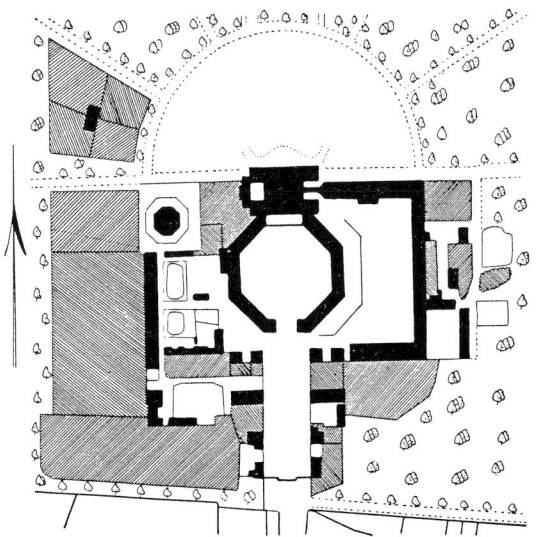

95-97. Odense Palace, Viborg Town Hall, and the palace in Roskilde, 1720-1733.

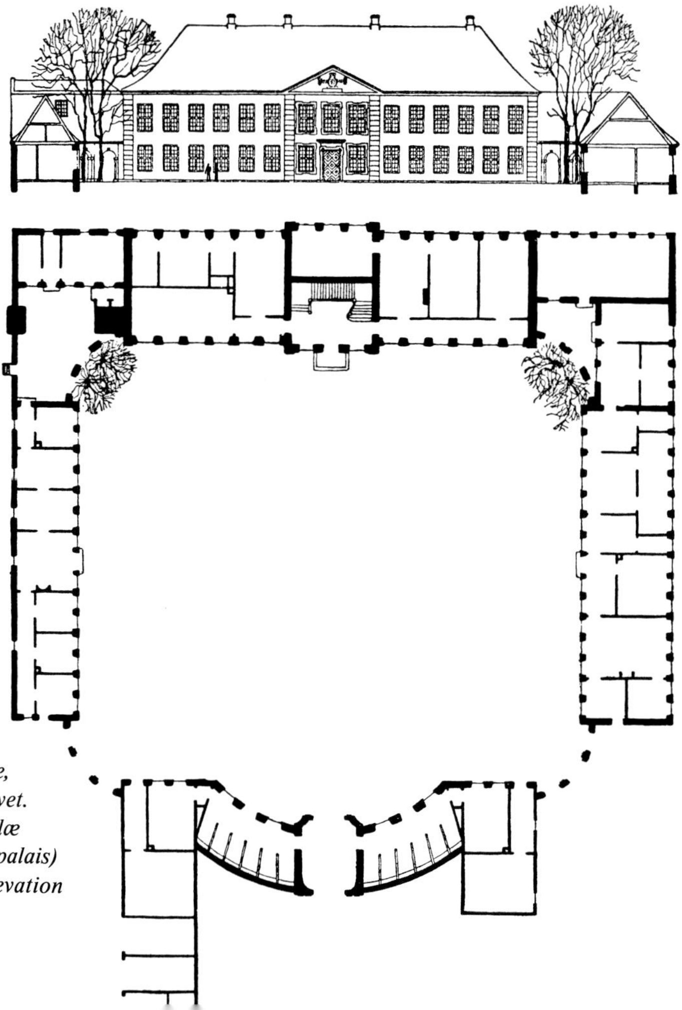

97. Roskilde, Stændertorvet. Det gule Palæ (the yellow palais) Plan and elevation 1:750.

On the basis of the old St. Hans Monastery, which had been converted to a royal residence in 1575 by Frederik II, Frederik IV, in 1720-23 rebuilt Odense Palace with a new royal wing toward north. The architect was J.C. Krieger. The wide facade with quoins, window architraves and triangular pediment seem somewhat prosaic. However already in 1789, the main wing was converted to a Lord Lieutenant's residence and the beautiful interiors were altered, for example a grandiose stairway in the vestibule disappeared. A rebuilding in 1841 by Jørgen Hansen Koch added the present classicistic doors and panels, as well as the portals facing the garden and the courtyard.

It was in Copenhagen, that many of Denmark's eighteenth century standards were set, as was the case in Viborg when the new Town Hall was to be built after the great city fire of 1726. Master builder, Claus Stallknecht built the still existing building, which with its quoins and extended centre portion, stairway, pediment and spire, was very similar to the town hall being built at the same time in Copenhagen. The style became almost a standard for new town halls built in the provinces during the rest of the century.

The Middle Age bishop's palace on Stændertorvet in Roskilde was so run-down in 1732 that the Court's master builder, Lauritz de Thurah was asked to build a new palace for the Royal Court. The Yellow Palace was practically completed the next year and is quite similar to Odense Palace, except that two lower side wings were added as well as a curved gate wing all of which were connected by an arched arcade.

96. *Viborg. The old town hall.*

95. *Odense, Kongens Have (the kings garden). Odense Palace.*

98-103. Conflagration buildings 1729-1737.

98. *Copenhagen. Gråbrødretorv 1-9.*

102. *Copenhagen. Fiolstræde 18, before restoration 1990-91.*

Below: Krieger's pattern drawings for brick houses, 1729.
Plans and facades 1:750.

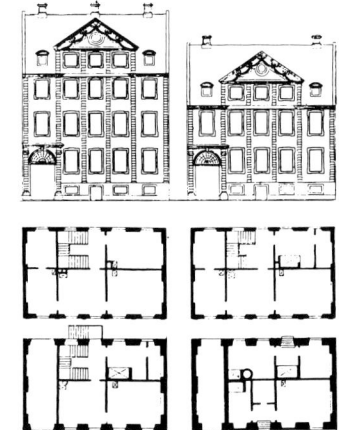

The greater part of Copenhagen burned down in the great fire of 1728 including the Middle Age quarter with its low, half-timber buildings and narrow lanes. Both the king and the municipal authorities saw the opportunity of straightening and widening the streets, and building new more fire resistant buildings. Therefore the Chief Master Builder, J. C. Krieger was commissioned to work out a series of standard building types for large spacious buildings with gable dormers, in both one, two and three storeys over a cellar. However a massive protest from the landowners made realization of the project difficult. A typical picture of Copenhagen after the fire is evident in the row of buildings along Gråbrødretorv Nos. 1-9, built between 1729 and 1732. They have brick facades facing the street, but with half-timber toward the court and neighbouring building. There is now a high cellar, three storeys and a gable attic, and the closely spaced, large windows are a fine source of light. An elegant but rare example of a richly decorated gentry house facade can be seen at Nybrogade 12, which master builder and architect Philip de Lange built for Court confectioner J.H. Ziegler in 1732. In order to stimulate the building trade, the ordinance prohibiting half-timber building was suspended between 1732-37, during which time the housing blocks were rapidly completed. Examples of half-timber buildings from this period can be seen at Gammel Mønt 41, Skindergade 13, Fiolstræde 18 and Toldbodgade 9.

100. *Copenhagen. Gammel Mønt 41.*

101. *Copenhagen. Skindergade 13. (Not shown).*

103. *Copenhagen. Toldbodgade 9. (Not shown).*

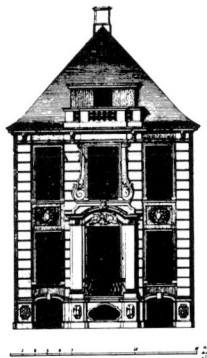

Above and left: **99.** *Nybrogade 12. The original facade. After Thurah: Hafnia Hodierna.*

113

104-106. Viennese baroque and French rococo, 1733-1745.

104. *Copenhagen. Christiansborg palace. The marble bridge and the two pavilions. Below: Riding grounds near Christiansborg palace.*

106. *Northwest Fyn, Margård. (Not shown).*

Since the middle Ages, the old Copenhagen Castle had been rebuilt and enlarged several times. However in 1731, it was torn down and Christian VI commissioned master builder E.D. Häusser to build a new grand castle, which both in size and furnishings was worthy of an absolute monarch. The enormous building work, formed as a four winged block, was erected between 1733-45. Here in the first Christiansborg Palace, Viennese baroque and French rococo had their debut in Denmark. Outstanding interiors were done by the best artists, men like Le Clerc, Eigtved and Thurah. However in 1794, the entire palace went up in flames and only the riding grounds complex with its stables, manage, and theatre, the Marble Bridge and its two pavilions designed by Eigtved were saved.

At about the same time, in 1743-44, Niels Eigtved built Prinsens Palace on Frederiksholms Canal, just opposite the palace. The three-winged scheme, with its low gate wing with vases, cartouches and recessed main wing became the first Danish rococo palace built according to French ideals. The palace is now part of the National Museum, and the preserved rooms in the main wing give an impression of the former Christiansborg interior.

In 1744-45, Eigtved built the small pleasure pavilion, Frederiksdal by Furesø Lake for Privy Councillor J.S. Schulin, the earliest example of a "maison de plaisance" in Denmark, with large and small rooms symmetrically organized along the main axis' vestibule and conservatory. The mansard roof is the result of an alteration carried out by J.G. Rosenberg in 1752-53, who while working on Frederiksdal also built Margård on northwest Funen, also inspired by French country estates.

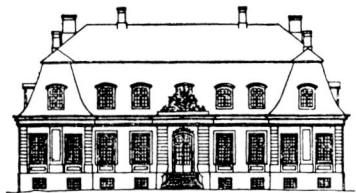
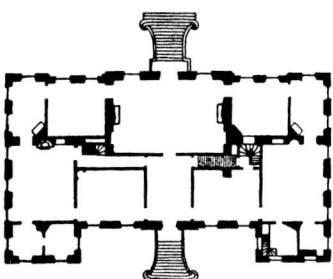

104. *Copenhagen. Frederiksholms Canal. Prinsens Palæ, now the Danish National Museum.*

105. *Frederiksdal near Furesøen. Plan and elevation 1:750.*

107. Eremitagen 1734-1736.

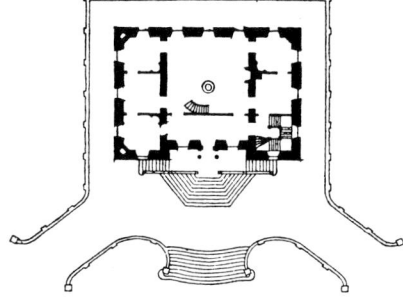

107. *Jægersborg Dyrehave park. Eremitage palace. Reconstruction of the original plan 1:750.*

In 1734-36, the Court master builder, Lauritz de Thurah created the small hunting manor, Eremitagen in Dyrehaven park, which became one of his major works. Despite its modest size, the building's tall, massive blocklike form dominates the plain on which its stands. The smooth banded, rusticated, massive ground floor lifts the richly decorated upper floor, the whole being gathered under the heavy mansard roof, which on the entrance side is interrupted by two side pavilions with segment gables. The south German baroque has a Danish offshoot here, and the sumptuous magnificence is carried on into the interior, where the rooms on the main floor are practically untouched, with marble, stucco and mirrors. It is evident that Thurah was not afraid to compete with Eigtved's more willowy rococo in the king and queen's chambers on the north side, which are quite different than the rest of the interior. The building was intended only for use by the royal hunting parties for food and rest after the hunt, and therefore the manor was equipped with a table, that with the help of an elevator system, could be lifted, fully set, from the kitchen up into the dining room. This enabled the royal visitors to dine without the presence of servants, "en eremitage", and from this the manor's name was derived.

Dronning Sophie Magdalenes Chamber.

East side 1:750.

Dining hall.

108-110. Ledreborg, Lerchenborg and Valdemar's Manor, 1743-1754

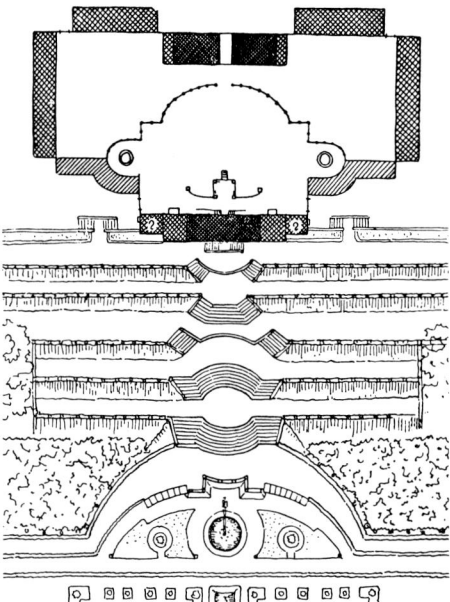

108. *Ledreborg near Lejre. Left: Plan 1:3000. Below: North facade with one of Thurah's pavilions in the background.*

The manor estate Ledreborg near Lejre has a special place in Danish architectural history due to its location and organization. In 1743, Privy Councillor J.L.Holstein commission J.C. Krieger to modernize the old Lejregård, and the main building was lengthened with three bays at each end and a uniform rhythm of pilasters on the facade with side and centre pavilions, emphasized by a pediment and balustrades. A chapel was placed at the west end, and to the east, a monumental stairway, while the centre of the main storey had a magnificent full-height cupola hall. From 1745, Eigtved worked with the design of the interior, while Thurah was commissioned in 1748 in connection with the design of the two elegant, curved pavilions, which created the transition from the main building to the three-winged farm yard. In 1799, the north wing was replaced by the present, tower-adorned gate building. The site was located on the edge of a river valley, and Krieger exploited this feature with an impressive, terraced garden on both sides of the river. These have been partially recreated.

Lerchenborg, near Kalundborg has certain elements in common with Ledreborg, but is more authentic in terms of source of inspiration: The long gone royal country estate. Hirschholm. This magnificent and exceptional complex, by Danish standards, was created in 1743-45 by the conversion of an old estate, and was laid out on a symmetrical axis from the garden via the main building and riding grounds to the large home farm. The architect may have been Eigtved as the facades of the main building and its beautiful interior seem to indicate.

A similar quality can be found at the large estate created by Holstein architect, G.D. Tschierscke, near Valdemar's Manor on Tåsinge around 1754. The 200 metre long, axis of symmetry culminates in a small tea pavilion by the water.

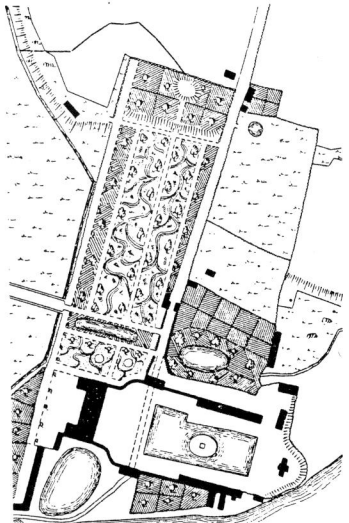

110. *Valdemar's castle on Tåsinge.*
Site plan, app. 1800.
Ca 1:8000.

109. *Lerchenborg near Kalundborg.*

111-112. Gammel Holtegård and Turebyholm, 1750-1757.

112. *Thurebyholm between Køge and Haslev.*

Lauritz de Thurah was also given the opportunity of realizing the new ideals of a countryside leisure home when he built Gammel Holtegård in 1756-57 as his own summer residence. The long, single-storey main building with its low end pavilions is covered by a hipped roof. The building's symmetry is observed in the placement of the dormers and chimneys, and the centre pavilion garden facade is discretely emphasized with balustrades, and the court facade, by a pediment added during this century. After an extensive restoration in 1976-83, Gammel Holtegård now functions as an archives and exhibition building for the borough of Søllerød.

In 1746, Lord Steward, Count A.G. Moltke received Bregentved manor estate from the king, and the following year he purchased the nearby estate Turebyholm, where in 1750-54 he commissioned Niels Eigtved to build a new main building. Today it is completely preserved, and the cool, restrained rococo interiors are typical of this architect. The garden room running through the centre of the building is marked on both facades with wide cartouche decorated pediments and large stone stairways with curved, wrought-iron railings. The main entrance facing east also has a stone stairway and a cartouche over the door.

111. *Gammel Holte, Attemosevej. Gl. Holtegård.*

113. Frederiksstaden, 1749-1757.

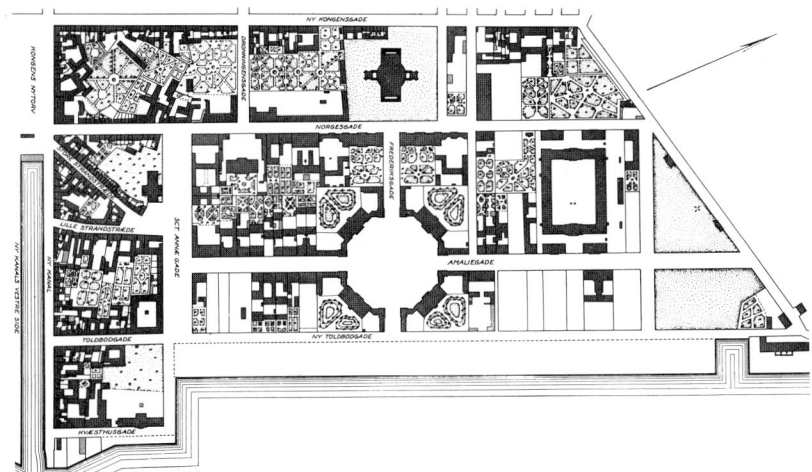

113. *Copenhagen. Aerial view of the Frederikstaden quarter with courtyard and the Marble Church in background. Plan after Geddes map 1757, scale: 1:10,000.*

113. *Copenhagen. Frederikstaden, Amaliegade* **17.** *Below: Dehn's Palace, Bredgade 54.*

In celebration of the 300th anniversary of the House of Oldenborg in 1749, Frederik V took the initiative to establish Frederiksstaden, a new city district in the large areas bordered by Skt. Annæ Plads, Bredgade, Esplanaden and Toldbodgade. Eigtved was responsible for the master plan and the artistic design. The rectangular area was laid out according to a simple cruciform plan with an octagonal square at the intersection of the two axes, Amaliegade and Frederiksgade. The objective was naturally, the ceremonial veneration of the absolute monarchy, underscored by Frederik V's equestrian statue in the centre of the square, and the monumental Frederiks Church that was never built, at the end of the short Frederiksgade. Therefore a number of stringent requirements were placed on the design of the buildings, so that the windows, cornices and building heights were at the same respective levels as was typical of many other urban complexes in Europe at that time. Eigtved was to plan or approve all building projects to assure the desired uniformity. The crowning achievement was the square's four palaces, Eigtved's most important work and the climax of the rococo period in Denmark. Other grand palaces were Berckentin's, the present Odd Fellow Palace on Bredgade 28 from 1755, and the twin palaces on both sides of Frederiksgade, Bernstorff's and Dehn's, Bredgade 40-42 and 54 from 1756, all built by J.G. Rosenberg. An important Eigtved gentry house is Amaliegade 17, from 1754-56. His Frederiks Hospital, Bredgade 66-72, the present Kunstindustrimuseum from 1752-54, is also worth mentioning. However the front buildings facing the street were done by Thurah in 1755-57, who at the same time built Amaliegade 25 for himself.

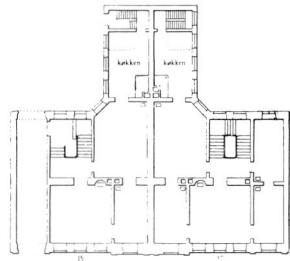

Above: Amaliegade 15-17. The original plan 1:750.

Below: Amaliegade 25.

Below: Frederik's Hospital, now Kunstindustrimuseet, Bredgade 66-72.

113. Amalienborg, 1751-60.

113. *Copenhagen. Amalienborg. A.G. Molkte's Palace, now Christian VII's Palais.*

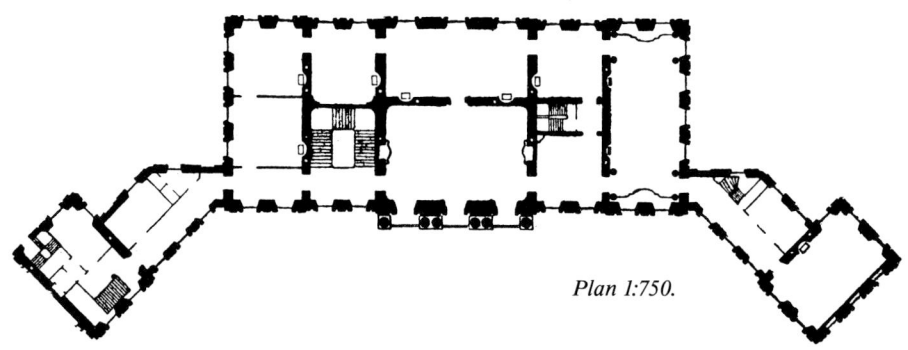

Plan 1:750.

The four palaces on Amalienborg Palace Square were planned from the beginning to be the magnificent gathering point for the Frederiksstad district and a perpetual memorial to the absolute monarch Frederik V, whose equestrian statue, a masterwork by the French sculptor Saly, graces the centre of the square. The king chose four of his most trusted men as "clients", Privy Councilors Moltke, Levetzau, Brockdorff and Løvenskjold, however the latter was forced to sell before completion to Anna Sophie Schack. The properties were free, but the clients were required to follow Eigtved's drawings as far as the exterior was concerned. Each palace consists of a main block connected with corner pavilions to which raised, low gate wings were added at a later date. The facades have slightly emphasized side pavilions and a prominent centrepiece with tall windows and a column-supported protruding cornice, which above the roof balustrade is decorated with the Counts' herald cartouches. Eigtved demonstrated his international calibre here and Amalienborg is Denmark's most distinguished example of rococo architecture. A. G. Moltke's Palace in the southwest corner of the square was built in 1751-54 under Eigtved's supervision as the most elegant private home in Denmark. Fortunately the piano nobile's magnificent rooms are still preserved, especially the grand hall facing the square. After the Christiansborg fire of 1794, the royal family bought the four palaces. Moltke's and Schack's were rebuilt by Harsdorff as residences for the king and the crown prince, which is why the connecting colonnade across Amaliegade was built. Brockdorff's Palace, just opposite Moltke's, was not rebuilt until 1828, when Crown Prince Frederik (VII) came of age. The fine, late classicistic, partially preserved interior, is by Jørgen Hansen Koch. Levetzau's Palace toward northwest was sold in 1794 to Crown Prince Frederik, who commissioned painter and architect N.A. Abildgaard to renovate the piano nobile, however part of this has been altered under later rebuilding work.

Above: Saly's equestrian statue on the palace square.

Above: Main stairway in Molkte's Palais.

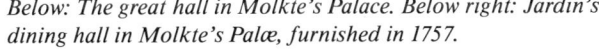

Below: The great hall in Molkte's Palace. Below right: Jardin's dining hall in Molkte's Palæ, furnished in 1757.

114. Buildings at Holmen, the Royal Dockyards, 1742-1772.

114. Copenhagen. Nyholms Hovedvagt guard station with mast crane in background.

114. Nyholms Hovedvagt guard station, east side and section, 1:750.

114. Copenhagen. Holmen. Arsenalgården and Kongeport portal.

 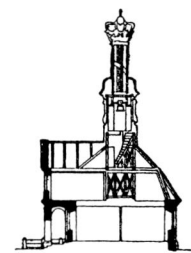

At the close of the seventeenth century, an enormous string of fortifications was laid out in the water stretching from Christianshavn in a large curve up toward Toldboden to protect Copenhagen's coastline. Within this so-called "Nyværk", three artificial islands were created, Nyholm, Frederiksholm and Arsenaløen, which have since served as a naval base and dockyard. In 1742-43 Nyholm's Hovedvagt guard station was built with the Dutch master builder, Philip de Lange as architect. The building's function required an open, covered loggia for the guard posts and a tower with a clock and bells. The resulting design was very personal and festive with a heavy, royal crown decorated spire. However the building that has become Holmen's symbol, is the large mast crane built by Philip de Lange in 1748-51. An impressive timber construction runs through the entire height of the structure, so that the brickwork is actually only a curtain-wall. An extensive restoration was carried out in 1984-85 by the Danish Defence Construction Service. Further south on the Arsenal island in 1741, Lange built Arsenalgården, the first of his building schemes on the Holmen. The two wings are connected by a richly decorated Royal Gate. The Hovedmagasinet (main storage house) and Takkelloftet (rigging loft) on Frederiksholm were also done by Philip de Lange in 1767-72, but they both had extra storeys added in 1858.

114. *Copenhagen. Holmen. Main store house on Frederiksholm.*

115-117. Buildings on Christianshavn, 1738-1781.

Top: Copenhagen Strandgade. **116.** *Asiatisk Kompagni, right in photo, and* **115.** *Christian's Church in background. Below:* **116.** *Eigtved's warehouse for the Asiatisk Kompagni.*

Christian's Church at the end of Strandgade was built in 1755-59 for Copenhagen's German community, under the name, Frederik's German Church. The drawings were done by Niels Eigtved, who died the year before Frederik V laid the foundation stone. Thus it was his son-in-law, G.D. Anthon who supervised the building work, and he is alone responsible for the beautiful tower. The church is unusual in that it is oriented according to its width, with the alter, pulpit and organ place above each other in the middle of one of the long walls, while the other three walls are covered with boxlike galleries similar to a theatre. The inspiration can have come from South German baroque churches or perhaps the Reformert Church in Copenhagen. The cellar is like a large burial vault with direct access from stairways in the end walls.

On Strandgade 25, Philip de Lange, in 1738, built a late baroque office building for the Asiatisk Kompagni, which in 1781 was enlarged with an identical companion piece. However the function was quite different, the rear of the building reveals that it is merely a warehouse. Along the harbour basin to the rear, Eigtved built a massive warehouse in 1748-50, and today, the entire scheme is part of the Foreign Ministry complex. A somewhat curious example of late rococo can be found at sculptor S.C. Stanley's Gård, on Overgaden oven Vandet 6, built in 1755-56. A later height increase of the side wings conceals the original building with a transverse pavilion between two short, deep side wings. This type is of English origin, as is the triple Palladian windows on the facade of the piano nobile.

117. Copenhagen, Overgaden oven Vandet 6. Stanley's Gård.

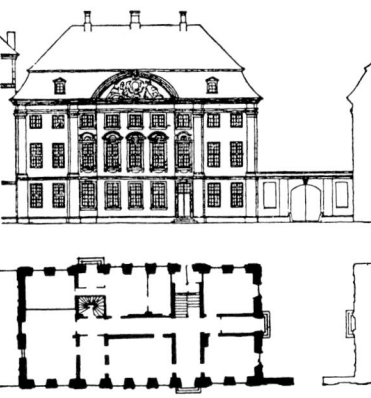

115. Copenhagen, Strandgade. Christian's Church.

Above: *116. Asiatisk Kompagni, plan and elevation 1:750.*

118-120. Nicolas Henri Jardin, 1759-1771.

Above: **119.** *Helsingør. Marienlyst Manor.*
Below: **118.** *Gentofte, Jægersborg Allé. Bernstorff Manor.*

With the death of Eigtved in 1754, the rococo period in Denmark ended. It was immediately succeeded by French classicism under the heavy influence of the new director of the Royal Academy, the French sculptor Saly, who called in his countryman, architect Nicolas Henri Jardin, and named him professor of architecture. Jardin's main job, beside teaching, was to carry out the prestigious project of building Frederik's Church. However he also found the time to do other projects. One of the first being the country estate, Bernstorff Manor from 1759, built for the foreign minister, Count J.H.E Bernstorff, which was typical of the current Louis XVI style with its simple basic form in two storeys, smooth banded, rusticated side and centre pieces, and a rectangular, symmetrical plan around a deep vestibule and an oval garden room. This protrudes from the facade in a semicircular bay, crowned by a small dome. Later rebuilding works created a mezzanine level under the dome and removed the vase decorated balustrade that topped the wall.

During the same period, 1759-63, Jardin rebuilt an old country manor for A.G. Moltke. Built about 1587 by Frederik II, the three-storey Marienlyst Manor lies against a slope, north of Elsinore. It was enlarged with four bays on each side with the original building remaining as a protruding centre portico. The facade was decorated with smooth banded rustication on the lower level, and oval medallions with festoons between the first and second floors, all crowned by a massive cornice with a balustrade to hide the flat roof.

Following this in 1765-71, Jardin built the Sølvgade Barracks in Copenhagen, a different formal and unostentatious scheme with a baroque influence. Classicism is evident in the grand arch at the main entrance, the high door pediments and the double-F in the plan, a gesture to Frederik V.

Above: Jardin's proposal for the completion of Frederik's Church, 1756.

120. *Copenhagen, Sølvgade 40. Sølvgades Barracks, now DSB's headquarters.*

121-123. French classicism in the countryside, 1765-1795.

121. *Liselund on Møn.* **123.** *Moesgård south of Århus, now the Prehistoric Museum.*

The cultivation of the noble simplicity in classical architecture and the impressive, romantic natural landscape were united in several country estates on Zealand at the end of the eighteenth century. The most refined example is the small country manor Liselund on Møn, built in 1792-95 by Andreas Kirkerup, with strong influence by the client, Prefect Antoine de la Calmette and his wife Lisa Iselin. Even though the centre axis was lengthened with a dining room, the "maison de plaisance" plan is recognizable in the central garden room surrounded by secondary spaces. However the large hipped, thatched roof, supported by wooden columns in front of the garden room and around the dining room, give the building the air of a romantic hermitage. The light, summerish elegance in the interior and furnishings is still partially preserved, as is the surrounding romantic park with monuments and small pavilions.

On Funen, A.G. Moltke modernized the manor estate Glorup as early as 1765, after it had been rebuilt as a baroque manor in 1743-44 by Philip de Lange. Moltke commissioned architect C.J. Zuber, a student of Jardin's, who may have aided him in the project. In addition to the very fine interiors, he altered the four-winged scheme with a new attic over the gate, a roof ridge turret formed as a classicistic temple, and a raised east facade with smooth banded rustication facing the courtyard. The garden was a composite of a French parterre garden and an English park, which can still be perceived.

Architect Zuber also built Moesgård south of Århus in 1776-78, where the main building with its oval garden room was strongly influenced by Bernstorff Manor. Today Moesgård and its more recent home farm complex, functions as a prehistoric museum, after an extensive restoration and renovation by C.F. Møller in 1964-70.

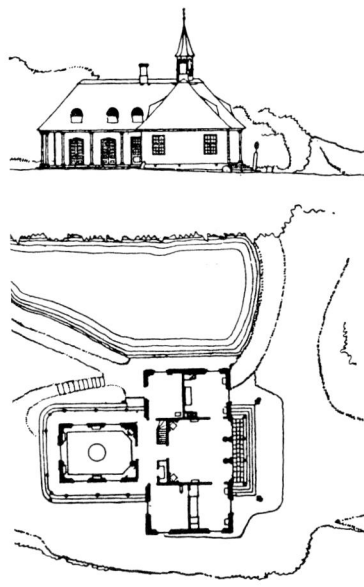

121. *Liselund. Northeast side and plan 1:750.*

122. *Glorup on Fyn. Gate wing.*

124. Christiansfeld, 1772-1826.

Christiansfeld was founded in 1772 by the Moravian Brethren, a protestant religious sect from the Sachsen area. The town was strongly supported by the Danish government, who hoped it would help industry and trade. The right-angled street grid was inspired by the sect's town, Gnadau near Magdeburg. The town plan is based on an 8 Hamburg alen module, about 4.58 metres. The parallel streets, Lindegade and Nørregade, are dominating features that border the church square. The first four houses, Lindegade 17, 25, 26 and 28 were built one year later in yellow Flensborg brick and set the tone for the sober and refined building culture that still characterizes the town. The architectural style is a mixture of Danish and Saxonian-Silesian traditions, where the lesenes and gable cornices represent the Danish, while the narrow hipped roof, the tall slender gables and the brick window architraves and bands can be found in the German Brethren towns.

Building work continued in 1774 with the Brother House and two years later, the Sister House where the unmarried members of the sect lived. The church was built in 1776 and the Widow House in 1779. At the same time a number of private homes were built, so that in 1782, after ten years of national subsidies, there were 36 buildings in the town. After a period of stagnation, building continued until 1826, when the town was almost completed.

Christiansfeld has preserved it special character both in whole and detail, and both the interiors as well as the exteriors display many signs of a great love and respect for good traditional craftsmanship. A visit to this town is a great experience and should include a side trip to Gudsageren, a very unusual cemetery.

124. *Christiansfeld. Lindegade 26.*

124. *Christiansfeld. The widows' house.*

124. *Christiansfeld. Gudsageren.*

124. *Christiansfeld. The church.*

125-126. Tønder and Møgeltønder, 1730-1830.

Even though Tønder is one of Denmark's oldest merchant towns, numerous fires have erased most traces of the Middle Age buildings. However the many preserved gable buildings of the traditional Slesvig type from the seventeenth, eighteenth and nineteenth century, no doubt reflect the historical conditions. The narrow, deep lots run from the main street to the rear streets, and the end of the house facing the street is traditionally divided up in a deep anteroom (the dielen), which was side by side with the sitting room (the dørns), and a kitchen behind. The rear and smallest part of the building usually houses the large living room (the piselen), so that there is room for a small courtyard with access from the dielen. The stable and coach house, etc. faced the street to the rear.

One of the most elegant houses in town is Digegreven's House, Vesterbrogade 9, built in 1777 for the wealthy mayor and lace dealer, Carsten Richten. The facade is dominated by two protruding bays and a magnificent rococo portal on the centre axis. The mansard roof is hipped toward the street and garden. The building at Østergade 25-27, nr. 25 also with two symmetrical bays, is typical of the townscape at the beginning of the last century, when both facades were redone in brick. Uldgade, with its many small, one storey gable buildings, is one of the most picturesque streets imaginable. No. 14, from the beginning of the nineteenth century, is a typical example. Slotsgade in the nearby town of Møgeltønder has preserved a number of exceptional brick long houses with great thatched roofs and excellent detailing, the oldest being from the 1730's in the west Slesvig tradition. The plans of many of these buildings are also extremely well-preserved.

126. *Møgeltønder. Slotsgade.*

Right: **125.** *Tønder. Digegreven's House, Vestergade 9.*

Below: **125.** *Tønder. Uldgade.*

127-130. Ærøskøbing, Ebeltoft, Sønderho, Varde 1645-1800.

127. *Ærøskøbing. Vestergade 29 (post office).*

127. *Ærøskøbing. Søndergade 32, Prior's House.*

129. *Sønderho on Fanø. Captain Brinch's House.*

Ærøskøbing, on the north side of the island of Ærø has a great number of well-preserved gentry houses from the eighteenth and the early nineteenth century. The interplay between the buildings, street proportions, paving and landscaping make the town one of the finest examples of a preservation worthy, intact merchant town milieu of a high architectural caliber. In addition to the picturesque, half-timber buildings from the seventeenth century, such as Søndergade 32 and 36, the large brick building on Vestergade 46, from 1784 (the chemist) and Vestergade 29 (the post office) illustrate the solid, substantial character of the provincial building culture.

Due to the modest town development in Ebeltoft, a number of old street areas are preserved, most noteworthy being the main street with the old Town Hall from 1789, which today serves as a museum, and the side streets, Overgade and Nedergade.

A quite different character can be found in the old seaman's town, Sønderho on the island of Fanø. Here the brick, thatched roofed long houses lie in large, irregular groups, breached by narrow, pathlike streets, protected by dikes and rows of dunes. The well-preserved Captain Brinch's house from 1772, near the northern dike, is one of the town's largest and finest.

Varde can not be characterized by old building traditions, but the Kampmann'ske Gård on Storegade 33 from 1781 (rebuilt 1797-98) is a very praiseworthy example of the modest yet pristine provincial classicism. The fine little house on Torvet 5 should also be mentioned.

128. *Ebeltoft. The old town hall.*

130. *Varde. Den Kampmann'ske Gård, Storegade 33.*

131. Eighteenth century Dragør.

131. Dragør. Bymandsgade near corner of Blegerstræde.

131. Dragør. Bymandsgade 34 (right in photo)

After having been a fishing village, Dragør became an important skipper town with many ships at sea during the eighteenth century. The street grid originated from a few Middle Age directional lines, but what makes Dragør special is that almost all streets run in an east/west direction while all the alleys run north/south. In principle, all the houses are placed on the north edge of the street and more or less joined together in rows, end to end, while the gardens face south and the neighbouring street. Thus the streets are edged by houses on one side only. Skipperstræde og Strandstræde are typical alleys, Strandgade and Von Ostensgade, typical streets. Most of the buildings are brick, one storey and with tile roofs, while many of the larger, ship captain's houses are in two storeys, often increased in height by later additions. A number of buildings in the town were the product of the very active master builder, J.H. Blichmann, who worked in Dragør during the last half of the eighteenth century. Examples of this are Badstuevælen 8 from 1785, Fogdens Plads 2, buildt around 1800, Strandstræde 8 from about 1784, Strandgade 16 erected before 1811, Dragør Kro Magstræde 3-5 from 1800-1806, and Zytfensgade 4 and 6, buildt 1775 and 1780, respectively. There are even preserved drawings of some of the houses in the Dragør Museum. The well-preserved, dense and low housing is in context with the street furniture, paving and planting to form a unique whole, with which a great deal of local effort is employed to preserve.

132. Svaneke, 1770-1861.

Among the towns on the island of Bornholm, Svaneke distinguishes itself by its location on the sloping rock-bound coast and with its harmonious form, precisely delineated against the surrounding open landscape.
During the Middle Ages, a fishing village grew up around the natural, narrow inlet. In the sixteenth century it was granted a municipal charter but Svaneke didn't really expand until the end of the eighteenth century, primarily due to the establishment of the now existing artificial harbour in 1806-16. A special feature of the town is the large number of half-timber farms, which cultivated the surrounding land up until the end of World War II. However during the nineteenth century, it was the merchant houses that dominated the townscape. Three of the largest lie facing the harbour: The present Hotel Østersøen, renovated in 1839 and heightened by an attic storey in 1889, Siemsens Gård from the 1770's and Smidtgården, Storegade 2, first rebuilt in 1855-65 and again more recently. Holstgården or Søllings Gård on the Torvet, from the 1820's is now a tavern, and is also well-preserved. Another characteristic feature is the high split stone bases, which due to the sloping rocky ground sometimes are a full storey high. This can clearly be seen in the harbour area and up on Kirkebakken, Havnebakken, Vigebakken and Hullebakken hills. Half-timber construction was employed far into the nineteenth century, and typical examples can be found at Kirkebakken 6 from 1834, and Svinget 6 from 1850. Brick houses came late to Svaneke, a beautiful example is Borgergade 11 from 1861, one of the few protected buildings in town. There is a fine view of the town from the high-lying Vestergade and Trappegangen.
Svaneke was awarded the European gold medal for town preservation in 1975.

132. *Svaneke. View from the stair passage.*

132. *Svaneke. Hullebakke/Henrik Hansens Gade 4.*

132. *Svaneke Harbour with the three large merchant houses.*

133-135. The C.F. Harsdorff period, 1777-1787.

134. *Copenhagen, Toldbodgade. The Blue Warehouse, The yellow warehouse and the Vestindisk Warehouse.*

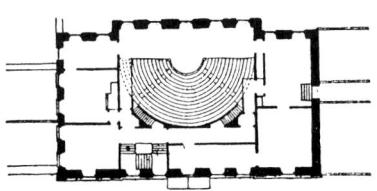

135. *Copenhagen, Bredgade 62. Academy of Surgeons. Plan and elevation 1:750. Right: Auditorium.*

One of Jardin's most talented students at the Royal Academy was C.F. Harsdorff, whose refined, French oriented classicism was first discernible at Moltke's burial chapel in Karise from 1766, and Frederik V's chapel in Roskilde, which was not completed until the 1820's. His mastery was evident in his first city building, Kongens Nytorv 3-5, called Harsdorff's Mansion, built in 1779-80. Here he succeeded in building on a difficult corner site by combining the facades of two buildings so that the pilaster decorated main building's outer left bay also functions as the outer right bay of the smaller building around the corner. The main building's protruding middle section is topped by a pediment supported by Ionic pilasters, with the volutes turned sideways in a rather unorthodox manner. The bend in the facade is elegantly resolved by the semicircular end of the dining room. This feature, an oval or rounded dining room, and accented side bays, won wide acceptance in the city, especially after the fire of 1795. At the same time, Harsdorff was also involved in quite different, robust warehouse projects in the harbour area for the great prospering commercial houses of the time: Vestindisk Warehouse from 1779-81 and the Blue Warehouse, built in 1781-83 and restored 1978-79 by Flemming Hertz and Ole Ramsgaard Thomsen. The Yellow Warehouse, lying in between, was built by G.E.Rosenberg in 1777-79. Its present form is the result of a restoration in 1978-79 by Hans Munk Hansen, brought on by extensive fire damage in 1968. The latter two warehouses are now converted to condominiums.

Another Jardin student was architect Peter Meyn, whose most important work was the Surgical Academy on Bredgade 62, from 1785-87. The somewhat heavy facade is dominated by the quoins on the side bays, the Ionic columns by the portal and the heavy attic storey. The large amphitheater auditorium with the fine, arched coffered ceiling has been preserved.

134. *Copenhagen, Toldbodgade. The Yellow warehouse.*

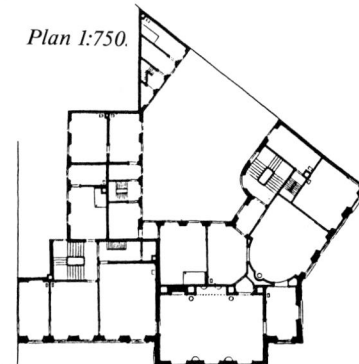

Plan 1:750.

133. *Copenhagen, Kongens Nytorv 3-5. Harsdorff's Hus.*

136-137. Harsdorff's last years, 1794-1799.

136. Copenhagen, Ved Stranden 14. Gustmeyer's Gård.

113. Copenhagen, Amaliegade. Colonnade on Amalienborg Square.

Many competent master builders took a further education at the Royal Academy, one of them was master mason J.M. Qvist. The fact that he was an avid student is evident in the fine building on Ved Stranden 14, built in 1796 for consul F.L. Gustmeyer. Harsdorff's influence is obvious, but a special feature is the recessed centre section behind the two Ionic columns and accompanying pilasters. The interior was recently rebuilt and restored by architect David Bretton Meyer in 1986. On the second floor, behind the columns, architect Hans J. Holm built a vaulted hall with a decorated ceiling in 1873.

About 1790, Harsdorff was introduced to the architecture of ancient Greece, which gave his final works a mature and serene beauty: The Colonnade across Amaliegade at Amalienborg (1794) and Erichsen's Palace, Holmens Kanal 2-4 (1797-99). The latter was the only private home in Copenhagen with an Ionic columned portico on a baselike lower storey. But in reality, the mansion is an L-shaped building with its main facade facing Holmens Kanal and originally part of a well-planned townscape accompanying the old Royal Theatre lying opposite. The piano nobile has preserved elegant interiors with a great hall, bedrooms and a dining hall with a semicircular end wall and richly decorated ceiling and walls. The interiors were designed by the French architect, J.J. Ramée in 1799-1801.

137. Copenhagen, Holmens Kanal 2-4. Erichsen's Palace.

137. Erichsen's Palace. Corner room facing Holmen's Kanal and Kongens Nytorv.

143

138-141. Country estates, 1800-1806.

140. *Copenhagen, Frederiksberg Gardens. The Chinese Pavilion.*

140. *The Chinese Pavilion. Detail.*

138. *Kgs. Lyngby, Nybrovej 401. Sophienholm. Now an exhibition building for the borough of Lyngby-Taarbæk.*

On the slope running from Nybrovej down toward Bagsværd Lake, the French architect J.J. Ramée, who designed the interiors of Erichsen's Palace on Kongens Nytorv in Copenhagen, built a country estate around 1800. It was called Sophienholm and the client was the wealthy Copenhagen merchant Constantin Brun. Ramée also planed the scenic English park with a Gothic porter's lodge, stable, a "Norsk House" and a Chinese pavilion. Sophienholm, with its simplified, cubistic, formal classicism and extremely low roof, represented the new architectural currents from France. The division into a luxurious centre building and two low side wings for guests and servants is typical of Ramée.

In 1806, he built the country estate Øregård on Strandvejen in Hellerup for the merchant, Johannes Søbøtker, where this subdivision is again evident. However, here he crowned the centre section with a low pediment. The plan is a typical "maison de plaisance", with the vestibule and garden room on the central axis. Apparently there were none of the usual, evocative pavilions in the park.

The Crown, of course, was also involved in these tendencies, and starting in 1798, Frederiksberg Have park was altered to the English style. On this occasion the Chinese Pavilion was built in 1799-1800 from drawings by Andreas Kirkerup, and the little Apis Temple, 1802-04, designed by painter and architect, Nicolai Abildgård. The columns are from the vestibule in Moltke's Palace at Amalienborg.

A year later in 1805, Abildgård built himself a fine little vacation house with a large garden called the "Sparrow's nest". This small, rectangular, stuccoed half-timber house is two storeys high with a thatched roof. No wonder that a century later it became a favorite archetype for the garden houses of neoclassicism and early modernism.

139. Gentofte, Ørehøj Allé 2. Øregård. Now an exhibition building for the borough of Gentofte.
Plan 1:750.

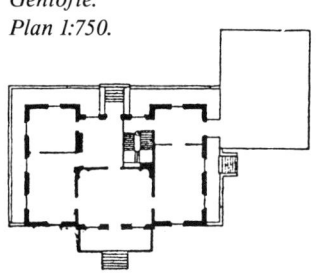

141. Virum, Spurveskjul 4. Abildgård's summer house, »The Sparrow's nest.«

142. C.F. Hansen's classicism, 1805-1822.

Harsdorff had a particularly capable successor in his pupil, Christian Frederik Hansen, who completely dominated Danish architecture in the late classicistic period at a level equal to his contemporaries abroad. After a promising career as a rural master builder in Holstein, where he built many manors and estates in Altona, he returned to Copenhagen at the beginning of the 1800's, where one of his first large projects was the new Town hall and Court House on Nytorv, built in 1805-15. The huge columned front and deep stair hall forms an effective introduction to the building's interior. The same theatrical staging is evident in the adjacent, narrow Slutterigade, which is bounded by two arched bridges in connection with the Arresthus (jail), which was built at the same time. Its facade is heavily symbolic with exaggerated, massive rustication and a powerful portal - woe be those who end behind these heavy walls. It is obvious here that romanticism emphasizes the expressive and evocative, with considerably stronger effects than Harsdorff favoured.

Opposite page: Entrance drive to Slutterigade from Nytorv.

Above: Entrance to the arresthus (jail) from Slutterigade.

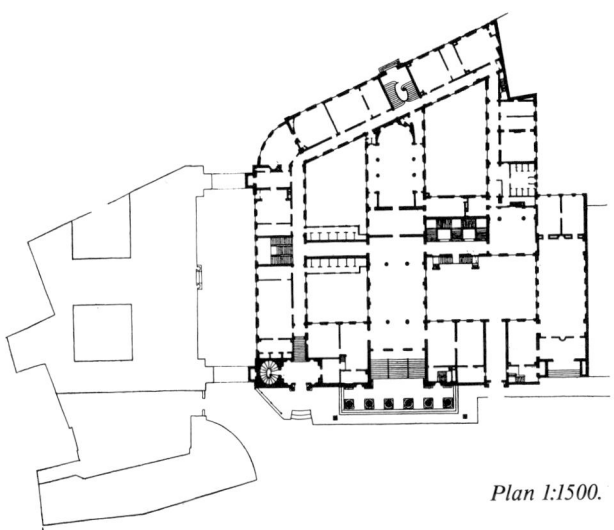

Plan 1:1500.

142. *Copenhagen, Nytorv. Town Hall and Courthouse.*

143-144. Country estates by C. F. Hansen, 1802-1822.

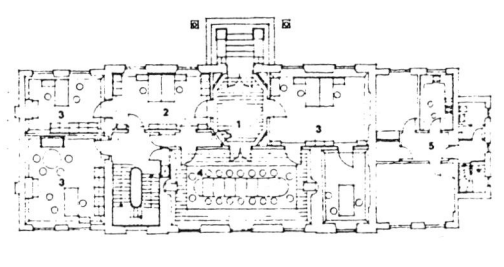

143. *Gentofte, Søholm Park 1. Søholm. Left: Vestibule.*

143. *Søholm. Plan 1:500.*

Before the Court House, C.F. Hansen built the Søholm estate on Emdrup lake in 1805-09. It is a simple rectangular building with a high cellar, two storeys, a low hipped roof and pediment with a billiard room and an observation loggia facing south. The building was faithfully restored in 1982-84 by David Bretton-Meyer.

Pederstrup on Lolland, built in 1813-22 for Prime minister, Count C.D.F. Reventlow is the only preserved C.F. Hansen manor estate in Denmark. The simple, modest main building is in one storey with a centre section that protrudes on both facades, and a pediment and attic level. In 1938-40, the building was freed from an unfortunate renovation that took place during the last century. It was converted to a museum supervised by architect Viggo Sten Møller. Recently in 1984-87 is was restored by architect Per Axelsen.

144. *Pederstrup northeast of Nakskov.*

144. *Pederstrup. Detail of dormer and pediment.*

145-146. Christiansborg Palace church. Hørsholm church, 1803-1822.

145. Copenhagen. Christiansborg Palace Church.

Right: Interior.

Below: Plan 1:750.

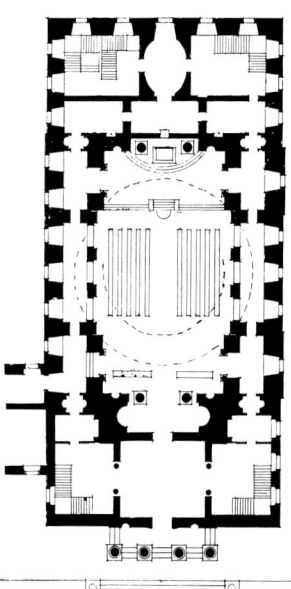

C.F. Hansen's greatest work took place between 1803-28 and was the rebuilding of Christiansborg Palace that had burned down in 1794. Although the current style of the time was pure classicism, he reused as many of the existing walls as possible and retained the same division of floors. Only the west wing facing the riding grounds was replaced by an open colonnade, and the tower was removed. The church was formed as a small, individual temple building with an elegantly detailed, classic portico facing the palace square. The low copper roof is crowned by a flat dome, which is inspired by Roman architecture, primarily Vignola's S. Andrea north of Porta del Popolo. The interior of the rectangular building is almost square, and the sedate, beautiful room is roofed by a coffered dome, supported by pendentives. The church was the only C.F. Hansen building that survived the palace's second fire in 1884.

In order to obtain building materials for the palace, Hansen was given permission to tear down Hirschholm Palace, including the palace chapel. As a replacement for this, Hørsholm Church was built in 1820-22. With its simple basic form: a porch and bell tower to the north, followed by a long house with side galleries and terminated by a chancel and apse to the south, the church appears as a miniature version of Our Lady Church in Copenhagen, though the barrel vault ceiling is only partly coffered.

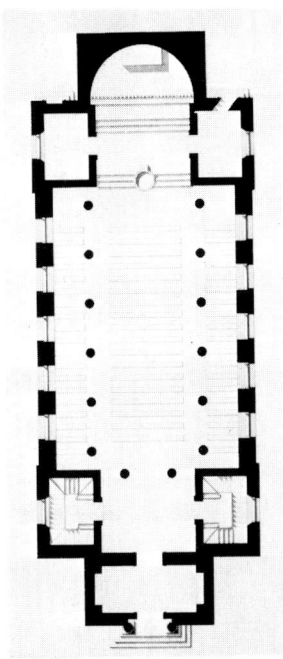

146. *Hørsholm Church. Plan 1:450.*

146. *Hørsholm, Kirke Allé. Hørsholm Church.*

147-148. Late classicism dies off, 1811-1836.

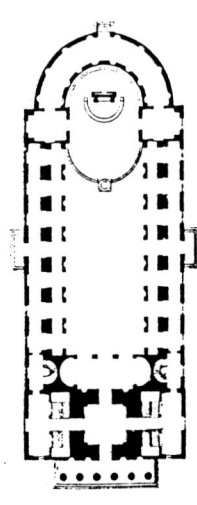

147. *Copenhagen, Frue Kirkeplads. Our Lady Church. Interior. Left: Facade toward Nørregade.*

Plan 1:1500.

The Copenhagen fires were a disaster for the city's churches. Our Lady Church, the Cathedral of Copenhagen, was totally destroyed both in 1728 and during the British bombardment in 1807. C.F. Hansen was commissioned to rebuild it in 1811-29, and he reused parts of the burned out baroque church's walls. It was no doubt a difficult problem to fit these into a classicistic concept, but the result is a powerful, simple building with a prismatic clarity, whose qualities were revived by Vilhelm Wohlert's restoration in 1977-79. This is especially true of the interior, where the lighting and furnishing emphasize the grandiose qualities of the space and Thorvaldsen's beautiful sculptures. The main entrance in the spireless tower is marked by a Doric portico facing Nørregade. The chancel is a semicircular, domed rotunda.

A number of buildings around the church are also by Hansen, such as Soldin's Stiftelse, Skindergade 34/Dyrkøb 1 from 1812-15 and the former Metropolitan School on Fiolstræde 4-6, built in 1811-15.

Copenhagen University was founded in 1479 and has always been located in the neighbourhood of Our Lady Church. The present main building was built in 1831-36 by a Hansen pupil, Peder Malling, in a semiclassicistic, semigothic style that heralded the coming unorthodox view of classicism. The entrance hall was decorated with frescoes by Konstantin Hansen and the Solemnity Hall has richly decorated walls and ceilings by C. Hilker.

Before this, Malling had built Sorø Academy's new, rather massive classicistic main building in 1822-27.

147. *Copenhagen, Frue Kirkeplads. Copenhagen University. Entrance hall.*

148. *Sorø Academy. (Not shown).*

147. *Copenhagen, Fiolstræde 4-6. The Metropolitan school.*

149. Thorvaldsen's Museum, 1839-1848.

149. *Copenhagen, Porthusgade 2. Thorvaldsen's Museum. Below: The vaulted entrance hall.*

After many years in Rome, the famous Danish sculptor, Bertel Thorvaldsen, decided to contribute all of his work and his extensive collection of art and antiquities to a museum in Copenhagen to be financed be a public collection and his own savings. Frederik VI donated a site behind the Palace Church where the four-winged royal coach yard was. In 1839-48, architect M.G. Bindesbøll converted the building to Denmark's first art museum, which was also outstanding in a European context. A great deal of the existing walls were reused, though to the west a large front hall was added with five, tall, tapered portals, which formed the main facade. Above this, the goddess of victory rushes forward in her four-in-hand, a bronze sculpture by H.W. Bissen from a sketch by Thorvaldsen. The tapered portals allude to the classic temple entrance and possibly to Thorvaldsen's initials AT, the A being for Albert. These are repeated all the way around the building, also facing the rectangular courtyard where the artist's grave is located. The most conspicuous exterior feature, aside from the rich colours, is the long pictorial frieze in coloured cement stucco from a sketch by Jørgen Sonne. Facing the canal, the fresco depicts Thorvaldsen's homecoming in 1838. Toward the palace church one can see the unloading of his works from the frigate Rota, and facing the palace their transport to the museum. The interior is richly decorated with mosaics and terrazzo floors, strongly coloured walls, which bring out the sculpture's white marble, and Pompeii inspired ceilings. In the basement, architect, professor Jørgen Bo designed a space for temporary exhibitions in 1968-73.

Plan: 1:1500.

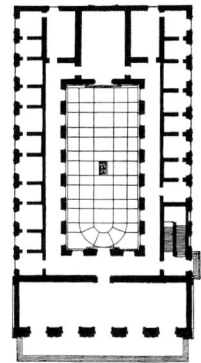

Below: The interior court with Thorvaldsen's grave.

150-153. M.G. Bindesbøll, 1850-1858.

150. *Copenhagen, Østerbrogade 57. The Medical Association housing scheme. Below: Drawing from 1853.*

151. *Vordingborg. Oringe National Hospital. Plan 1:2500.*

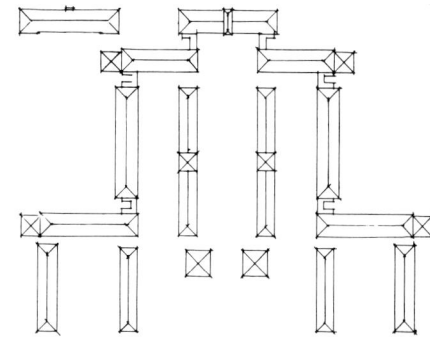

The Lægeforeningens Boliger (The Danish Medical Association's Housing) on Østerbrogade were built as a result of the serious Cholera epidemic in Copenhagen in 1853. They were one of the first examples of inexpensive, healthy housing for poor families, who would otherwise have to survive under indescribably terrible conditions within the city's walls. In 1854-56, M.G. Bindesbøll designed the housing scheme which consisted of two, parallel, two-storey wings (A-H), divided four and four on each side of a wide avenue with small gardens in front and wash houses and toilets behind. The units were small and Spartan but this was compensated for by the access to fresh air, light and common areas. Ever since, the scheme has been a constant source of inspiration in the development of the best in Danish housing. The scheme was later expanded to over twice its size by architect Vilhelm Klein.

The same matter-of-fact, strongly simplified architecture is also evident in other Bindesbøll buildings such as the Oringe National Hospital, built in 1854-57. The modest, uniform yellow brick buildings are organized in a simple, symmetrical plan around a three-storey main building, with low, men and women's wards on each side. Another example is the Agricultural College's first buildings on Bülowsvej in Copenhagen, built in 1865-58.

When a project demanded, Bindesbøll freely employed different styles. This is true of Hobro Church from 1850-52, which is characterized by late Gothic, yet also contains a number of original features. The tower is located over the east chancel, which together with the west end and the three chapel-like side-buildings along the long walls are decorated with pinnacles.

153. *Hobro Church.*

152. *Copenhagen, Frederiksberg. Bülowsvej 13. The Agricultural College.*

154-155. J. D. Herholdt and The University Library, 1857-1861.

When the Copenhagen University library was forced to move from the Trinitatis Church loft, a design competition was arranged, which called for a fireproof building with a continuous stack room, circulation room and reading room, etc. It was to be of brick and iron, and have facades that were in keeping with the surroundings. J.D. Herholdt won with a project that also introduced a romantic, historicized style with the use of numerous sketchbook motifs from the north Italian Middle Ages. The library was built in 1857-61, and as opposed to the other buildings around Frue Plads square, the facades are of red brick, with many brickwork details that express a new interest in structural honesty. The vertical divisions and pointed gables over each window bay emphasize the context with the University's main building, just as the gable toward Frue Plads is clearly conceived as a pendant to the scholarship foundation building's end wall on Nørregade. A sense of integrity is also evident in that each semicircular arched window bay has a matching pair of columns in the interior. These tall thin, cast iron columns give the library hall a cathedral-like atmosphere, despite its modest size.

The combination of italien motifs and danish brick, became an artistic break through for Herholdt, who continued his success with a.o. Grøns Pakhus, Holmens Kanal 7, from 1860-62.

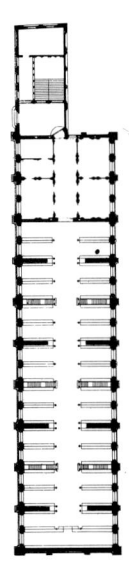

154. *Copenhagen. The University library. Plan 1:1500.*

155. *Copenhagen, Holmens Kanal 7. Grøns Warehouse. Renovated in 1990-91 by architect Niels Brøns. Facade 1:450.*

Right: **154.** *Copenhagen, Fiolstræde 1. The University Library. Library hall; above: The end facade facing Krystalgade.*

156-158. Early historicism, 1859-1869.

156. *Copenhagen, Øster Farimagsgade 5. The Municipal Hospital. The centre section with church and operating rooms.*

156. *The Municipal Hospital. Plan 1:2000.*

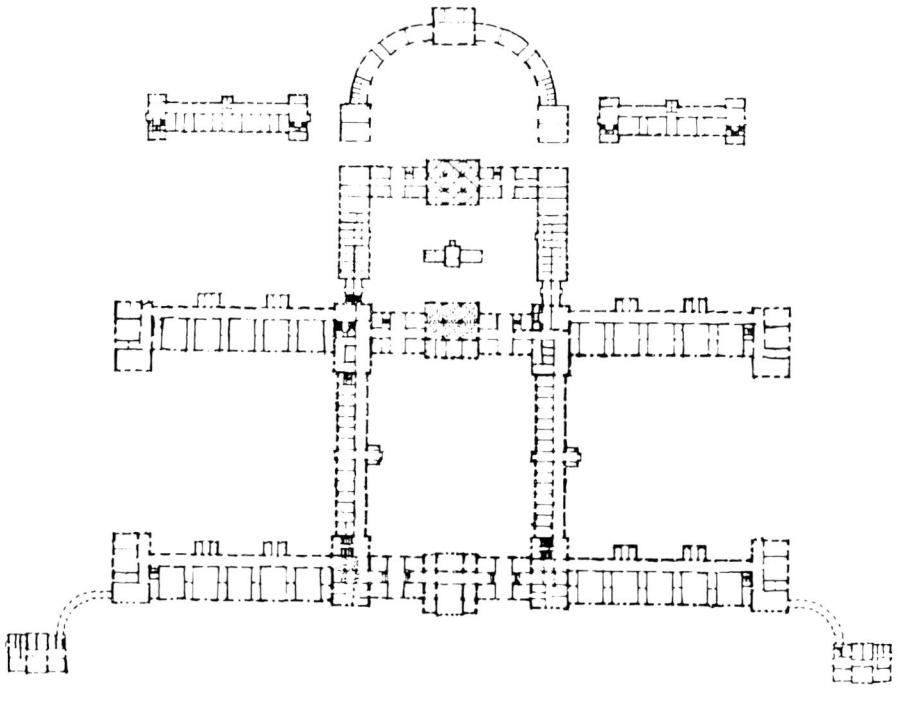

As a replacement for the Public hospital that had been torn down on Amaliegade, Copenhagen's Municipal hospital was built in 1859-63 on the former demarcation terrain just outside the old ramparts. The plan of this large complex is reminiscent of a rambling baroque palace, however this is offset by the facades' Greek Byzantine style and the long row of two-bay, ten-patient wards, separated by a single-bay service room. The symmetrical scheme is divided up in men's and women's wings, with all wards having solar exposure. The architect was Christian Hansen, who worked and lived in Athens for a number of years. His special insight in Byzantine architecture is evident in the hospital church, centrally placed under the dome. The fact that he also mastered more conventional styles, such as Italian Renaissance, is evident in the former Zoological Museum on Krystalgade 25-27 in Copenhagen, built in 1863-69.

The rebuilding of the fire damaged Frederiksborg Palace brought architect Ferdinand Meldahl great fame. He was thus a natural choice to supervise the rebuilding of the Frijsenborg manor estate, which was converted to a French/Dutch inspired Renaissance scheme in 1862-66. The result was one of Meldahl's most successful manor estates, with fine proportions and detailing. Many of the greatest artists of the time participated in the decoration of the interiors.

158. *Frijsenborg near Hammel.*

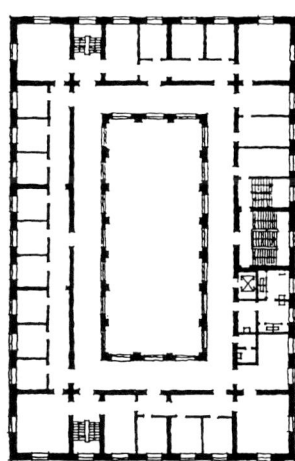

157. *Zoological Museum. Plan 1:750.*

157. *Copenhagen, Krystalgade 25-27. The former Zoological Museum.*

161

159. Historicistic church restorations, 1864-1892.

159. *Viborg Cathedral after restoration, old photo.*

15. *Bjernede Round Church, old drawing; below: After restoration.*

With the adoption of church inspection law of 1861, the concept of restoration became an accepted principle in Danish architecture, as the law required that major alterations should respect the church's original style, and that efforts should be made toward restoring that style. This gave both positive and negative results. The reestablishment of the centre tower on Maria Church in Kalundborg in 1866 and the restoration of the Chapel of the Magi at Roskilde Cathedral could be considered positive, whereas the rebuilding of Viborg Cathedral is somewhat unsuccessful. Despite the poor condition of the cathedral, so much of the old twelfth century Romanesque cathedral still remained that a more faithful restoration should have resulted. Instead the decision was made to tear the remains down and build a new church, as close as possible to the ideal that had been envisioned, inspired by the cathedral in Lund, Sweden. Only the crypt and the lower part of the apse still remains. The project was supervised by N.S. Nebelong 1864-71 and continued by H.B. Storck until its completion in 1876.

One of Storck's later works, the restoration of Bjernede Round Church near Sorø in 1890-92, with its dry, academically correct reconstruction, completely did away with the charming little building with its mitrelike roof. The violent criticism that followed helped to broaden an understanding of architectural values in later additions to historical buildings.

160-162, Building society houses in Copenhagen, 1865-1903.

Housing for the impoverished portion of the population has traditionally been left to private initiative, even though public institutions often have to alleviate the worst results of this. In the middle of the last century, the housing conditions for the working class in Copenhagen were so bad, that neither speculation or private charity (such as the Medical Association's housing) could do anything of significance with the problem. Therefore an interest in relieving the problem arose in the worker's own ranks, and several housing associations were established after 1865. The Workers' Building Society came into being that year, with the purpose of building a number of small row houses for members' dues and the loans that could be managed. After ten years, the tenant was given the deed to the house, and after 24 years he was debt free. Each house had two flats, so that one could be leased to another member. This housing form was chosen as the healthiest and most pleasant, and the owner-occupant form was to strengthen self-esteem, well-being and family life. The first houses were built in 1867-71 on Sverrigsgade on Amager with H.S. Sibbern as architect. However the most well-known are the 480 houses between Øster Søgade and Øster Farimagsgade, the so-called "Potato Rows", designed by Frederik Bøttger. The facades are of red and yellow brick, decorated with arches, bands and gables. These features are repeated in the 393 houses, built in the Kildevældsgade area of Østerbro in 1892-1903, where Bøttger built his 1000th house.

160. *Copenhagen. Building Society housing on Sverrigsgade on Amager. (Not shown).*

161. *Copenhagen, Øster Søgade. Kartoffelrækkerne housing.*

163-165. Vilhelm Dahlerup, 1872-1894.

163. *Copenhagen, Kongens Nytorv. The Royal Theatre.*

164. *Copenhagen, Vesterbrogade 3, Tivoli. The Pantomime theatre.*

The oldest Royal Theatre was built on Kongens Nytorv by Niels Eigtved in 1748, but due to several rebuilding projects and additions it had become completely obsolete. Therefore an architect competition was arranged in 1870, which was won by architects Vilhelm Dahlerup and Ove Petersen with a joint project that was realized in 1872-74. It was a magnificent theatre, inspired by the same spirit as the great ideals in Vienna and Paris, with resplendent stairways, foyers and sumptuous ornamentation in stucco, gilding, brocade and velvet. The style could be called Renaissance and was inspired by motifs from the Sapienza (university) in Naples. The main facade as well as the lower part of the side facades are sided with sandstone and limestone. A sort of tambour with a flat domed roof surrounds the theatre room and stage. The proscenium and the Acropolis drop curtain were copied from the old theatre. After this festive tour de force, Dahlerup was commissioned to design the Pantomime Theatre in Tivoli in 1874, possibly his best work. Dahlerup had never been in China, but nevertheless, the building was more Chinese than any other known example. Generally speaking, he was at his best when he was free to work with various styles, on projects that were not restricted by conventions. An example of this is the Søpavillon on Peblingsøen from 1894, built of wood for the Copenhagen Ice Skaters Association.

163. *The Royal Theatre foyer.*

165. *Copenhagen, Gyldenløvesgade/Peblingesøen. Søpavillonen.*

166. Ny Carlsberg Brewery, Jesus Church, 1880-1901.

The founder of Carlsberg Brewery, I.C. Jakobsen was one of the first to move his firm out of the old city. For this purpose he employed N.S. Nebelong as architect to build the new factory complex in Valby. His son, Carl Jacobsen, founded his own brewery in 1879 on an adjacent site, which grew up during the years 1880-83 with Vilhelm Dahlerup as architect. A prominent feature was the tower building facing Pasteursvej, and the double portal, Dipylon along side, both built in 1892. The most unusual building work was Dahlerup's Elephant Tower from 1901, that was to house the cooler and water tank, spanning Ny Carlsberg Vej, and supported by four massive granite elephants.

The Jesus Church on Kirkevænget, not far from the brewery, is the Jakobsen family burial church, and also Dahlerup's work. The basilica was built in 1884-91 as a restatement of early European church architecture, and contains Byzantine as well as Roman and early Christian features. The long house surrounds the raise, twelve-sided chancel, beneath which there is a low, circular crypt. There were no limits in terms of expensive materials, when dealing with the furnishings, which a number of artists participated in. The free-standing bell tower was built in 1894-95.

Above: Tower facing Pasteursvej.

Opposite page: **166.** *Copenhagen, Ny Carlsberg Vej. Ny Carlsberg Brewery. The Elephant Tower.*

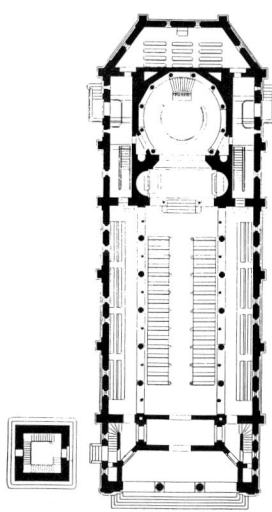

Plan, ca 1:750.

166. *Copenhagen, Valby, Kirkevænget. Jesus Church.*

167-169. Ferdinand Meldahl, 1873-1894.

Since work on Jardin's marble church project was ceased in 1770, Frederiks Church on Bredgade lay as a half-finished ruin. However the task that the absolute monarchy could not manage was finally taken over by finance and industrial magnate, C.F. Tietgen. He bought the ruins from the Ministry of Finance in 1874 with the commitment to complete the church and in 1894 it was consecrated. The architect was Ferdinand Meldahl, who in an ingenious way, combined the existing walls with a domed building in Roman baroque, strongly inspired by St. Peters Cathedral. The square around the church was edged with elegant buildings with flats for the well-to-do, so it was not a case of pure philanthropy.

Meldahl was also the director of Tietgen's Copenhagen Building Society, established in 1872, and was thus responsible for the fashionable buildings on Hovedvagtsgade and Ny Østergade, which replaced some of the city's worst slums. However other architects were employed to design the buildings. This was also the case with the buildings surrounding Søtorvet, which were built in 1873-76 by Vilhelm Petersen and Ferdinand Jensen on the old rampart terrain. The large luxurious buildings, with their towers, spires, domes and stucco facades in French Renaissance style create a festive northern entrance to the city.

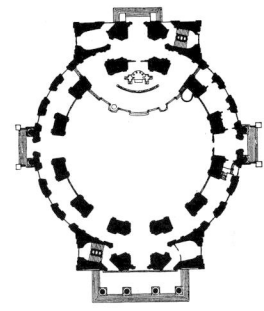

167. Marble Church. Plan 1:1500.

Opposite page: **167.** *Copenhagen, Frederiksgade. Frederik's Church, also called Marble Church.*

168. *Copenhagen. Hovedvagtsgade. (Not shown).*
169. *Copenhagen. Søtorvet.*

170-171. The National Museum of Art. The Glyptotek, 1889-1906.

171. *Glyptoteket. The facade of the Antiquity section facing the street, by the Glyptoteket.*

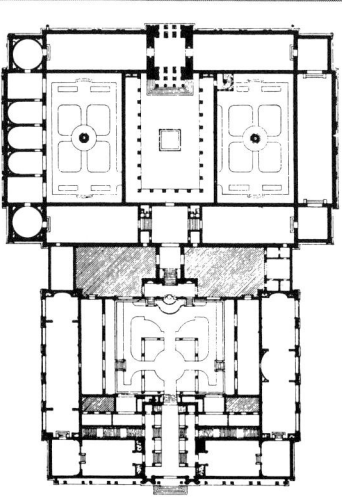

171. *Copenhagen, H.C. Andersens Boulevard/ Dantes Plads. Glyptoteket.*

171. *Glyptoteket. Plan 1:1500.*

As a result of the Christiansborg fire in 1884, the royal collection of paintings lost its home, and a competition for a new National Museum of Art was arranged. The winner was Vilhelm Dahlerup and Georg E.V. Møller. Their monumental project was built between 1889 and 1896 on part of the old ramparts near Sølvgade. This powerful statement in natural stone and brick is emphasized by the triumphal archlike entrance and the spacious two-storey hall. However from the very beginning there was a lack of space. Unfortunately a rebuilding project in 1966-69 by Eva and Nils Koppel removed the grand stairway in the entrance hall, which had been inspired by the ambassador stairway at Versailles.

The brewer Carl Jakobsen was both a skilled and avid art collector. He decided to donate his large and famous collection to the Danish state, and to build the Glyptotek on Dantes Plads square to house it. The oldest part, facing the square, was built in 1892-97 from drawings by Vilhelm Dahlerup and consists of three wings surrounding a glass-roofed conservatory, which was added in 1904-06. The festive facade is inspired by Venetian Renaissance and decorated with polished granite columns, statues, mussel shell ornaments and a terra cotta patterned brickwork. The new section was built in 1901-06 by Hack Kampmann in the classicistic style and houses the antiquity collection. The center section of the west wing is emphasized by a columned loggia, crowned by a triumphal pyramid, inspired by the ancient mausoleum on Halikarnassos.

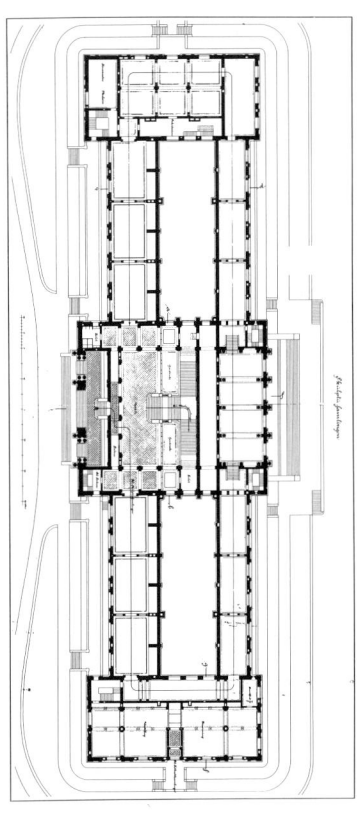

170. *Copenhagen, Sølvgade 48-50. The National Museum of Art.   Plan 1:1500.*

172-175. Nyrop and neoromanticism, 1885-1913.

173. Copenhagen, Bispebjerg Bakke 19-35. Bispebjerg Hospital.

175. Hørsholm, Rungstedvej 47. Villa for Agnes Nyrop.

174. Vallekilde Folk High School near Svinninge pr. Holbæk.

During the time of Herholdt, there arose an increasing interest in a nationally influenced, romantic architecture as a counterweight to the prevailing Europe oriented style that Meldahl and Dahlerup advocated. Though not especially romantic, H.B. Storck's, Abel Cathrines Foundation on Abel Cathrines Gade 13, from 1885-86, was the first work that pointed in that direction. Here Herholdt's red brick architecture blends with baroque forms in a firm, personal whole. A distinct Danish tone, explicit and with an air of friendly cheerfulness is now discernable. However the man who seriously created a Nordic and Danish direction in architecture was Martin Nyrop. Based on the hereditary traditions and high quality craftsmanship, he sought a character of honesty and trustworthiness in his buildings, where construction, details and choice of materials formed a synthesis. As far as possible this choice was confined to local materials and they achieved a force due to the fact that their natural colours and structure were allowed to dominate the character of the surface, occasionally reinforced by special treatments. For Nyrop, the details were a decisive factor in achieving the results he sought, though he managed to maintain a sense of the whole. This is especially apparent at Bispebjerg Hospital, built in 1907-13, even though the forms employed here are simple and objective. This is also true of the addition to Vallekilde Højskole from 1907-08. On a completely different front, Nyrop made great advances in the development of the small Danish house as can be seen in the house built in 1891 for his sister Agnes, on Rungstedvej 47 in Hørsholm.

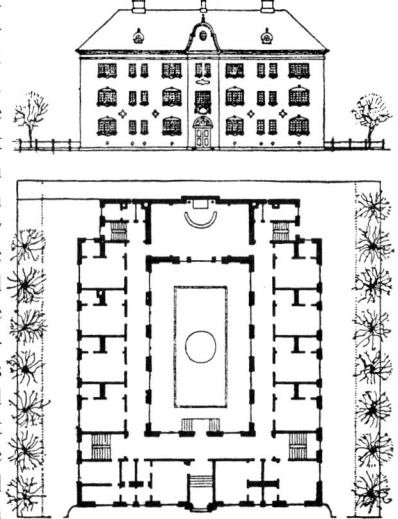

172. *Abel Cathrine's Foundation. Plan and elevation 1:750.*

172. *Copenhagen, Abel Cathrines Gade 13. Abel Cathrine's Foundation.*

176. Copenhagen's Town Hall, 1892-1905.

176. *Copenhagen, Town Hall Square. Copenhagen Town Hall. Main Hall.*

Facade detail.

Copenhagen tripled its population during the nineteenth century and C.F. Hansen's old town hall and court house was soon too small to house the increased administrative needs. After a public and a closed competition for a new town hall, Martin Nyrop was commissioned and the huge building complex slowly grew between 1892-1905. The simple plan is based on a rectangle in which the centre court is divided by a transverse wing, creating two courts: A large open one and a smaller one with a glass roof. All of the ceremonial rooms are placed around the roofed court, and this part of the building appears as a dominate block facing the Town Hall Square. Behind this are the lower office wings, with corridors facing the open courtyard and a beautiful long hall, that opens up through the entire height of the building near the rear entrance. The city council hall and rooms, the marriage hall and the City Archives are housed in the transverse wing, which is the symbolic core of the building, while the sumptuous assembly hall faces the town hall square. The tower, the city's highest, is placed asymmetrically opposite the transverse wing, inspired by the town hall tower in Siena, and strongly contributes to the building's character of sound unassuming democracy and civil government. The town hall was a breakthrough for a more democratic architectural attitude, which with a synthesis of freely chosen ideals, provides a spontaneous, lively narrative world of motifs, unburdened by classic wisdom. A high level of craftsmanship and solid materials characterize the detailing, just as the amazingly uniform decoration was carried out by a number of the best painters and sculptors of the time.

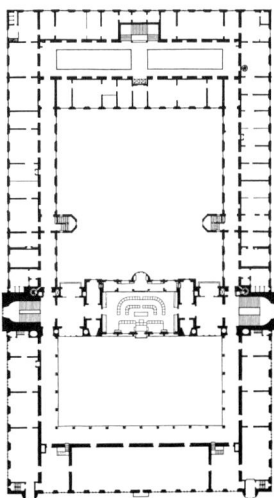

176. *Copenhagen Town Hall. Plan 1:2000.*

176. *Copenhagen Town Hall seen from Vesterbrogade. Old photo.*

177-180. Ulrik Plesner and the neobaroque, 1896-1910.

177. *Copenhagen,
Åboulevarden 12-18.
Åhusene housing scheme.*

177. *Åboulevarden 12-18.
Plan and elevation 1:750.*

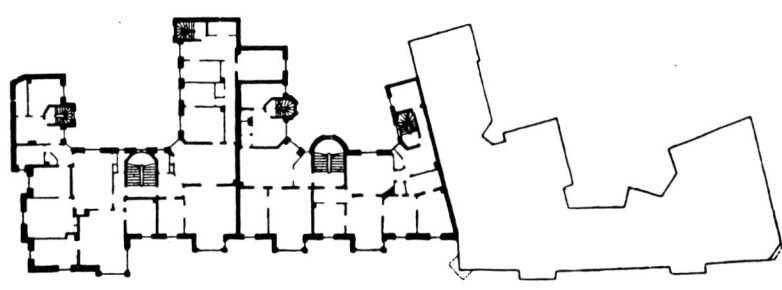

As was the case with Nyrop, Clemmensen, Borch and other architects involved with national romanticism, the basis for Ulrik Plesner's work was the traditional Danish architecture. However there is also a notable interest in English architecture, but unlike earlier practice, he didn't directly employ motifs from sketchbooks and surveys. The picturesque and well-formed baroque also attracted him, but without his losing a firm grip on the whole. This is clearly apparent in his housing projects, the first in the Åhusene, on Åboulevarden 12-18 from 1896-98, where the richly varied facade overhangs, bays, gables and dormers were pioneer work in this area. The traditional block pattern was in a state of fragmentation, the period of stucco ornamentation was past, and the red, undecorated brick facades were the dominant feature.

In collaboration with Aage Langeland-Mathiesen, Plesner later built the related buildings around Danas Plads (1908-09), and together they won a competition for the Student Union building at H.C. Andersen's Boulevard 6, which was completed in 1910. Here, English inspiration was strangely mixed with Christian IV's Renaissance, and admiration for his friend, Thorvald Bindesbøll, who often assisted Plesner with facade decorations. A good example of this is the building on Gammel Torv 8, which is also from 1908.

180. *Copenhagen, Gammel Torv 8.*

Left: **179.** *Copenhagen, H.C. Andersens Boulevard 6. The Student Union.*

Below: **178.** *Copenhagen. Housing scheme near Danas Plads.*

181-183. Copenhagen's Main Station. Saint Andreas Church. Elias Church, 1898-1911.

A rational organization of the Copenhagen's railway connections with the outside world required the establishment of a new Main Station, which was built in 1904-11, opposite the Liberty Memorial on Vesterbrogade. It was designed by the National Railway's head architect, Heinrich Wenck. The materials are red brick and granite, and many of the details and the strongly constructive division of elements, reveal an intense preoccupation with Nyrop's Town Hall. The departure and arrival hall, with its impressive timber structure, has been undergoing renovation since 1978 by DSB's Building service and the architectural firm, Dissing & Weitling.

During this period, a number of new churches were built in Copenhagen as the old parishes grew too large. This was why Martin Borch built Saint Andreas Church in 1898-1901 on the corner of Øster Farimagsgade and Gothersgade, in a virtuous juxtaposition of national Romanesque forms. Martin Nyrop built Elias Church on Vesterbro Torv in 1906-08, strongly inspired by the Hvide family's twin-towered churches in Tveje Merløse and Fjenneslev.

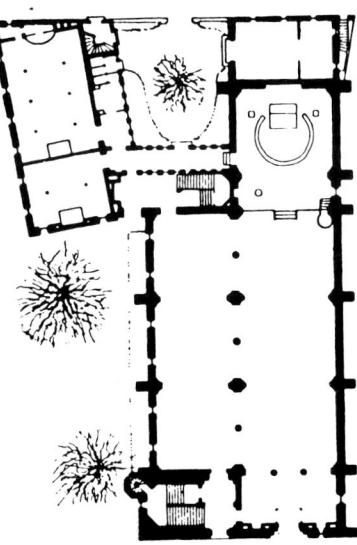

Left: **181.** *Copenhagen, Vesterbrogade. Main railway station.*

182. *Copenhagen, Øster Farimagsgade. St. Andreas Church. Plan 1:750.*

Left: **183.** *Copenhagen, Vesterbros Torv. Elias Church.*

182. *St. Andreas Church.*

184-186. Århus Theatre. Århus Custom House. the National Library, 1895-1902.

184. *Århus, Bispetorvet.*
Århus Theatre.

185. *Århus Harbour.*
Customs house.

At the end of the nineteenth century, Århus had become the country's second largest city and thus was in need of a decent, reasonably sized theatre. Hack Kampmann was commissioned as architect and in 1898-1900, on Bispetorv Square, he built a festive and strongly personal building, distinguished by his great decorative talent. Both the interior and exterior ornamentation plays on national motifs in the field of drama, flora and fauna. The vaulted blue dome of the theatre hall is decorated with ceramic swans and gulls. In 1953, C.F. Møller expanded the theatre rearward filling out the rest of the pointed city block. The most recent renovation was in 1981-82 by the same architects.

Shortly before the theatre was built in 1895-97, Kampmann built the Custom House building in the harbour area and it was given a somewhat more imaginative form than was customary with that type of building. At the junction of the two angular wings, the entrance is marked by a fortresslike tower, flanked by lower, octagonal towers.

Kampmann's National library on Vester Allé 12, built in 1898-1902, could be considered a minor masterpiece. The relatively simple block is decorated in a personal style with details gathered from all over the world, yet still manages to avoid appearing foreign in context. The handsome reading room has three skylight domes decorated with stucco and Danish poet's names.

186. *Århus, Vester Allé 12. The former National Library, now the commercial archives.*

186. *The National Library. Reading room.*

186. *The National Library. Entrance door.*

187. Skagen, 1891-1924.

187. *Skagen. Thorvald Bindesbølls Fish warehouse on the harbour.*

187. *Skagen. Harbour building.*

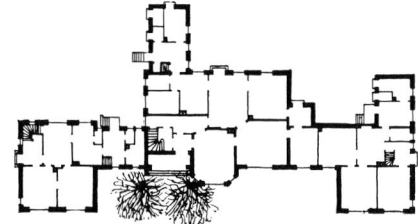

Plan, 1:750.

Despite its Middle Age origins, only a few houses remain from the early nineteenth century in Skagen. The majority of buildings in the town were built at the end of the 1800's and the beginning of this century in a style typical of the traditional old building methods: Low, yellow-washed houses with white-washed cornices, and white edged, red tile roofs. This very uniform style is due to a number of architects who came to Skagen after the town had been discovered by the Skagen-artists in the years following 1870. First and foremost was Ulrik Plesner who built the post office (1909), Klitgården (1914), the railway station (1914 and 1924), the hospital (1916 and 1923), Skagen's Bank (1918), and numerous smaller homes in addition to repeated renovations and additions to Brøndum's Hotel (1891, 1897, and 1909). When the fishing harbour was established in 1904-07, Plesner built the harbour building with offices and official's living quarters in 1905, a typical example of his Jutland inspired, modest building style with beautiful red brickwork.

The fish warehouses in the harbour were built in 1905-07 by the prolific, decorative talent, architect Thorvald Bindesbøll. His inspiration was not doubt garnered from Norwegian harbour towns like Bergen and Trondhjem.

On Højen (the hill) in Gl. Skagen, architect Knud V. Engelhardt built a summer cottage in 1917 that attracted much attention with its high, tarred foundation that terminated at the window sills. The meticulously detailed project was approved as a house type by the Society for Better Building Practices.

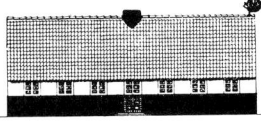
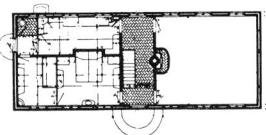

187. *Gl. Skagen, Højen. Summer house by Knud V. Engelhardt. Plan and elevation 1:400.*

Left bottom: **187.** *Skagen. Klitgården.*

188. Villas in the Ryvang district.

188. Copenhagen.
Svanemøllevej 56.
Carl Brummer.

Right: **188.** Svanemøllevej 56.
Plan 1:750.

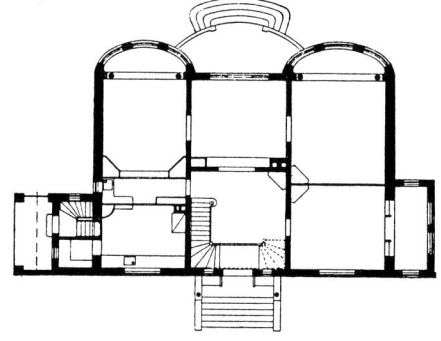

188. Copenhagen. Lundevangsvej 11.
Carl Brummer.

188. Copenhagen. Vestagervej 7.
Carl Brummer.

During the last half of the nineteenth century, the villa became the preferred housing form for many of the well-to-do. In the suburbs of Copenhagen and other large cities, large and often uncontrolled garden housing areas grew up, where different styles competed for attention over the property line fences. The Ryvang district, between Ryvangs Allé and Strandvejen in the Northern suburbs of Copenhagen was originally laid out with modest subdivisions for the wealthy gentry. In the early 1900's, a number of large villas were built here, which were not only designed by some of Denmark's most talented architects, but also represented the owners' need to manifest their influence and position in society. One of the most popular architects was Carl Brummer, who was highly knowledgeable in the area of German and English villa design, and also a virtuoso with neobaroque forms in red, hand-moulded brick, which was popular at the time. One of his earliest villas is at Svanemøllevej 56, built in 1904 with the entire street facade based on a portico motif. Lundevangsvej 11, from 1908 features an asymmetric, well-composed facade pulled out to the street line, and has a large, softly sweeping, hipped, tile roof. During the same year, Vestagervej 7 was built by the little traffic circus at Engskiftevej. Other noteworthy houses in the area are the painter J.F. Willumsen's house on Strandagervej 28 from 1906 and Ryvangs Allé 6, from the same year by Anton Rosen.

188. *Copenhagen.*
Ryvangs Allé 6.
Anton Rosen.

188. *Copenhagen.*
Strandagervej 28.
J.F. Willumsen.

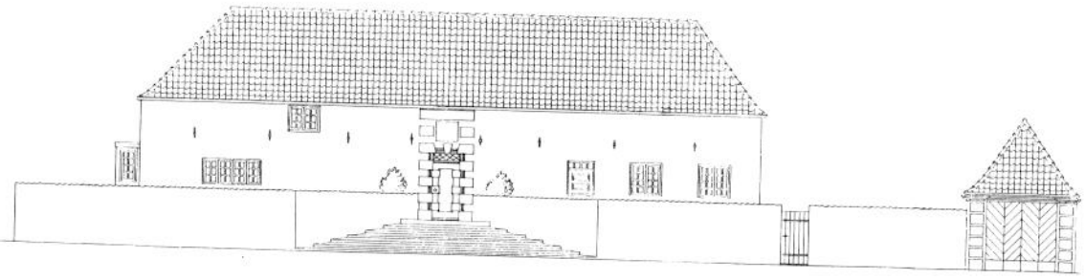

188. Copenhagen. Gl. Vartov Vej 16. Povl Baumann. Below: Plan 1:400.

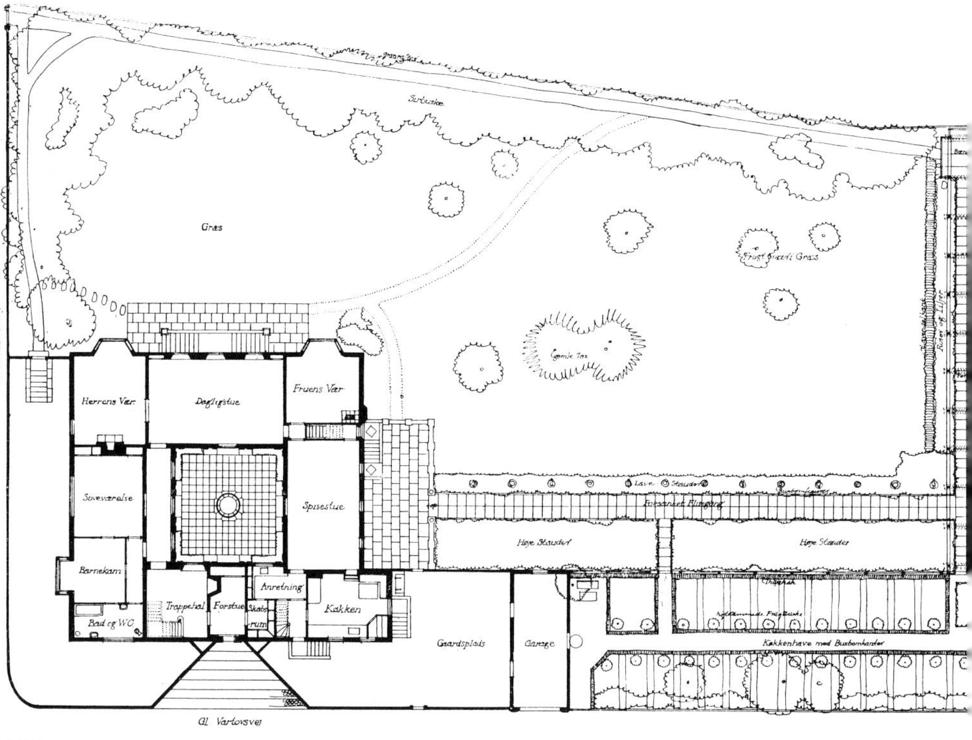

188. *Copenhagen. Gammel Vartov Vej 22. Aage Rafn. Street facade.*

188. *Gammel Vartov Vej 22. Plan 1:400.*

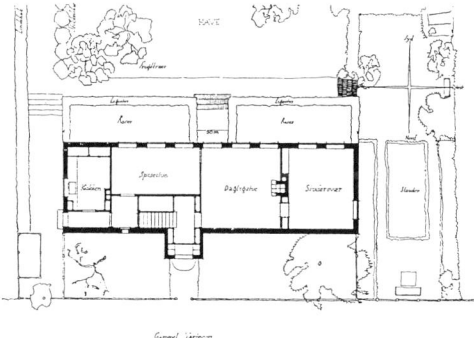

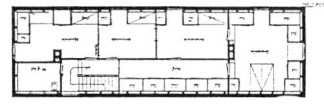

A home of an entirely different character is Povl Baumann's low, four-winged villa on Gammel Vartovvej 16 from 1916, an undecorated but exclusive villa behind its own garden wall. Here neoclassicism's formal and ordered proportions have received a very personal interpretation.
On the other hand, the villa at Gammel Vartovvej 22, built by Aage Rafn in 1919-20 is more strict and matter-of-fact. The street facade is completely free of windows.

189-193. Anton Rosen, 1906-1917.

Anton Rosen is an individualist in Danish architecture, creative, open to international trends and free of, but at the same time sensitive to, traditional practices. One of his most substantial works is Tuborg's old administration building on Strandvejen 54 from 1914-15, which is now used for formal activities. The combined hotel and commercial building at Vesterbrogade 34 from 1906 is an early example of American influence, with curtain wall facades. The commercial building at Frederiksberggade 16 on Copenhagen's pedestrian street, Strøget, was built in 1907 and is one of the few "Jugendstil" inspired buildings in Denmark. His major work in this genre is without a doubt, the Palace Hotel on the Town Hall Square, which Rosen built in 1907-10. The hotel's 65 metre high tower is decorated with four mosaics depicting the four periods of day and night. The facade is worthy of a major city hotel, and Rosen's unrivalled, creative talent was strongly expressed in the interior and furnishings, which today are all but lost. The complex stretches all the way through the block to the Grand cinema on Mikkel Bryggersgade. Rosen also designed a number of housing schemes including the beautiful garden village, Gerthas Minde in Odense, from 1912-17.

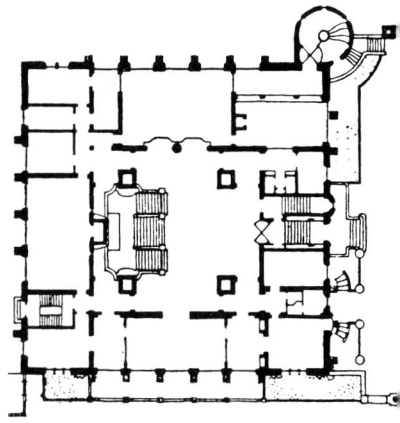

189. *Tuborg's old headquarters building. Plan and elevation 1:750.*

Opposite: **192.** *Copenhagen, Town Hall Square. Palads Hotel.*

189. *Copenhagen, Strandvejen 54. Tuborg's old headquarters building.*

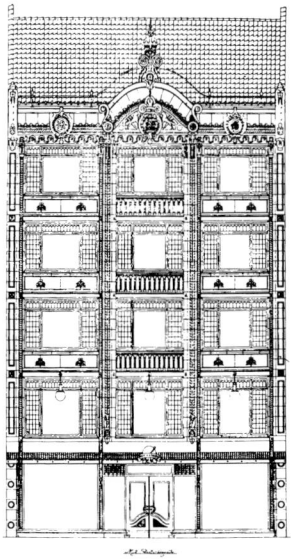

190. Copenhagen. Vesterbrogade 34. Above: Facade.

Opposite: **192.** Copenhagen. Frederiksberggade 16.

193. Odense. The garden village Gerthasminde, Gerthasvej.

194-196. The museums of neoclassicism, 1912-1917.

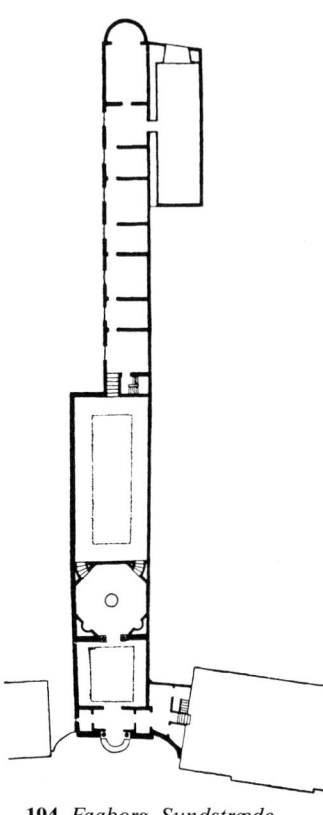

194. *Faaborg Museum. The octagonal domed hall. Plan 1:750.*

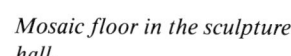

194. *Faaborg, Sundstræde. Faaborg Museum.*

Mosaic floor in the sculpture hall.

In 1910, the industrialist, Mads Rasmussen acquired a large collection of paintings by the artist group, "Fynboerne" and exhibited them for the public in his private home in Fåborg. In 1912, he decided to build a museum for these artworks on a long, narrow neighbouring property, and commissioned architect Carl Petersen. Petersen was a pioneer in his field and a strong advocate of the simplified expressiveness inherent in C.F. Hansen's classicism, and thus rejected the other, worn-out historical styles. However he was just as interested in a new spatial and form attitude, based on the textural effects of materials. Fåborg Museum, completed in 1915, was not only his major work, but also one of the most important buildings in twentieth century Danish architecture. The monumental entrance is pulled back from the street and with its sweeping side areas, beautifully effects the transition to the neighbouring buildings. Following the vestibule, there is a small exhibition space and then an octagonal domed room with Kai Nielsen's large black granite sculpture of Mads Rasmussen. This is followed by a large exhibition space, and all of these rooms are lit by skylights. After this, comes seven small niches with side lighting and this progression ends in the archive room with frescos by Johannes Larsen and furniture by Kaare Klint. Next to this is a sculpture hall with a large window facing the garden. The colour of the walls and the mosaic floors are strongly inspired by Thorvaldsen's Museum. A renovation and addition by Niels F. Truelsen was carried out in 1985.

This period saw the building of other museums. A. Høeg Hansen built a small art gallery on Mørksgade 13 in Århus in 1917, and Viggo Norn designed the Horsens Museum in 1915.

195. *Århus, Mørksgade 13. The Art Building.*

196. *Horsens, Sundvejen. Horsens Museum.*

Below: **194.** *Faaborg Museum. The large Painting hall.*

197-198. Ivar Bentsen and Marius Pedersen, 1913-1929.

198. *Holbæk.
Bakkekammen 23.*

198. *Holbæk.
Bakkekammen 50.*

197. *Svinninge pr. Holbæk.
Northwest Zealand's Power
Station.
Turbine Hall.*

The sudden wave of interest in classicism after the first decade of the century spread rapidly and also influenced Ivar Bentsen's power station in Svinninge from 1913. However it was rarely combined with such good proportions and artistic freedom as here. The original complex consisted of three buildings around a long square with a lawn and flower beds in the centre: A turbine hall with the end facing a two-storey, supervisor living unit and a one-storey director and accountant living quarters at right angles to this. The materials were flamed, red and yellow industrial brick and the elegantly formed pilasters are emphasized by alternating courses in each colour. The turbine hall is the dominant feature of the scheme with its protruding centre part and the slightly mannered side entrances with tall keystones. The facade itself is a study in geometric rules of proportion. Classicism is present in the triangular pediments and cornice bands, alternating with more baroque features in the placement of the pilasters and the barrack like character of the official living quarters. The elegant treatment of the brickwork was inspired by P.V. Jensen Klint.

In 1911, Ivar Bentsen built a home for himself at Bakkekammen in Holbæk (Møllevangen 1). In the years before 1920 he collaborated with Marius Pedersen and influenced the appearance of the entire neighbourhood with a number of exceptionally well-designed villas in the same gentry-like, classicistic, craftsman influenced tradition, which the Better Building Practice encouraged during these years. Good examples are Bakkekammen 23 (1911-12), the non-commissioned officers' housing 10-24 (1913), No. 50 (1915), No. 47 (1916), No. 27 (1919), No. 49 (1922) and Marius Pedersen's own house at No. 45 from 1929.

198. *Holbæk. Møllevangen 1.*

197. *Svinninge. Northwest Zealand's Power Station. Supervisor housing.*

199-200. The Gudhjem line railway stations and Hegel's country estate, 1914-1916.

199. *Gudhjem Station.*

199. *Østerlars Station. Street facade and nearby warehouse.*

Below: **199.** *Østermarie Station and post office. Right: Bay window facing the platform.*

When the final stretch of railway line was to be established on Bornholm, a competition was arranged that was won by the young architects, Aage Rafn and Kay Fisker. Their station buildings, built in 1915-16, expressed a completely different attitude than what was customary at the time: Gone was the heavy, pretentious architectural style, and instead the buildings were based on the local traditional building culture with long, relatively narrow buildings with whitewashed brick, tarred wood trim and recycled tiles on hipped roofs. The practical considerations were the most important, but when the situation demanded, a personal classicism was employed, combined with high quality craftsmanship. Every detail was well-designed, from the position on the site to the furnishings and the sign on the men's room door. The largest station was Gudhjem, which now functions as a museum, with an addition from 1990 by Niels F.Truelsen, while Østermarie and Østerlars stations have well-preserved exteriors. The strange, tall wooden pavilion at the whistle stop at Christianshøj is now converted to an exhibition space. A degree of English country house inspiration can hardly be denied, especially in the wood shingled bay at Gudhjem.

This style was popular in the years preceding World War I as can also be seen at Hegel's country estate on Strandvejen 859 in Springforbi, designed by Henning Hansen in 1914-15.

199. *Almindingen. The whistle stop near Christianshøj.*

200. *Copenhagen, Springforbi, Strandvejen 859. Hegel's country estate. Architect Henning Hansen.*

Plan 1:500.

201-203. Better Building Practices, 1915-1930.

201. *Copenhagen, Grøndalsvænge Allé/Godthåbsvej. Garden house society, Grøndalsvænge.*

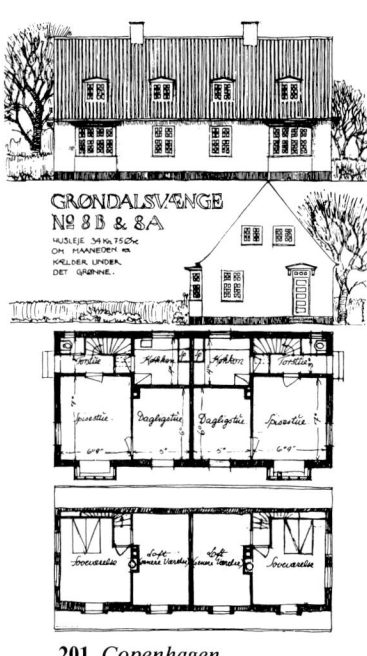

201. *Copenhagen. Grøndalsvænge. Two-family house. Plan and elevations 1:400.*
Right: Site plan.

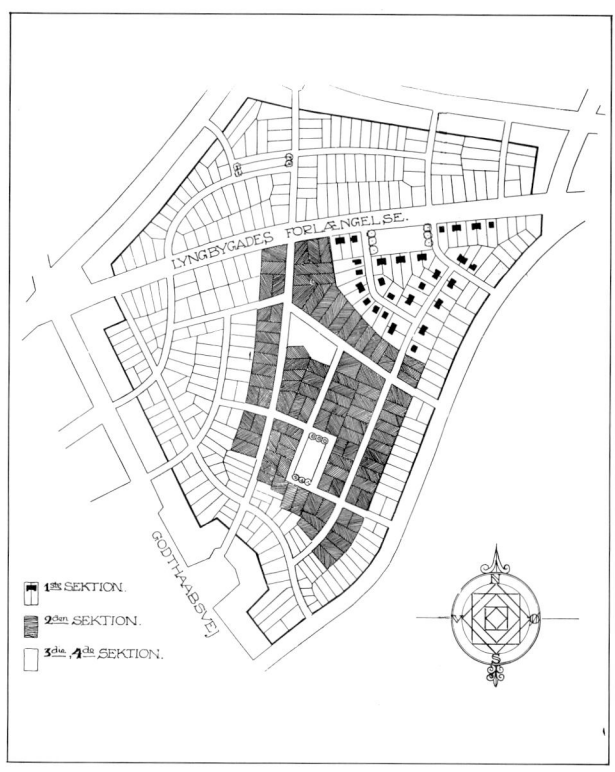

As early as 1907, the Danish Architect Association took the initiative to establish a "Design aid service" in order to reduce the amount of unsightly, home-made buildings being erected throughout the country. Their objective was to produce designs for inexpensive, practical and sound houses, or improve existing projects and offer free assistance. A result of this work was the establishment, in 1915, of the National League for the Advancement of Better Building Practices in rural areas. As it was a question of combining the best of former high-quality craftsmanship traditions with a rational optimal use of every available square metre, and calm, well-proportioned facades, the current neoclassicism seemed made to order to build the "little Danish house" for the average citizen. Architect Harald Nielsen was one of the leaders in these efforts and during the years between the two world wars, thousands of Better Building Practice houses were built throughout the country. Many housing associations also needed help in establishing well-functioning garden towns, where the consideration for a pleasant whole, balanced the tendency to individualism. A good example of this is Frederiksberg Municipality's Functionaires Housing Association on Finsensvej/Ved Grænsen, built in 1914-19 by K.T. Seest and H. Koch. Another is the Garden Home Association, Grøndalsvænge between Hillerødgade and Gothåbsvej, built in 1914-20 by Poul Holsøe and Jesper Tvede. The Grøndalsvænge scheme was inspired by the leading town planner of the time, Camillo Sitte, but also by the winning projekt in a 1908 town plan competition for the outer districts of Copenhagen, done by city surveyor Carl Strinz, Bonn.

202. *Esbjerg, Skjoldsgade. Villa by Harald Peters, 1921.*

203. *Sæby, Skovallé 20. Villa by Harald Nielsen, 1915.*

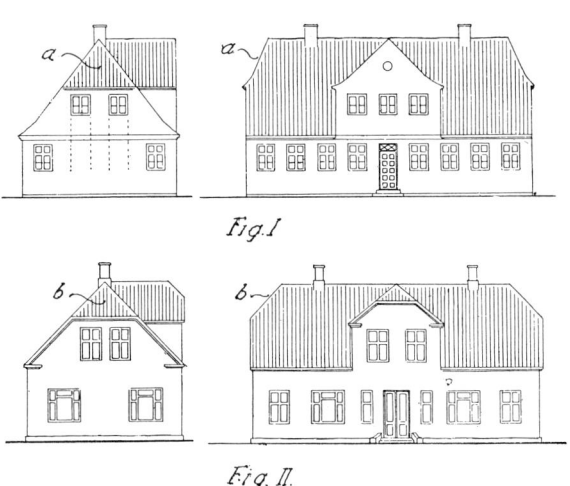

Ill. from The Society for Better Building Practices annual report, 1919: »Figure 1 shows a house with a firm and fitting exterior. The size and form of the roof are related to the height of the walls. The profile of the house is firm and distinct. The gables are hipped, and the roof height is the same as the pediment... in short: The building's «mass» is firm and distinct in form ... Figure 2... shows a weakness in form, which is all too common in many houses being built throughout the country«.

204. Tibirke Bakker, 1916-

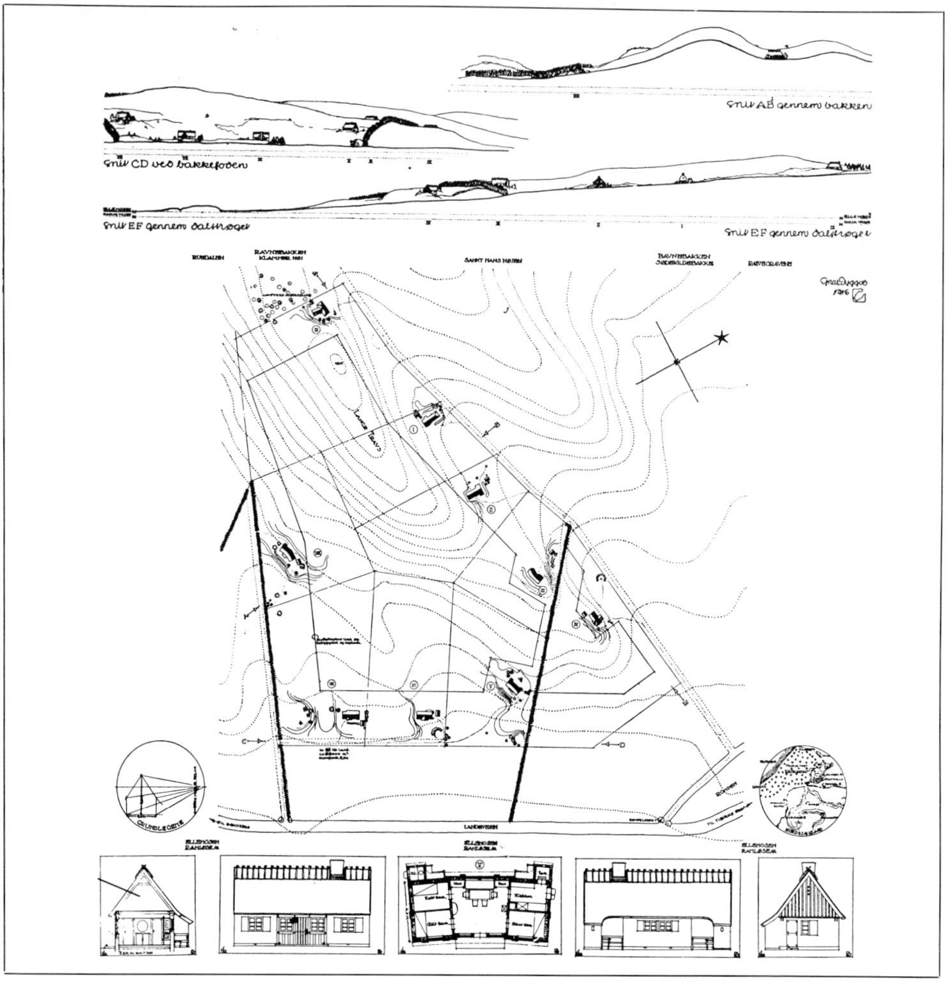

Above: **204.** *Tibirke Bakker. Ejnar Dyggve's development plan from 1916. Plan 1:5000.*

Below: **204.** *Tibirke Bakker. Langetravs 11-15. Ejnar Dyggve.*

Tibirke Bakker in North Zealand is a quite unusual landscape compared to the rest of Zealand, due to its heather blanketed, sandy hills and spread groups of vegetation. The scenic beauty is primarily the result of more than seventy years of careful planning and the buildings as well as the landscape is strictly controlled by ordinances and preservation laws.

In 1916, architect Ejnar Dryggve worked out an alternative development plan for an area around Lange Travs. A new feature of this plan was that it attempted to preserve the character of the landscape. All buildings should be placed in the valley areas along the edges of the site, while the hill tops should be preserved as protected common areas.

A fencing-in of the rather large parcels was not allowed and there were restricted building lines that determined the placement of the houses on the site. Codes restricted building heights to one-storey with thatched, pitched roofs. In this way the Tibirke Bakker area became Denmark's first example of a planned vacation house area, that up until today still has retained much of its original character.

Between 1916 and 1920, Ejnar and Inger Møller Dyggve designed a number of houses here, such as Klammerhøj 8, Langetravs 9, 11-15 and Silkebjerg 7 and 11. Carl Petersen and Ivar Bentsen also had commissions here, the former at Bakkedalen 1, rebuilt in 1919, and the latter, in collaboration with Harald Nielsen, at Johs. V. Jensens Vej 3, built in 1913 for the famous author, for whom this street was named. One of the most beautiful houses, Bakkedalen 11, from 1915, was designed by Mogens Clemmensen. During the thirties, several well-known architects built houses for themselves in this area. Bentsen in 1932 on Silkebjerg 3, Vilhelm Lauritzen in 1937 on Langs Diget 15, and Knud Thorbal the same year at Langetravs 5. Throughout the years, new parcels have been laid out and new houses built. One of the newest is on Silkebjerg 8, from 1976 by Susanne Ussing and Carsten Hoff.

204. *Tibirke Bakker. Detail of Silkebjerg 7. Ejnar Dyggve.*

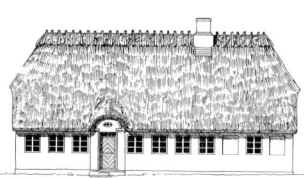

Above: Johs. V. Jensens Vej 3. Elevations, 1:400. Ivar Bentsen and Harald Nielsen.

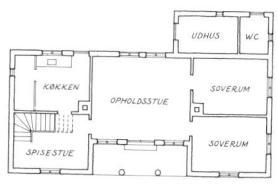

Bakkedalen 11. Mogens Clemmensen. Drawing by Thorkel Dahl. Plan 1:400.

205-207. The Police headquarters. Saint Lucas Church, Århus, The Workers Assembly Building, Horsens, 1918-1926.

205. *Copenhagen, Otto Mønsteds Gade/Polititorvet. Politigården. The round court.*

Below: *Main facade facing Polititorvet.*

205. *Politigården. Plan 1:1500.*

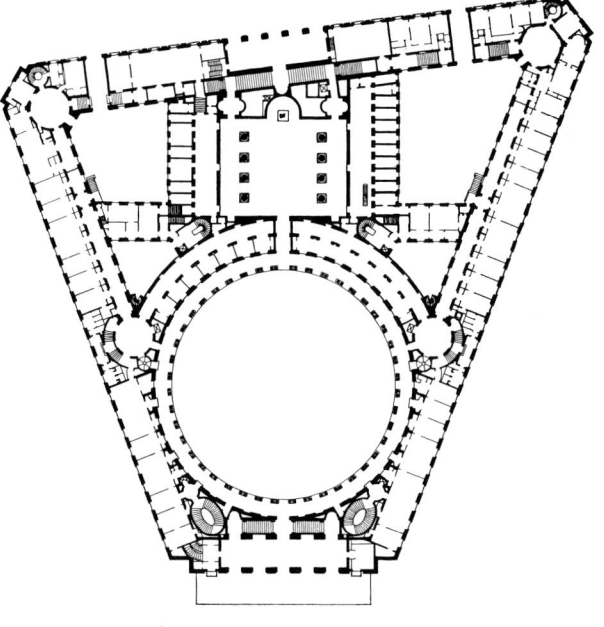

The job of designing a new main headquarters for the Copenhagen Police was given to architect Hack Kampmann in 1918. After his death in 1920, work was continued by his son, Hans Jørgen Kampmann together with Holger Jacobsen and Aage Rafn, the latter being credited with the final result. The site was a dismal fill area near Kalveboderne. Therefore the facades were kept as neutral as possible with grey-black stucco and uniform rows of high, identical windows with white reveals. To make up for this somewhat drab approach, the interior courts were magnificent, a large circular one, 45 metres in diametre, and a smaller square one. The large courtyard was surrounded by 44 pairs of columns with the horizontal lines strongly accented by three overhanging cornices. The small courtyard is partially covered and dimly lit, completely dominated by the vertical lines in the eight enormous columns, a deliberate contrast to the round courtyard. This powerful interplay of contrasts: dark and light, high and low, horizontal and vertical is a characteristic feature of the Police Headquarters building, and all interior details are meticulously carried out in an effectual, and artistically exceptional free play with classicistic motifs. On its inauguration in 1924, the Police Headquarters was considered one of the most outstanding works within this genre, but at the same time it represented the culmination of a theatrical formalism that had completely lost any sense of rationality.

A simpler, but academically dryer form idiom is present in Kai Gottlob's Saint Lukas Church in Århus, built in 1921-26 as the result of a competition in 1918. The Workers Assembly Building in Horsens, built in 1926 by Viggo Norm, is inspired by the Police Headquarters, simple in the exterior, but rich in its interior colouring.

206. Århus. St. Lukas Church.

207. Horsens, Kildegade. The Workers Assembly Building.

Below: 205. Politigården. The square court.

205. Politigården. Oval stairwell.

208-210. Neoclassicistic schools, 1923-1926.

208. Copenhagen, Gentofte, Gersonsvej 32. Øregård School.

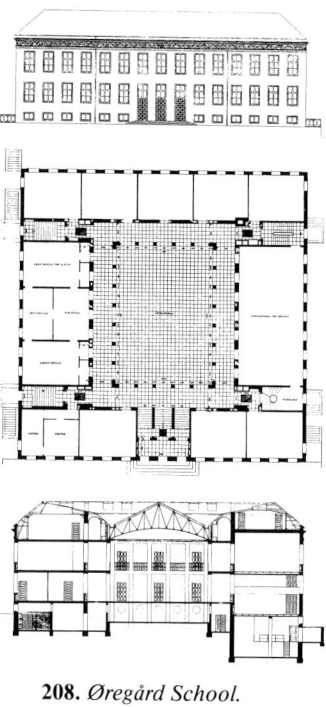

208. Øregård School. Plan, section and elevation 1:750.

208. Øregård School. The aula.

In 1920, Edvard Thomsen won a closed competition for Øregård School on Gersonsvej 32 in Hellerup. It was built in 1923-24 in collaboration with G.B. Hagen and was the first example of a pure aula school in Denmark. A school in which all classrooms are oriented into a roofed court that functions as an assembly hall. The competition project's formalistic classicism was forced to surrender to an architecture with more emphasis on the structural aspects. This is especially evident in the simple, neutral interior. However the solid volume, with grey stucco facades and high, regular rows of windows with pronounced reveals is a typical classicistic feature, especially the decorative frieze under the roof cornice, with its Pompeiian inspiration. A renovation and addition was carried out in 1977-80 by Gehrdt Bornebusch.

A more orthodox neoclassicism was employed at Randers State school in 1923-25, a four-winged scheme, with two storeys surrounding a school yard bordered by a colonnade. Two of the wings are extended on both sides by one-storey wings. The architect was Hack Kampmann assisted by his son Christian, who continued the work after his father's death. At the same time, Viborg Cathedral School was built with the same form idiom, but in this case, one of the wings was replaced by a colonnade similar to C.F. Hansen's Christianborg. The school opened in 1926 and an addition was built during the 1950's by architect Leopold Teschl.

209. *Randers, Hassagers Boulevard. Randers State School.*

210. *Viborg, Gl. Skivevej. Viborg Cathedral School.*

211-212. P.V. Jensen Klint and Kaare Klint, 1916-1940.

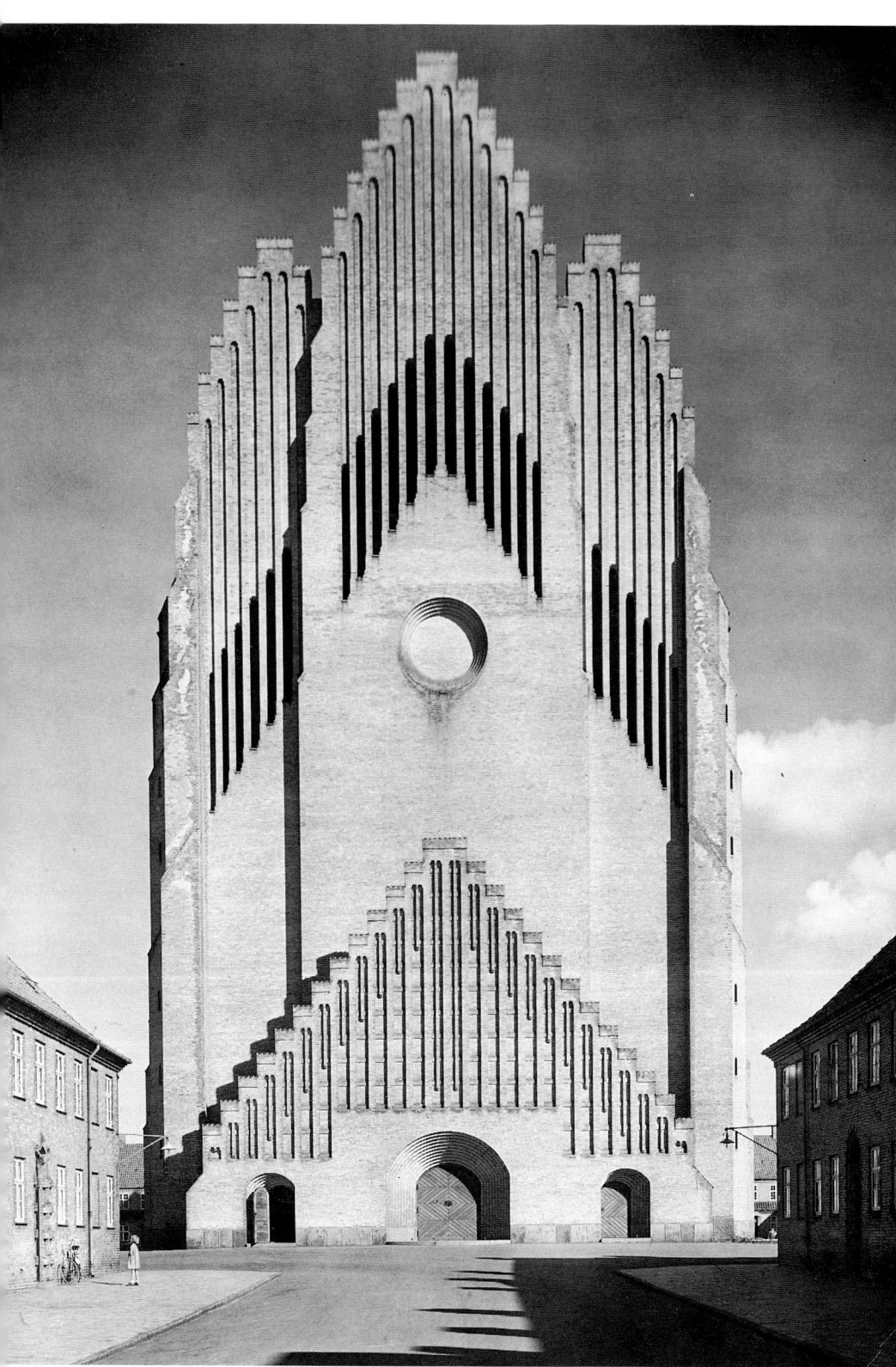

Although architect and engineer, P.V. Jensen Klint only won second prize in a 1913 competition for a Grundtvig Memorial, which he had designed as a tower rich with decorative blindings, he was chosen anyway to built the monument as he had included a church in his project. It wasn't until 1921 that the site was designated on Bispebjerg Hill and in 1927 the tower was completed. In 1930, Jensen Klint died and his son, Kaare Klint completed the church nave and crypt with the final consecration taking place in 1940. Grundtvig's Church is a three-aisle, vaulted church with a tower of the same width as the nave. There is also a low, wide porch in front. The material is light yellow, hand-moulded brick laid in a cleverly designed bond, in which the headers coincide in every fifth course. Combined with the high-quality brickwork, this bond gives a calm and distinctive wall surface. Architecturally, the church is a magnified restatement of the Danish village church. With its strong inspiration from the late Gothic, market town churches, it is one of the final examples of the Nyrop period's national romanticism, but with many original features both in combination and detail. The buildings surrounding the church were also designed by Jensen Klint between 1924 and 1926 in collaboration with Charles I. Schou and Georg Gøssel.

Prior to the Grundtvig's Church project, in 1913 there was a competition project for a church in Århus, which was very similar. It was built in 1916-20 in Odense's Saint Hans Country parish and is now called Fredens Church.

212. *Odense, Skibhusvej. Fredens Church.*

Opposite page: **211.** *Copenhagen Bispebjerg, På Bjerget. Grundtvig's Church*

Below left: Grundtvig's Church. Interior.

Below: Grundtvig's Church. Plan 1:750.

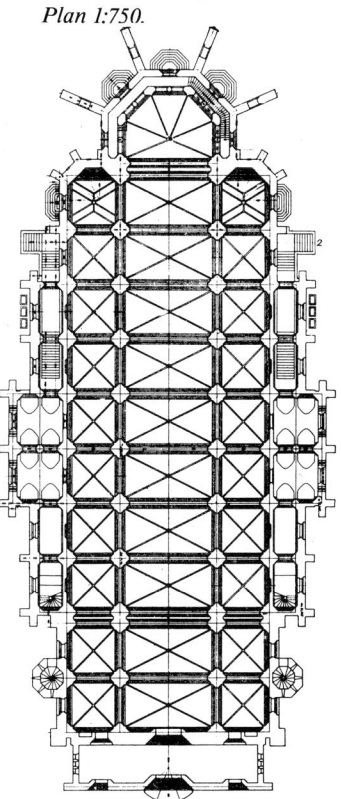

213. Studiebyen, 1920-1924.

213. *Copenhagen, Gentofte, Rygårds Allé. Studiebyen. Gate house.*

213. *Studiebyen. Site plan.*

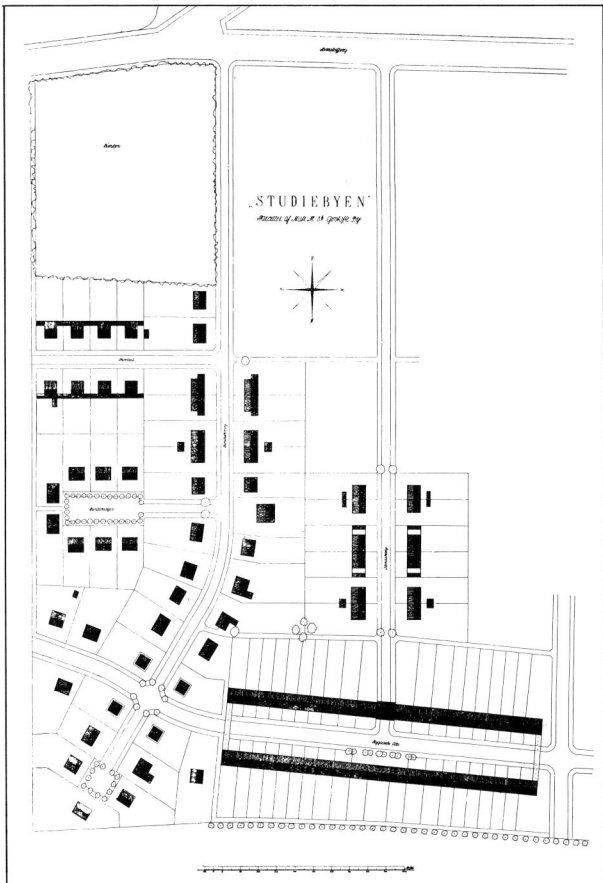

The following architects were involved in the design of Studiebyen: Peter Nielsen, August Rasmussen and V. Rørdam Jensen (gate house and row houses), as well as Ivar Bentsen and Thorkild Henningsen, Svend Møller and Georg Ponsaing, Edvard Thomsen, Anton Rosen, Poul Holsøe, Ole Falkentorp, Kay Fisker etc.

The period following World War I was epoch-making for Danish housing. A decent housing standard for all became a task of national importance, and the housing associations rendered an extraordinary service in improving the standard of multi-storey housing. The garden home for the low level income group was just as important, and for this reason KAB, Copenhagen's Public Housing association, built Studiebyen on Rygårds Allé in 1920-24, where a group of well-known architects were allowed to experiment with a variety of housing forms: Villas, two-family houses and row houses, in order to illustrate the adventages and disadventages of the various types and compare thier economy. Different technical solutions were tried, and dispensations from the building regulations were granted. Alternative building materials and insulation were tested in search of the most inexpensive practical solutions. The invited architects were asked to draw 2 houses opposite each other, in order to acheive a visually calm street.

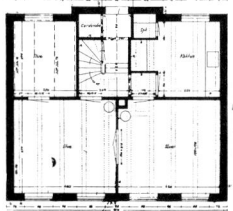

213. *Studiebyen. Lundeskovsvej 8. One-family house by Jesper Tvede.*

213. *Studiebyen. Lundekrogen. Two one-family houses by Kay Fisker.*

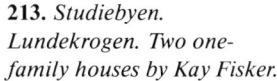

214-221. Bakkehusene and Thorvald Henningsen's row houses, 1921-1928.

214. Copenhagen, Hvidkildevej. Bakkehusene.

Below: Site plan. Plans, section and elevation.

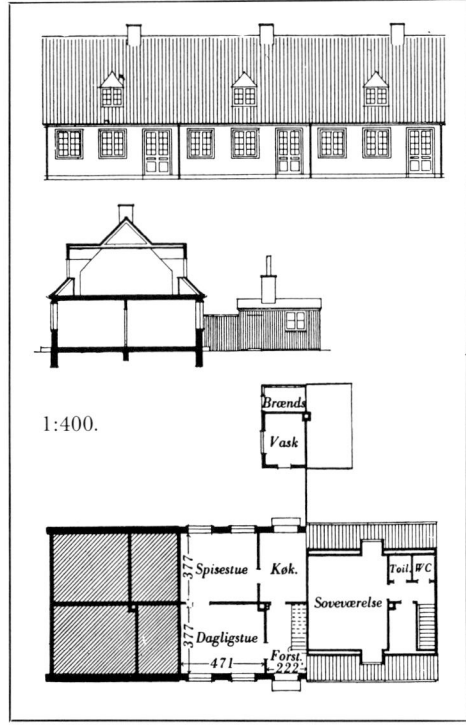

At the same time, in 1921-23, KAB commissioned Thorkild Henningsen and Ivar Bentsen to built the Bakkehusene scheme on Hvidkildevej. The long low blocks they designed were a revival of the provincial town's continuous street facades, with the addition of a front and back yard. However the relatively small houses were invaded by the upper middle class, and Henningsen's subsequent row houses on Sallingvej (1923), Hulgårdsvej (1924), Sundvænget (1925), Bernstoffsvej (1927-28) and Fuglebakken (1928) are therefore somewhat larger. However, he succeded in building a few blocks more in keeping with the original intentions of inexpensive garden dwellings for the working class. These are the row houses on Saltværksvej in Kastrup and Damvænget by Roskildevej in Rødovre from 1928. Thorkild Henningsen also revived the veranda and the sheltered out-door seating place, and the basis for a popular, national housing form was established.

215. *Row houses near Sallingvej.*

218. *Gentofte, Bernstorffsvej. (Not shown).*

221: *Rødovre, Damvænget. (Not shown).*

220. *Kastrup, Saltværksvej. (Not shown).*

Below: 217. *Row houses on Sundvænget in Hellerup.*

Right: 219. *Row houses on Fuglebakken, Egernvej.*

Below: 216. *Row houses at Hulgårdsvej.*

222-223. Classicism's large housing blocks, 1919-1929.

222. Copenhagen, Hans Tavsensgade/Struenseegade. Housing blocks. Right: Plan 1:1500.

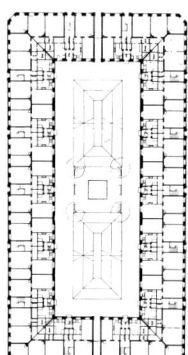

223. Hornbækhus. Plan 1:1500.

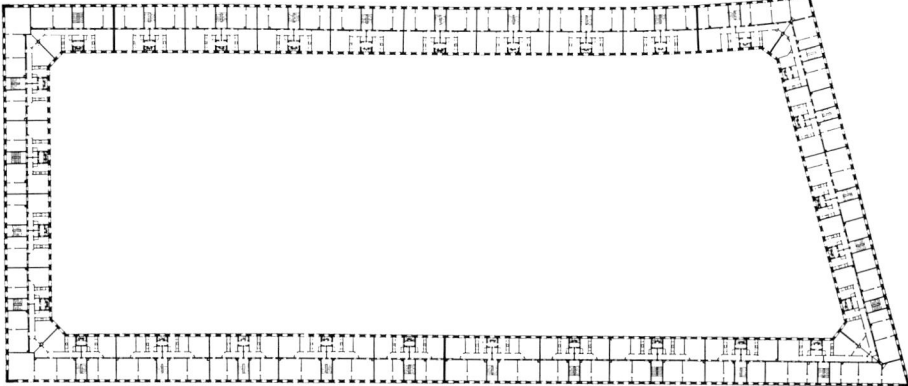

The housing shortage during and after World War I was countered by both National and local efforts. A state initiative resulted in the establishment of a rent control board and a housing commission in 1916, and a National Housing fund in 1922-28. The classicistic multi-storey flat block, with its economical, uniform rhythm was a major component in the development of housing projects and the breakthrough came with Povl Baumann's municipal housing schemes on Hans Tavsens Gade and Struenseegade in Nørrebro, built in 1919-20. The facades were built on a modular system based on the fixed size of the window bays. The austere financial conditions limited the size and number of flat types, but all had toilets. This type became a standard, and the so-called "kilometre style" influenced a number of the housing projects built in the years that followed.

A good example is Hornbækhus on Borups Allé 5-23, built by Kay Fisker in 1922-23 with national housing funds. The large five-storey block contained 290 flats and all living rooms faced the street, while the kitchens and bedrooms faced the courtyard, with no regard for compass orientation. However this block was the first in which the courtyard was laid out as a green, and it was planned by landscape architect, G.N. Brandt.

223. *Copenhagen, Borups Allé 5-23. Hornbækhus.*

Facade detail of Hornbækhus.

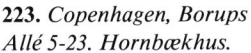

213

224-225. Classens Have and Solgården, 1924-1929.

224. *Copenhagen, Classensgade 52-68. Ved Classens Have. Plan 1:1500.*

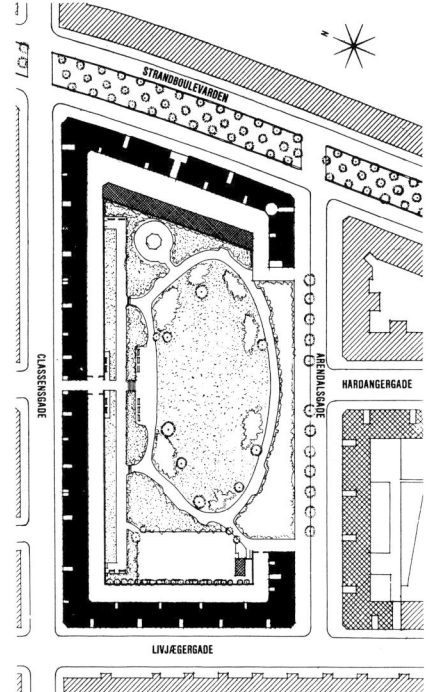

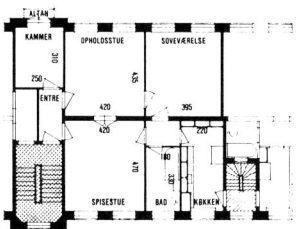

224. *Ved Classens Have. Four rooms. 1:400.*

The following year, the housing project Ved Classens Have, Classensgade 52-68 by Carl Petersen, Povl Baumann, Ole Falkentorp and Peter Nielsen, revealed even newer trends. Here the five-storey block was only half closed around a municipal park, a forerunner for more open planning schemes. However, a high wall still blocks the direct access to the garden. The final break came in 1929, with Solgården on Skt. Kjelds Gade 16-20 by Henning Hansen. Here the southeast corner of the block is open and the entrance doors, as well as the living rooms, are oriented toward the central park. The housing scheme consist of 181 flats from 1 to 4 1/2 rooms, some of them equipped with small nurseries for large families. The flat plans show some experimentation, and both types appear with and without the traditional rear stairway.

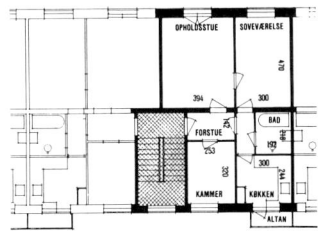

225. *Solgården. Three rooms. 1:400.*

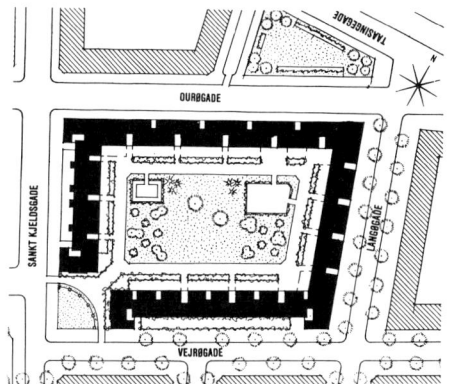

225. *Copenhagen, St. Kjelds Gade/Vejrøgade. Solgården. Left: Plan 1:1500.*

226-227. Vodroffsvej 2 and Vestersøhus, 1929-1939.

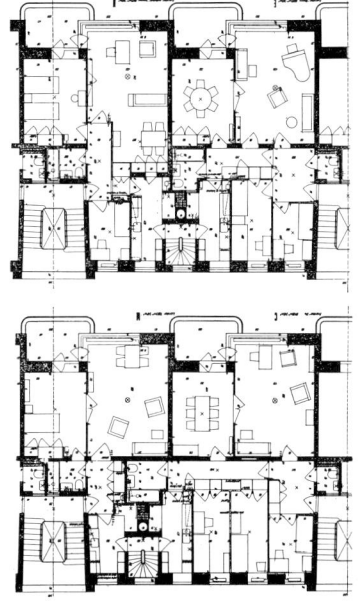

227. *Copenhagen, Vester Søgade. Vestersøhus. Left: Detail of entrance. Below: Furnished flat plans, 1:400.*

The clear and simple form ideals inherent in neo-classicism, combined with its rational and economical building methods, were a logical prelude to modernism. With modernism, all superfluous ornamentation was removed in preference to highly functional housing plans, oriented to the sun and with every square metre judiciously employed. The architectural merits were now determined by proportions, general control and optimum housing functions. Honesty in structure and materials replaced style and decoration. A transitional phenomenon can be seen in the housing scheme on Vodroffsvej 2 in Copenhagen, built in 1929 by Kay Fisker and C.F. Møller. The preliminary drawings revealed a connection with the past in terms of closely spaced windows and mullions, and broad architraves. However the completed project is built up of horizontal bands of windows and walls, in red and yellow brick. The bay windows and balconies have returned to bring light and air into the flats, yet the units are still characterized by the living needs of the past.

The same two architects built the large, seven storey block of flats, Vestersøhus, on the other side of St. Jørgen's Lake. Here the bay window balcony motif was developed to near perfection, with large, semi-recessed, semi-protruding balconies intimately tied to the corner windows. The material treatment and detailing of the facades is beautifully executed, and the balconies and roof terraces give the building a rhythmic, sculptural quality.

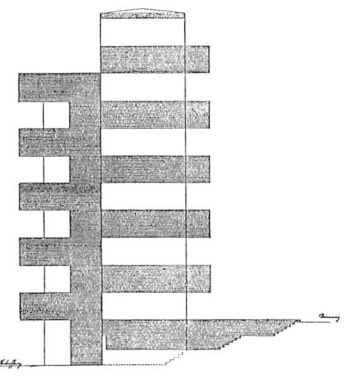

226. *Vodroffsvej 2. Concept drawing of split level between the street and the lake.*

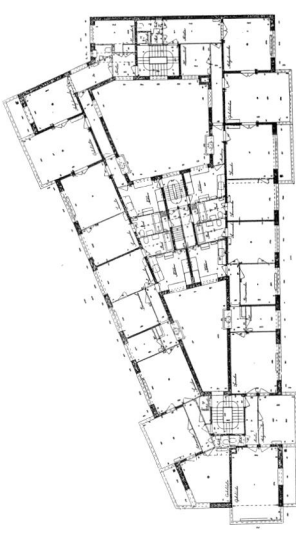

226. *Copenhagen, Vodroffsvej 2. Plan 1:750.*

228-229. Blidah Park and Storgården, 1932-1935.

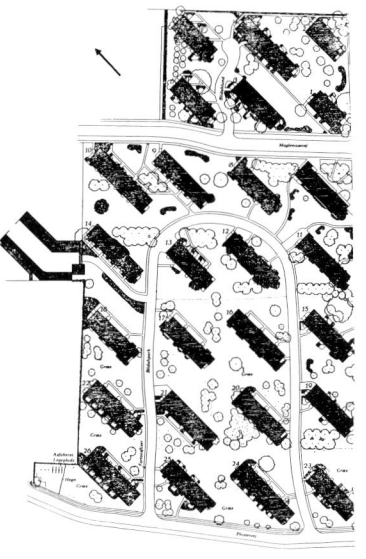

228. *Copenhagen, Hellerup, Strandvejen 221. Blidah Park.*

Plan 1:4000.

The Blidah housing scheme was built in 1932-34 on a site previously occupied by large old villa gardens, where the fine old landscaping, in many cases, was influential in determining were the blocks of flats where placed. It was the first real park housing scheme, with freestanding, parallel blocks, surrounded by green common areas. Due to solar orientation and views, the blocks were placed on north/south axes and staggered in relation to one another. This plan solution became the norm for many of the park housing schemes developed during the thirties and forties. The scheme consisted of both large and small flats, and again, the balcony motif was employed, both as a supplement to the flat and also as a prominent facade element. The blocks north of Maglemosevej were designed by Ivar Bentsen, Jørgen U. Berg and Acton Bjørn. The blocks along Phistersvej were designed by Kooperative Arkitekter. The three northernmost blocks, south of Maglemosevej, are by Edvard Heiberg and Karl Larsen, and Ivar Bentsen designed the two southernmost blocks facing Strandvejen, while A. Skjøt Pedersen designed the rest. The latter blocks, are somewhat characterized by early modernism's infatuation with ship forms.

The next step in the development can be seen at Storgården on Tomsgårdsvej 78-110, built in 1935 by Povl Baumann and Knud Hansen. Here a long block has replaced the planned block scheme, and a supple building form follows the slight curve of the site. The main facade with the living rooms faces south offering a view to the playground and green areas. The unending rows of leisure balconies strongly contribute to the monumental character of the scheme.

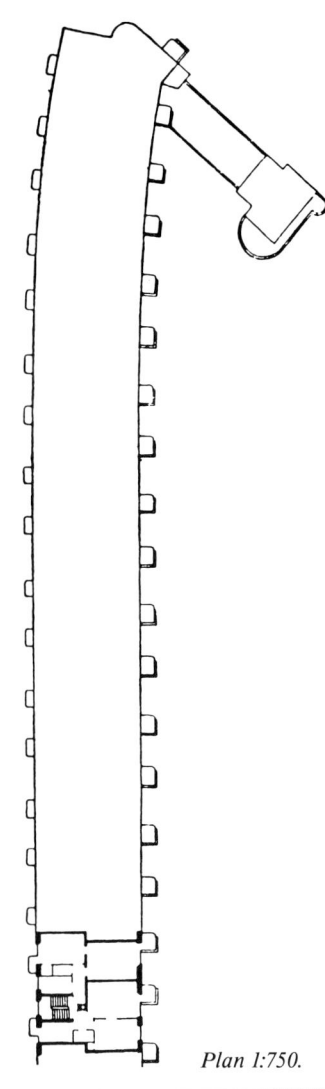

229. *Copenhagen, Tomsgårdsvej 78-110. Storgården.* Plan 1:750.

230. Bella Vista and Bellevue, 1934-1937.

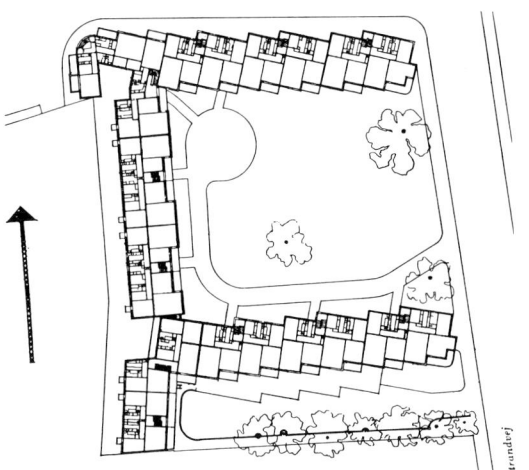

Plan 1:1500.

230. *Copenhagen Klampenborg, Strandvejen 407-33. Bella Vista housing scheme.*

International modernism with its smooth white surfaces, flat roofs and large areas of glass was clearly the source of inspiration for Arne Jacobsen's housing scheme, Bella Vista on Strandvejen 407-33 in Klampenborg from 1934. But the architect's absolute artistic talent has imbued the three-winged scheme with a personal tone that makes it a major work in Danish architectural history. By staggering the flats in the side wings he manages to give them all a private balcony and a view over the strait. However, the white surfaces conceal the fact that this is a traditional brick building with steel beams over the wide window openings. The scheme was enlarged around 1960 with a block of flats and a row of atrium houses.

A little bit further along Strandvejen, Arne Jacobsen had already, in 1931-32, planned the Bellevue sea bath facilities for the borough of Gentofte. In 1936-37 it was augmented with the Bellevue Theatre, a light, spacious building planned for summer revues. The walls were covered with striped canvas, giving a tentlike, summerish ambience. The roof can be rolled open so that shows can take place in the open when weather permits. South of the theatre was a large restaurant that was later converted to housing.

230. *Bellevue Theatre. The open roof in the theatre.*

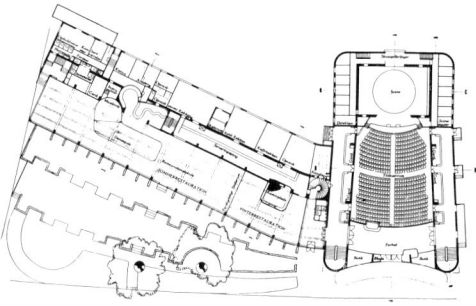

230. *Bellevue-complex. Plan 1:1000.*

230. *Copenhagen Klampenborg, Strandvejen 449-451. Bellevue Theatre.*

231-236. Modernistic commercial buildings, 1930-1937.

233. Copenhagen, Gammel Torv 6. Stellings Hus.

232. Copenhagen, Banegårdspladsen 2-4. Hotel Astoria.

New materials and structural systems such as reinforced concrete, steel framing, steel windows and numerous sheet materials were soon widely accepted, especially in the area of commercial building, which was more receptive to new ideas than the housing sector. One of the few large steel frame structures in Denmark, is the commercial building, Vesterport at Vesterbrogade 8 in Copenhagen, built in 1930-32 by Ole Falkentorp and Povl Baumann. The decks are of reinforced concrete and the street facades are sided with copper. The symmetrical arrangement of the main facade with its tall central section has a clear classicistic reminiscence, whereas the interiors and the long gone elegant penthouse nightclub were distinctively modernistic. Across the street in 1934-35, Ole Falkentorp solved the difficult task of building Hotel Astoria, on the several metre wide, narrow site between the railway hollow and Reventlowsgade. It is a reinforced concrete structure with projecting upper floors that house two rows of hotel rooms and a central corridor.

Clearly inspired by the Swedish architect Gunnar Asplund, Arne Jacobsen built the commercial building at Gammel Torv 6 in 1937 for the firm, A. Stelling. The upper storeys of the reinforced concrete structure are sided with glazed, grey stoneware tiles, while the lower shop levels are sided with green enameled steel sheets. The building has been thoroughly detailed and fits well in scale and materials with the other buildings in the area, a fact that was not generally recognized when it was built. Other reinforced concrete structures from this period are the Berlinske Tidende building on Pilestræde from 1928-30, A.C. Bangs Hus on Østergade 27 from 1932-34, and Svane Apothecary on Østergade 18 from 1934. These were all designed by Bent Helweg-Møller and bear witness to his great decorative talent.

234. Copenhagen, Pilestræde 34. Berlingske Tidende. Renovated 1990-1991 by Knud Peter Harboe.

235. A. C. Bangs Hus, Østergade 27 (Not shown).

236. Svane apothecary, Østergade 18. (Not shown).

Below: 231. Copenhagen, Vesterbrogade 8. Vesterport.

237-239. Municipal buildings, 1931-1937.

237. Copenhagen, Halmtorvet. Kødbyen.

238. Copenhagen, Vanløse Allé 44. Kathrinedals school.

The great housing exposition in Stockholm in 1930 heralded the breakthrough for modernism in Scandinavia. Among the first architects who experimented with it in Denmark was Copenhagen's municipal architect, Poul Holsøe and his staff. Reinforced concrete was employed in a number of technical facilities, and the city acquired streamlined trams and busses. The new, great Kødby, meat market on Halmtorvet, built in 1931-34 is also characterized by white, smooth and cubistic, reinforced concrete blocks, which clearly symbolize the modern hygienic attitudes that had been adapted at that time. The only decorative elements were the various company signs, and this was the first time that advertising was subject to a deliberate design treatment. The associated architects were Curt Bie and Tage Rue.

A typical example of the large aula schools that were built after Øregård primary school, is Katrinedal School on Vanløse Allé from 1934 by Kai Gottlob. This archetype was further developed at the School by the Strait on Samosvej 50 from 1937, in which the rectangular aula was ellipse formed by the balcony railings and roof lantern. Next to this, Gottlob built a school for the delicate children. This scheme had quite a different character, with a two-storey classroom wing, six octagonal classrooms and an open two-storey space. The entire south facade is of continuous glass.

237. *Kødbyen. Detail.*

239. *Copenhagen, Samosvej 50. The School near the Strait. Aulaen. Left: Plan 1:1000.*

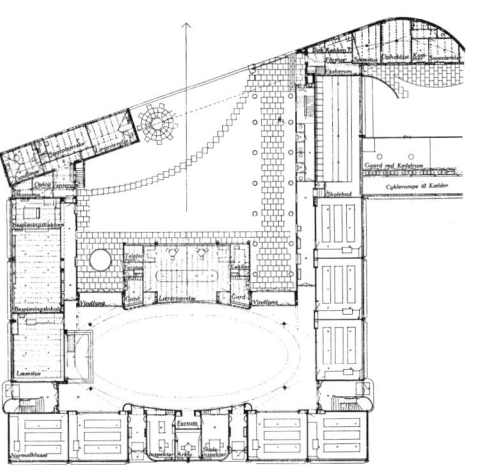

239. *School for delicate children, sleeping hall.*

240-241. Crematoriums 1927-1937.

240. Copenhagen, Roskildevej 59-61.
Søndermarkens Crematorium.

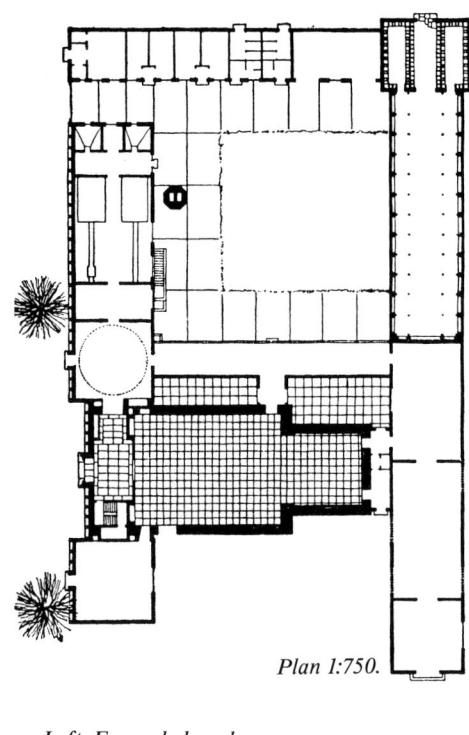

Plan 1:750.

Left: Funeral chapel.

In 1926, Frits Schlegel and Edvard Thomsen won a competition for a crematorium and chapel at the new Søndermark Cemetery on Roskildevej 59-61 in Frederiksberg. However a completely different project was realized in 1927-30, one which heralded the arrival of modernism in church architecture. No repressive traditions restricted the solution of these contemporary problems. The funeral chapel was formed as a dark nave with high clerestory windows, connected by a large opening to a bright chancel with a catafalque. The cubistic central section is surrounded by low wings, which toward the southwest form a four-winged court. The materials are red, hand-moulded brick and copper roofing.

The real breakthrough did not occur until 1937 with Frits Schlegel's crematorium chapel at the Mariebjerg Cemetery near Lyngby, where concrete also emerged. The building has a visible reinforced concrete frame filled out with pale, hollow concrete block. The north and south facades have fenestrations with cruciform glass prisms. The chapel has white walls and ceilings. The chairs are arranged in a semicircle around the secluded chancel and catafalque. The transition from the monumental, well-proportioned block to the scenic cemetery, designed by G.N. Brandt is toned down by a series of light pergolas. As in many of Schlegel's other buildings, there is a noticeable inspiration from the French architect Auguste Perret.

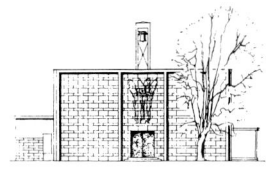
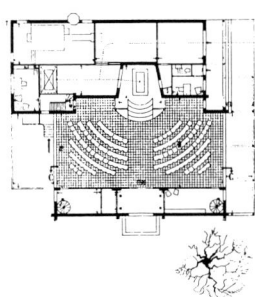

241. *Mariebjerg Crematorium. Plan and elevation 1:750.*

241. *Copenhagen, Mariebjergvej. Mariebjerg Crematorium.*

242. Mogens Lassen on Sølystvej, 1935-1938.

242. Copenhagen Klampenborg, Sølystvej 9-11.

242. Sølystvej 9-11. Interior.

242. Sølystvej 9-11. Plans of basement and ground floor, 1:400.

Mogens Lassen is one of the Danish architects who most clearly was inspired by Le Corbusier, yet managed to retain his own personal, creative expression. This is especially evident in the three reinforced concrete houses on Sølystvej 5, 7 and 9-11, built near the site of the old Christiansholm Fort, on a slope along one edge of a small ravine, with the main entrances located at first floor level. Nos. 5 and 7 were built in 1935, the latter being symmetrical both in plan and facade, with the kitchen and dining room on the entrance level on one side of the central stair tower, and the living room on the other. The bedrooms on the upper floor have access to a balcony-loggia, while the lower level is on level with the garden. Mogens Lassen built No. 5 for himself in three storeys with a roof terrace. As with the other houses, there are no windows toward north, whereas the nonbearing south facade has sliding windows from wall to wall.

No. 9-11 was built in 1938 at a spot where the slope is not as high. The house has thus only two storeys and follows the curve of the road. It also differs from the others with a distinct division in three sections with individual roofs. These sections contain the kitchen and living room, and the bedrooms for parents and children, the latter two being separated in order to preserve a beautiful tree. All rooms have direct and intimate access to the outdoors, as opposed to the first two. The materials and structure are both imaginative and well-chosen.

242. *Sølystvej 5.*

242. *Sølystvej 7 with No. 5 in background.*

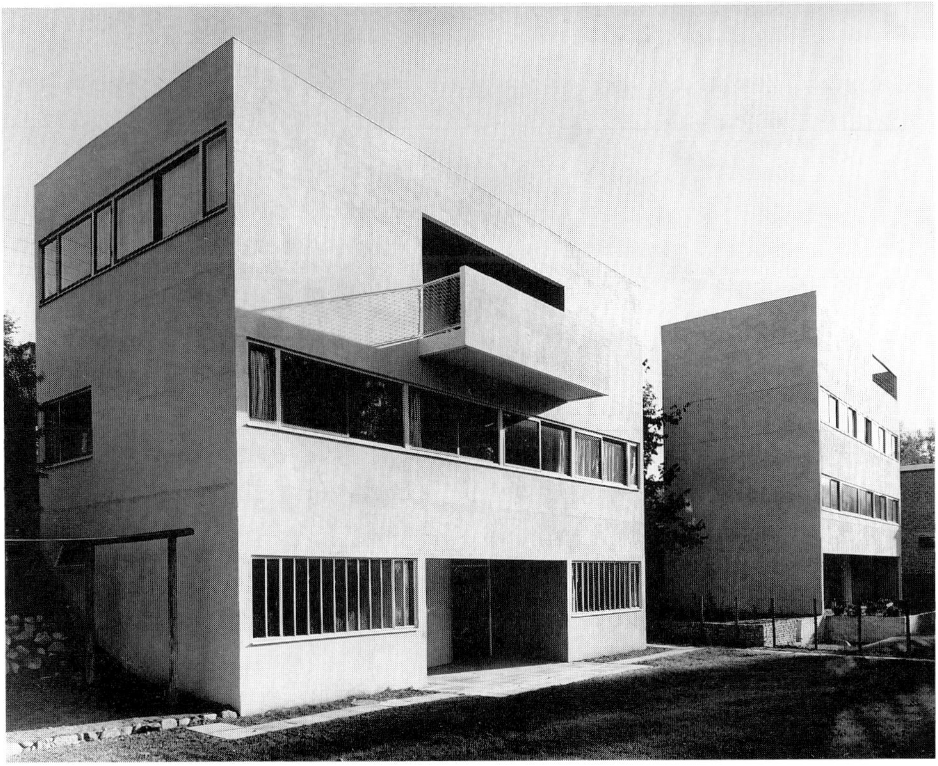

243-244. Århus University and Nyborg public library, 1932-1946.

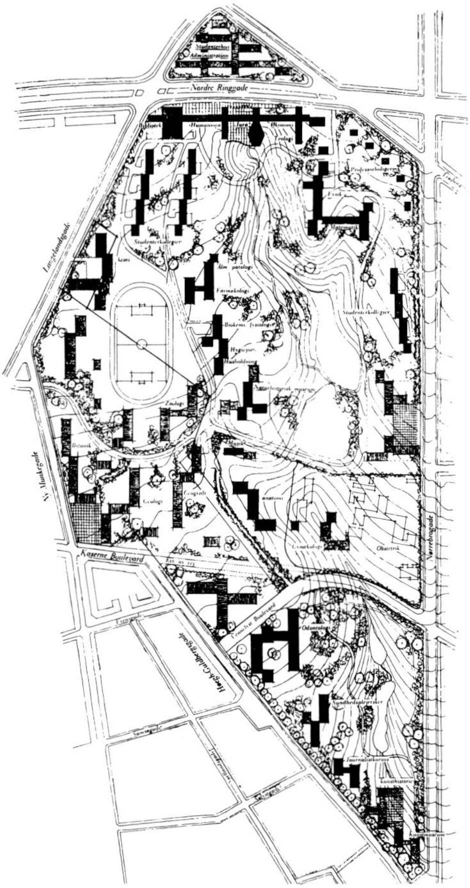

243. *Århus, University park. Århus University.*
Left: Plan 1:6000.

243. *Århus University. Physics/Chemistry Institute, built 1932.*

In 1931, Kay Fisker, C.F. Møller and Poul Stegmann together with landscape architect C. Th. Sørensen won the competition for a new university in Århus. Their project combined modernism's basic ideals with the best of the Danish tradition's form and material attitudes. The site is a fantastic one, on a rather hilly area north of the city with a valley and several ponds. The buildings spread out, though generally oriented in a north-south direction along the border of the site in order to emphasize its scenic character. The individual faculties, laboratories, dormitories and housing have each been given their own characteristic form with regard to their function. However they are bound together by a common scale of materials in yellow brick and roofing tile, as well as their crystal sharp, intersecting volumes with thirty degree roof slopes without eaves, and the large closely spaced, flush window openings. Building work was started in 1932 and continued up until recently. After 1942, C.F. Møller worked alone in realizing the original main plan, though with skillful variations in each individual building. The main building, with the hexagonal, prismatic aula facing the park is thus C.F. Møller's own work and was built in 1942-46. On a completely different level, but in the same spirit as Århus University, is Nyborg public library, built in 1938-40 by Flemming Lassen and Erik Møller as the result of a public competition. Lying on a little peninsula east of Nyborg castle, the one-storey wing modestly respects its neighbour and fits well into the townscape on the opposite side. The firm control of the whole and the detailing makes the library a prominent example of the modern tradition.

243. *Århus University. The aula seen from the park.*

Below: **244.** *Nyborg, Torvet. Nyborg Public library.*

245. Århus Town Hall, 1938-1942.

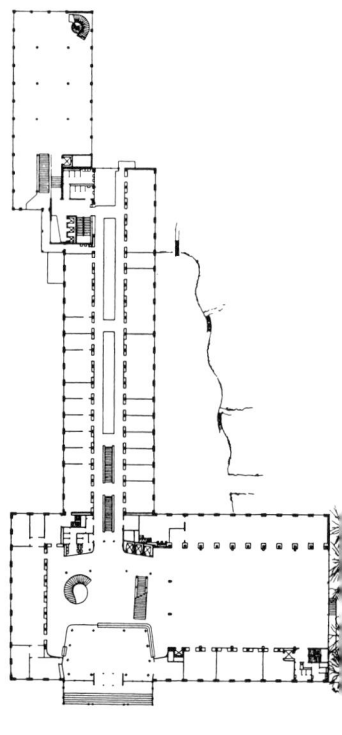

245. *Århus, Town Hall Square/Park Allé. Århus Town Hall, plan 1:1500. Below: Stair in Town hall lobby.*

Arne Jacobsen and Erik Møller won a competition in 1937 for a new town hall in Århus. After minor changes brought on by a public debate that demanded a more formal character, it was built in 1938-42. The tower, entrance and marble siding were the changes required of the architects. Otherwise the project was basically the same as the competition proposal. The town hall is built of reinforced concrete and divided up in three sections: The town hall with its city council hall and formal chambers opening onto a neighbouring park through a large wall of windows, a tall office wing with a centre corridor that opens up through the entire height of the building, and a low wing by the tower that houses the service areas. Gunnar Asplund's town hall in Göteborg, Sweden has clearly influenced the scheme, though it has its own identity through its light and bright sense of a whole, and the careful and thorough detailing.

245. *Århus Town Hall. Interior.*

246-247. Søllerød Town Hall and Lyngby Town Hall, 1938-1942.

246. *Copenhagen Søllerød, Øverødvej 2. Søllerød Town Hall.*

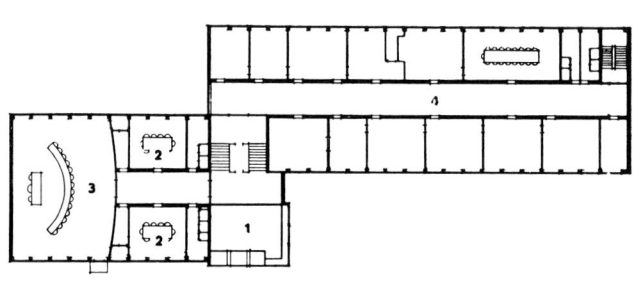

247. *Lyngby Town Hall. Plan 1:750.*

The light, marble siding is repeated at Søllerød Town Hall, which Arne Jacobsen and Flemming Lassen built in 1940-42 as the result of a competition. The building has a reinforced concrete frame filled out with cinder block and consisting of two connected wings, of which the northernmost contains a lobby, meeting room and council hall, while the south wing houses offices. The same architects also designed an addition in 1967.

In 1938, Hans Erling Langkilde and Ib Martin Jensen won the competition for Lyngby Town Hall, which was completed in 1941. The five-storey office building curves around a triangular front plaza. The town council hall is expressed on the Greenland marble facade by two-storey windows.

247. *Lyngby Town hall. Stairway.*

246. *Søllerød Town Hall. Plan 1:750.*

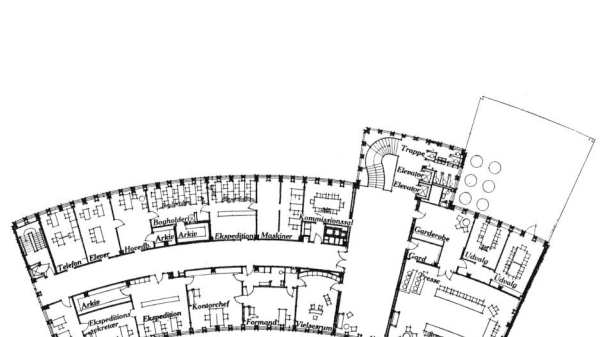

247. *Copenhagen Kgs. Lyngby, Lyngby Torv. Lyngby Town Hall.*

248-249. The Broadcasting House and Gladsaxe Town Hall, 1937-1945.

248. *Copenhagen, Rosenørns Allé 22. Broadcasting House. Below: Studio 1, concert hall.*

Vilhelm Lauritzen was commissioned in 1934 to design a new Broadcasting House. Work started in 1937 and the studios and office building were finished in 1941. The large concert hall or Studio 1 was built in 1939-45. These three functions are clearly separated in the plan so that the two staggered office wings, with centre corridors, face Rosenørns Allé as does the main entrance. The concert hall faces Julius Thomsens Gade and the lower studio block lies as a connecting link between them. All of the buildings are built of reinforced concrete and sided with pale yellow ceramic tiles, however the staggering of the blocks and their precise intersections help to soften the somewhat schematic modernism. Other aids are the colour scheme and the many good details, such as G.N. Brandt's lush roof garden adjacent to the canteen. The main feature of the Broadcasting House is the large concert hall with its untraditional, trapezoidal plan and wavy ceiling, the form of which was arrived at from acoustical considerations. The scheme has been expanded on several occasions, including a five-storey office wing facing Worsaaesvej.

Lauritzen also designed Gladsaxe Town Hall in 1937 as the result of a competition. The angular, three-storey office building has side corridors and continuous window bands. Interior concrete columns allow a greater flexibility in changing the location of office partitions in relation to the facade. A side wing was added in 1953. In 1985-86, Knud Munk built an addition with a town council hall and an office wing.

249. *Copenhagen Søborg, Rådhus Allé. Gladsaxe Town hall.*

248. *Roof garden by the canteen.*

248. *Broadcasting House. Plan and elevation 1:1500.*

248. *Roof garden.*

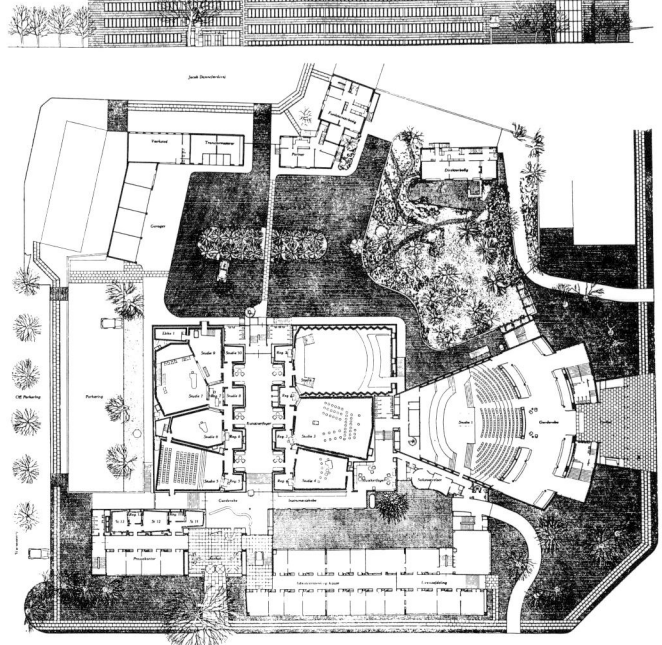

250-251. Bispeparken and Grundtvig's School, 1937-1942.

250. Copenhagen,
Tagensvej/Tuborgvej/
Frederiksborgvej.
Bispeparken. Block 3.

250. Bispeparken. Plan
1:5000.

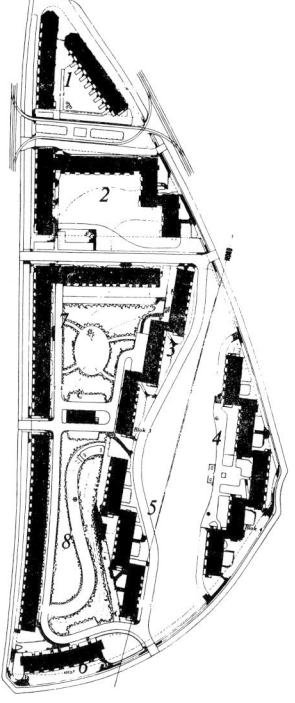

Above: Bispeparken block 5.
Below: Bispeparken block 6.

238

Between 1940 and 1942, on a site south of Grundtvig's Church, bordered by Tagensvej, Tuborgvej and Frederiksborgvej, the Public Housing Society built the Bispeparken high-rise housing scheme, which is typical of the large park schemes and green common areas of the forties. The blocks are freely placed on the site, but still allow a large green that opens to a view of the church. The many, basically small flats are dominated by the thirties' balcony-bays, which in most cases are roofed and oriented toward the sun when possible. The site plan was done by Ivar Bentsen and the Kooperative Arkitekter (Edv. Heiberg and others), while Kaare Klint and Valdemar Jørgensen designed Block 1; Knud Thorball and Magnus Stephensen, Block 2; Heiberg and Harald Petersen, Blocks 3 and 5; Fr. Wagner, Block 4; Knud Hansen, Block 6; and Vagn Kaastrup, blocks 7 and 8.

Farther south, at the end of the green wedge, lies Grundtvig's School on Magistervej 4, from 1937-38, built by Municipal architect Poul Holsøe and F.C. Lund. It is a symmetric scheme with all the normal classrooms placed in a south oriented, three-storey wing, while the aula, flanked by the special classrooms lies in the centre, facing north. The entire north wall of the aula is one large window offering a view of the church. The somewhat fragmented plan is an indication of what was to follow in the next decade.

251. *Copenhagen, Magistervej 4. Grundtvig's school*

251. *Grundtvig's school. The aula.*

252-254. The row houses and linked houses of the forties.

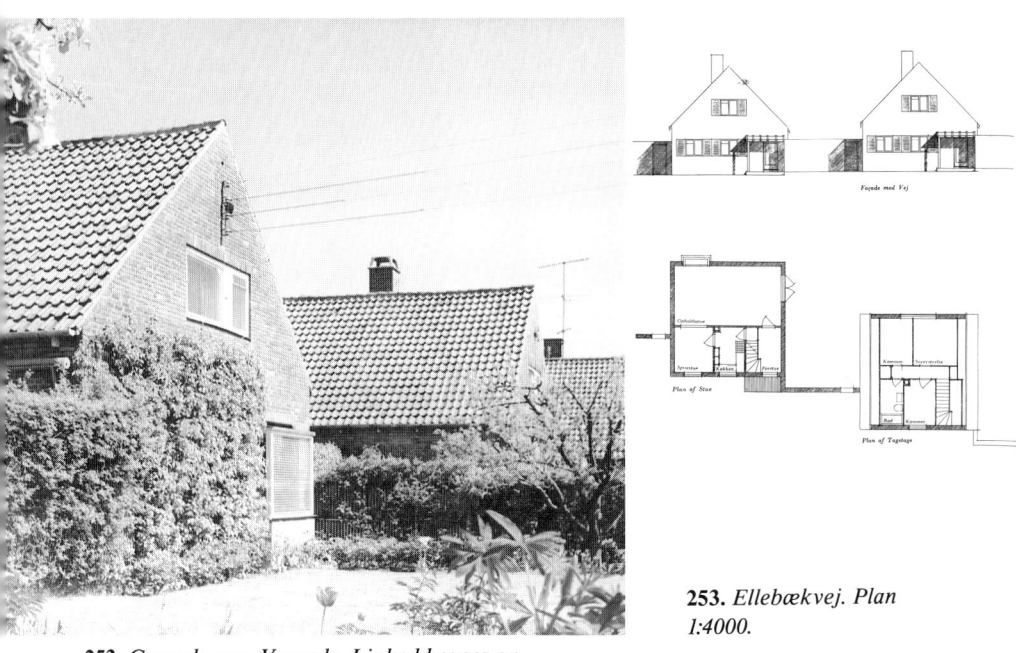

253. Copenhagen, Vangede. Linked houses on Ellebækvej by Arne Jacobsen.

253. Ellebækvej. Plan 1:4000.

252. Copenhagen, Utterslev, Grønnemose Allé 21-49. Atelier houses.

252. Atelier houses. Plan 1:1500.

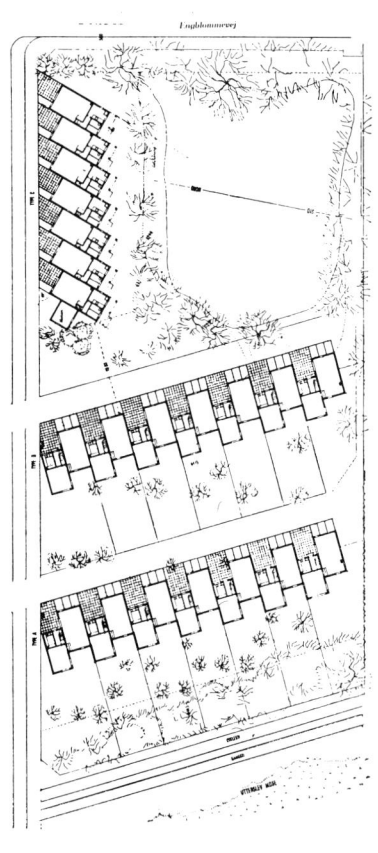

The price increases, lack of materials and shortage of housing that followed in the wake of World War II influenced the building industry during the decade up until the fifties. A return to traditional building methods was necessary and made it a virtue of necessity to appreciate the simple solutions and fine details of brickwork in which the shortage of steel brought a renaissance in bricked arches over the reduced window openings. The void of large projects stimulated an interest in the smaller ones, especially the most economical building types, such as the row house and linked house. Among the more untraditional examples are Viggo Møller-Jensen's Atelier Houses on Grønnemose Allé in Utterslev, built in 1943, for painters and sculptors. The three rows of houses lie by a large pond, and the individual units are staggered thus forming sheltered terraces and work courts. The houses had to be as inexpensive as possible and had mortar-brushed walls, asbestos-cement roofing, tarred wood on the balconies and fences, and were originally heated by wood stoves.

A new variation of the row house was the so-called linked houses, which were separated from each other by small connecting units that contained the secondary facilities. They were not as economical as the row house, but offered a greater variation in the row structure. Good examples of these are Arne Jacobsen's scheme on Ellebæksvej in Vangede from 1943 and Eske Kristensen's on Skjoldagervej in Jægersborg from 1943-44.

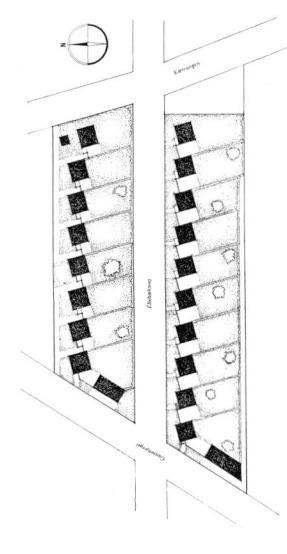

253. *Ellebækvej. Plans and elevation 1:750.*

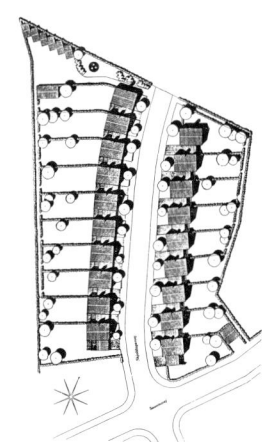

254. *Skjoldagervej. Plan 1:4000.*

254. *Copenhagen, Jægersborg. Linked houses on Skjoldagervej.*

255-256. Voldparken and Mother Help, 1949-1956.

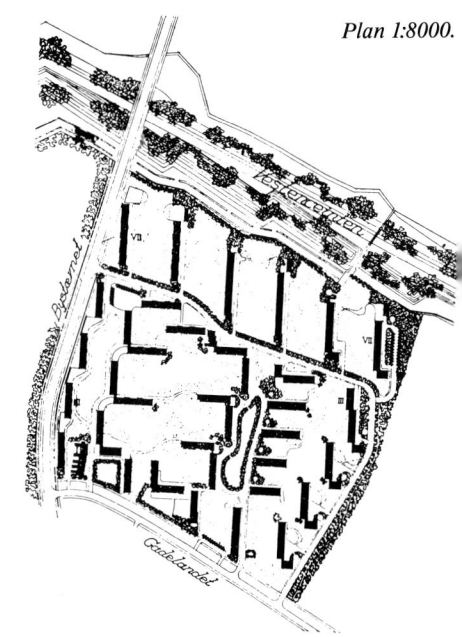

255. *Copenhagen, Husum, Arrildsgård, Kobbelvænget. Voldparken.*
Left: Facade detail.

Plan 1:8000.

After the war, work was started on the design of Voldparken, an enormous building scheme, considering conditions at that time. It lies adjacent to the West Enceinte in Brønshøj and contains about 1400 flats as well as shops, day-care centres etc. The site plan was done by architects Edvard Heiberg, Karl Larsen, Municipal Architect F.C. Lund, Viggo S. Jørgensen and Kay Fisker. The blocks nearest the embankment are seven storeys high and those to the south are three storeys with large common areas in between. Despite its general impression, Kay Fisker's block toward the east is the most pronounced with its large hipped asbestos cement roof and wide band of balconies with asbestos cement siding. The landscaping was planned by C.Th. Sørensen and the scheme was carried out in 1949-51. Near Kay Fisker's housing block, lies his Voldpark School. The yellow brick and grey asbestos cement roofing and siding are repeated here. The school is a fine example of Fisker's ability to tie large building schemes together with simple means, in this case the large roof surfaces, deep shadows and precise building masses. The school's two main, staggered wings are connected by a unique stairway with a double system of straight runs with intermediate landings. The scheme was built in two stages, in 1952 and 1956.

The plan type with staggered wings is repeated in one of Fisker's best works: The Mother Help building on Strandboulevarden 127. The seven-storey wing has a centre corridor that is expressed in the high, clear cut, end walls, which makes the rows of rooms on either side appear as individual wings. It was built in 1953-54.

256. *Copenhagen, Strandboulevarden 127. Mother Help. Below: Plan 1:750.*

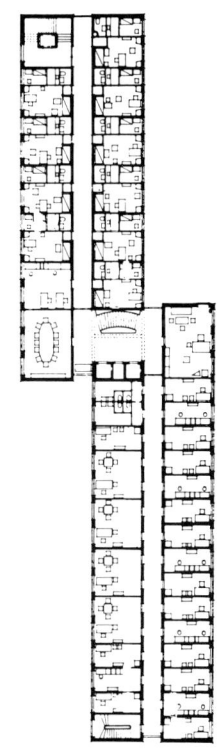

255. *Voldparkens School. Main entrance.*

257-258. Søndergårdsparken and Søholm, 1946-1955.

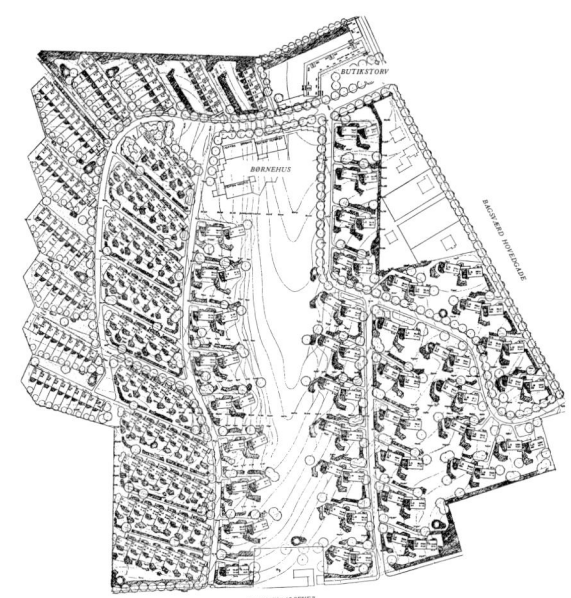

257. *Copenhagen Bagsværd, Ibsvej, Keltisvej, Kaaresvej and Sigmundsvej. Søndergårdsparken. Plan 1:6000.*

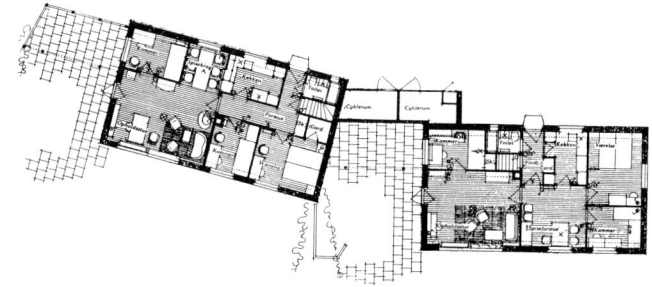

257. *Søndergårdsparken. Plans of individual buildings. 1:400.*

Near the corner of Gammelmosevej and Bagsværd Hovedgade in Gladsaxe, lies Søndergårdsparken, an open park housing scheme built in 1949-1950 and one of the post war era's most successful housing areas. The exceptionally mixed scheme consists of about 200 single, and one and a half storey row houses and individual buildings, built of yellow brick with white-washed window reveals, all lying around a large common area. The open areas around the buildings, with the exception of sheltered areas, are not subdivided in private gardens except along the row houses, instead they comprise a large, scenic common green. There is also a shopping centre, day-care centres, and homes for the aged. The architects were Poul Ernst Hoff and Bennet Windinge.

Nearby his older, major work, Bellavista, Arne Jacobsen was commissioned in 1946-55 to build the row- and linked house scheme, Søholm on Strandvejen 413. The view of the strait and the desire for a distinctive facade expression seen from Strandvejen was the basis for the form of this dynamic and characterful, rhythmically staggered row of houses. In order to offer the best possible views, the living rooms are placed on the first floor with open connection to the lower dining area. Insulating glass was used here for the first time, with reference to England. The unusual roof form is due to the high windows that catch the evening sun.

258. *Søholm.*

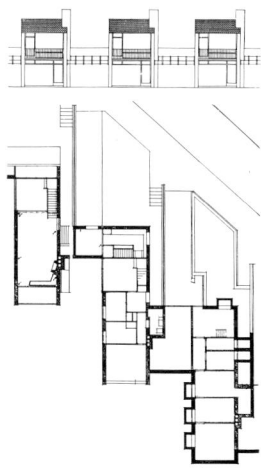

258. *Søholm. Plans and elevation 1:750.*

258. *Copenhagen Klampenborg, Strandvejen 413. Søholm.*

259-262. New school types, 1948-1958.

259. *Esbjerg, Grådybet. Grådyb School.*

Below: **260.** *Copenhagen Vigerslev, Rødbyvej 2. Hansted School.*

In 1949, architects Peer Hougaard Nielsen and C.J. Nørgaard Petersen won the competition for the Grådyb School in Esbjerg, which with a few alterations was built in 1951-54.

The school is in one storey with a rectangular plan in which the classrooms face inward toward a richly varied system of courtyards, while the corridors are oriented outward. A number of hexagonal, special classrooms cut into the large green yard toward south. Next to the main entrance on the west, is a trapezoidal assembly hall with a stage. This type represents a transitional form between the yard school and the atrium school.

Municipal architect F.C. Lund and Hans Chr. Hansen built Hansted School on Rødbyvej 2 in Vigerslev, in 1954-58 for the municipality of Copenhagen. This unusual scheme is L-shaped with low, one- and two-storey wings in which the classrooms are paired along individual stairways. A series of prominent saw toothed roofs give a special rhythm to the courtyard facade. Much attention has been given to daylighting conditions in which diffused and direct light are interspersed through high and low skylights. In contrast to this, the facades are relatively simple with yellow brick, dark brown wooden mullions, grey asbestos cement, and fixed windows with small, inserted, operable sections.

Munkegårds School on Vangedevej 178 in Gentofte, which Arne Jacobsen built in 1948-57, introduced a new type of school that combined the comb system with the atrium principle. By letting a row of parallel comb systems grow together, a network of classrooms emerges on one side with corridors on the other and closed, intimate courtyards in between. A two-storey block with an assembly hall, teachers rooms, etc. is placed in the centre of the large scheme.

On a beautifully overgrown site at Ordrup Krat, architects Hans Erling Langkilde and Ib Martin Jensen built the Skovgårds School 1949-51. The long wings fits well with the surroundings, and all the classrooms are oriented toward garden areas.

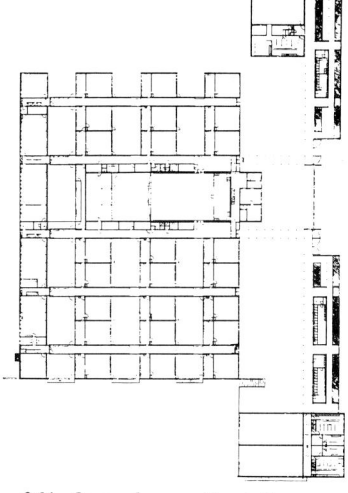

261. *Copenhagen, Gentofte, Vangedevej 178. Munkegårds School.*
Above: Plan 1:750.

262. *Copenhagen Gentofte, Skovgårdsvej 56. Skovgårds School.*

263-264. Bellahøj and Høje Søborg, 1949-1956.

263. Copenhagen, Bellahøjvej. Bellahøj. Site plan 1:10.000.

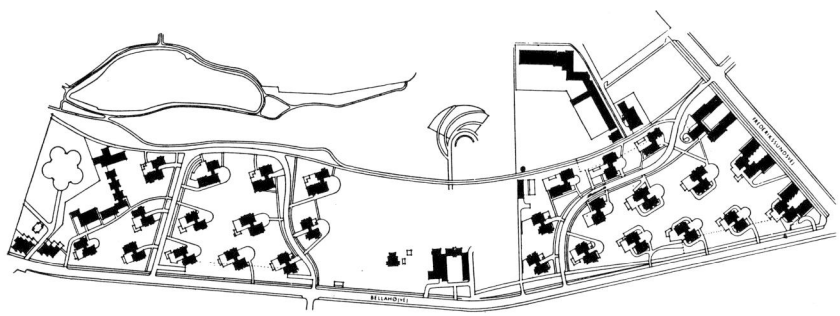

The Municipality of Copenhagen arranged a competition in 1944 for a large housing scheme on the site of the old Bellahøj country estate from 1792. The winning project by Tage Nielsen and Mogens Irming proposed a high-rise scheme that could enjoy the exceptional view over the city and the Øresund strait, while still retaining the parklike character of the site. After a number of revisions, the project was taken over in 1950 by four large housing associations, each with its own architect, though with a common set of general directives for the final design. The northern part was designed by Eske Kristensen and Edvard Heiberg, Karl Larsen, Ole Buhl and Harald Petersen. The southern part was done by Dan Fink, A/S Dominia's architect department and the Municipal Architect's Department. The eight- and ten-storey towers are each formed as twin, horizontally and vertically staggered blocks, tied together by a stairway and containing about 1300, relatively small flats with up to three and a half rooms. The scheme also has a shopping area and different common facilities. In terms of building methods, the Bellahøj scheme was an innovation with its bearing walls of non-reinforced concrete and facades cast with light reinforcing.

The Høje Søborg housing scheme on Søborg Torv, built in 1949-51 by Poul Ernst Hoff and Bennet Windinge was the first real collective scheme, planned for singles and families in which both parents worked. Therefore the apartments are rather small, but in return, there are a great variety of service functions: A permanent doorman, cleaning centre, a shop, restaurant, day-care centre, hobby room, party rooms and a roof garden.

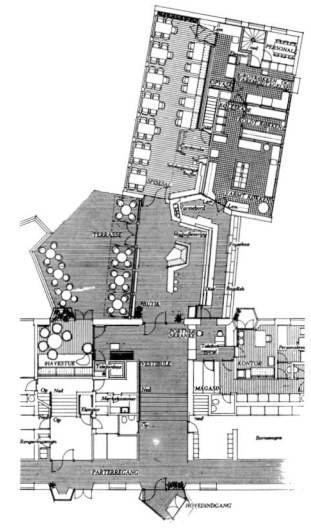

264. *Høje Søborg. Plan of common house, 1:600.*

264. *Copenhagen, Søborg Torv. Cooperative housing Høje Søborg.*

264. *Høje Søborg. Plan 1:1800.*

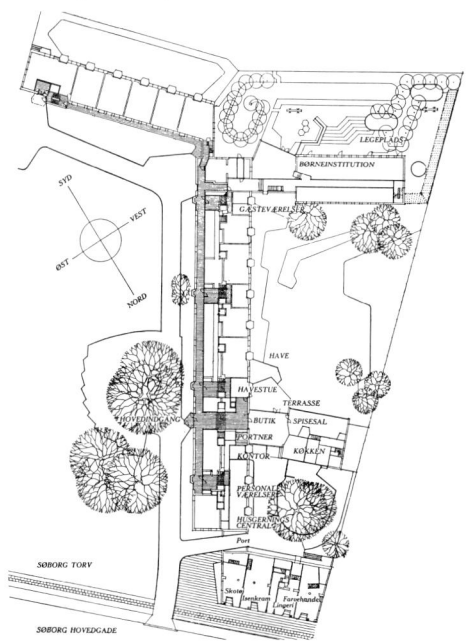

249

265-268. Post war single-family houses, 1950-1959.

265. *Hellebæk, Gammel Hellebækvej. Jørn Utzon's own house, 1952. Plan 1:750.*

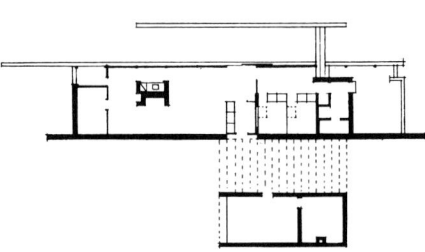

Left: **266.** *Copenhagen Gentofte, Smutvej 14. Erik Christian Sørensens own house, 1955. Plan 1:750.*

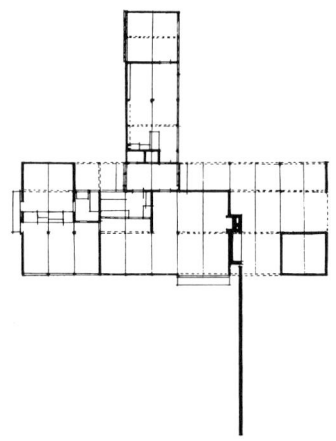

The lack of large projects during the war years sharpened the architects' interest in single-family houses, and the strict economical limitations gave rise to a new type: The one-storey house without basement and a low, thirty degree roof slope. These prismatic long houses in red or yellow brick won widespread popularity throughout the country during and after the war, due in part to a advantageous state loan system. During the fifties, inspiration from American and Japanese architecture, including Frank Lloyd Wright and Mies van der Rohe, led to a more differentiated plan with intimate contact between interior and exterior and the surrounding landscape, with exposed brick in the living rooms, natural wood paneling and visible wooden columns and beams. The real freedom in plan solutions came with the introduction of the flat built up roof, and the large insulating glass windows enabled the construction of outer walls as large continuous glass surfaces from floor to ceiling. The open plan offered a better use of the available space, greater flexibility and good opportunities for expansion. Of these individually designed and built houses, a distinctive type house production developed during the fifties, which not only offered fixed prices and high quality, but also a guarantee that the user got more for his money. The area of the single-family house increased from under eighty to over ninety square metres in the period from 1950 to 1960.

267. *Søllerød, Vangebovej. Government-subsidized housing, 1950. Architect Mogens Frisendal.*

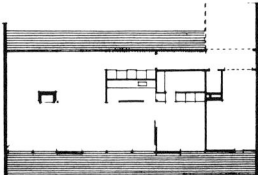

268. *Hørsholm, Strandvejen 68. Halldor Gunnlögssons own house. Interior and exterior. Above: Plan 1:750.*

269-270. F.L. Smidth & Co. and Tårnby Town Hall, 1952-1959.

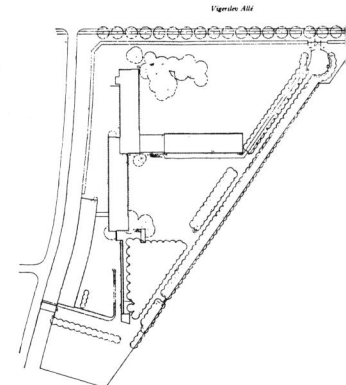

269. *F.L. Smidth & Co. Plan 1:5000.*

269. *Copenhagen Valby, Vigerslev Allé 77. F.L. Smidth & Co. A/S. Left: Detail of facade.*

One of Denmark's few, really large corporations, F.L. Smidth & Co. A/S, after many years of overcrowded conditions on Vestergade in Copenhagen, decided to move out to a site adjacent to their factory on Vigerslev Allé in Valby. Here Palle Suenson built an administration building in 1952-57 divided up in an eight-storey wing with drafting rooms and archives, connected to a four-storey wing that housed the accounting department, etc., as well as a perpendicular two storey wing for the executive offices. The latter two had pulled back roof levels with a wide eaves and flat roof. Despite the fact that the firm's principle business is building cement factories all over the world, they wanted a maintenance free facade in red brick. This was the basis for the narrow brick pillars of thin Flensborg brick that run from the foundation to the roof. The deep recessed windows with bronze frames, of which every other was operable, are screened from direct sunlight most of the day. A remarkably fine balance between the horizontal and vertical lines was achieved.

As the result of a design competition in 1953, Halldor Gunnlögsson and Jørn Nielsen were commissioned to build Tårnby Town Hall in 1957-59. It is two storeys high and based on a rectangular plan with two courtyards: an exterior one with a pool and an iron sculpture, and an interior one with a balcony and large stairway. The lanternlike superstructure with side lighting has broad eaves that seem to float over the hall. The plan's fixed grid is indicated by the uniform spacing of windows. The exterior siding is Norwegian marble. The refined, exclusive detailing in the interior is underscored by Poul Kjærholm's furniture.

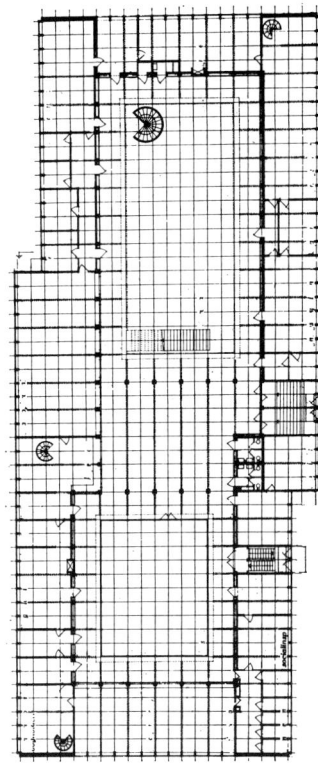

270. *Taarnby Town Hall. Plan 1:750.*

270. *Copenhagen Taarnby. Amager Landevej 76. Taarnby Town Hall.*

271-273. Kingo Houses, Søllerød Park and Nærum Vænge, 1951-1961.

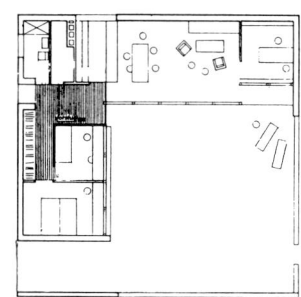

271. *Helsingør, Kingosvej.*
Jørn Utzon.
Kingo houses. Plan 1:400.
Site plan 1:5000.

Below: Courtyard

272. *Søllerød. Søllerød Park. Eva & Nils Koppel.*

With his Kingo Houses in Helsingør, built in 1958-60, Jørn Utzon created a remarkable innovation to the conventional linked house scheme. The basic element was a square courtyard house in which the L-shaped house and courtyard were edged by a screen wall. These units were linked together in a rather untraditional pattern, decided by the slope of the site, the solar orientation and the view. The result is an organic whole due to the traditional choice of materials, with yellow brick, red tile shed roofs and stained wood trim. The rolling terrain with a small pond offered an unusually attractive common area between the closed housing units. The access roads are discreetly held to the edges of the site, and the spaces between the buildings have a somewhat urban character. The Kingo Houses had a great influence on many courtyard and individual houses in the years that followed.

The Søllerød Park housing scheme was built in 1955 on an old park area, with Nils and Eva Koppel as architects. The two and a half storey blocks have single-storey flats on the ground floor and one and a half storey flats on the upper with access from a common balcony corridor. The nonbearing facade elements are of charcoal grey concrete elements and black impregnated wood.

Palle Suenson's Nærum Vænge from 1951-61 is both a sound and well-defined housing scheme, that with its yellow brick walls and large red tile roofs continues the Danish functional tradition.

273. Nærum. Nærumvænge. Palle Suenson.

274-277. Arne Jacobsen, 1953-1960.

274. *Copenhagen, Vesterbrogade/Hammerichsgade. SAS Royal Hotel. The inspiration is Skidmore, Owings & Merrill's Lever House in New York.*

Below: **275.** *Copenhagen, Nyropsgade 18. Office building for A. Jespersen & Søn. Plans and section 1:750.*

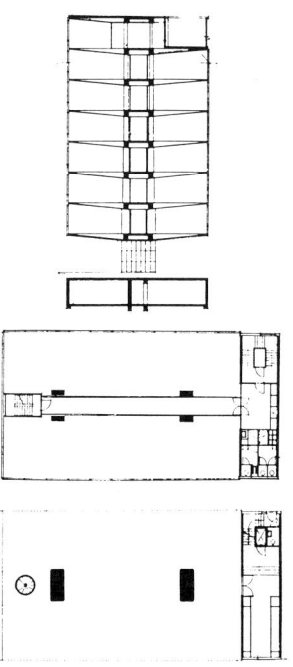

The twenty storey high SAS building with the Royal Hotel, built in 1960, was Copenhagen's first real skyscraper, strongly inspired by the New York prototypes. The tall block rises from a wide, long two-storey building that forms a base and houses the lobby, restaurant, tickets offices and administrative offices. Despite its large volume, the building has a sense of lightness and elegance, primarily due to the thin aluminium mullions and the pale glass spandrels, and avoids appearing as a dominant foreign object in conflict with its surroundings. Arne Jacobsen designed all the individual elements in the building, down to the furniture and tableware. Unfortunately the artistic whole has not been maintained in the many alterations that have occurred since.

An office building with a similar lightness and elegance, but of a far smaller scale, was built by Arne Jacobsen as early as 1953 for A. Jespersen & Søn on Nyropsgade 18. The building has an open ground level and is supported by two enormous, rectangular reinforced concrete columns. These continue up through the seven storeys and bear the cantilevered decks, with curtain wall facades, elegant glass screens. The vertical end wall element on the right side houses the stairway, elevator and rest rooms.

The same structural system with curtain walls was also employed at Rødovre Town Hall from 1955, one of the best examples of his uncompromising attention to details.

On Rihimäkivej in Aalborg, Arne Jacobsen built a little factory. With its clean cut, precise building forms, it is a beautiful example of his refined, perfectionistic architectural attitude, which is evident even in his smaller projects.

276. *Rødovre, Rødovre Parkvej 150. Rødovre Town Hall. Stairway.*

Below: **277.** *Aalborg, Rihimäkivej. Carl Christensen's Motor factory.*

278. Louisiana, 1958-1991.

278. *Humlebæk, Gl. Strandvej 13. Louisiana. Exhibition space with a view of Humlebæk pond. Below: Siteplan.*

In 1958, wholesaler Knud W. Jensen opened the old family country estate, Louisiana in Humlebæk as a completely new form of museum with music and exhibitions, a cultural centre primarily for modern art and exhibitions of international caliber. The old estate building is connected to a building scheme designed by Jørgen Bo and Vilhelm Wohlert with a quite untraditional form: An irregular row of long connecting corridors between transverse halls, that wind around the existing great trees and terminate on a high plateau on the edge of the coast. The delicate glass galleries and the sound exhibition blocks are carefully placed on the scenic site and offer a natural, direct contact between interior and exterior. The rolling site is exploited with split levels and the combination of scenic views, skylights, sidelights and artificial lighting offers excellent conditions for the architecture to actively participate in the exhibition experience, a quite different experience than one is accustomed to in the more self-effacing museums. A characteristic example of this is in the high exhibition space with its large window wall facing Humlebæk Pond. The long sequence of richly varied exhibition spaces ends in a cafeteria and a hearth room with an extraordinary view over Øresund Strait. This section was enlarged in 1976-77 with a theatre and concert hall built into the slope running down to the water. Several years later a compact south wing was added to the main building, to house the permanent collection. All buildings are of white painted brick, both inside and out. There are heavy, laminated timber beams in the halls that bear the flat roof and skylight lanterns. A subterranean addition under the park was opened in 1991 and houses an exhibition of graphic art.

Interiør of the latest addition.

278. *Louisiana.*

279-282. School buildings, 1956-1960.

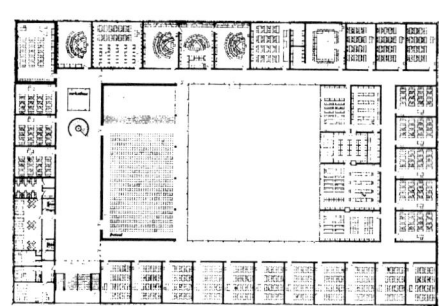

279. Århus Åbyhøj, Fenrisvej. Århus State School. Plan 1:1500.

Plan 1:1500.

281. Skive, Søndre Boulevard/Egerisvej. Skive High School.

Århus State School on Fenrisvej was built in 1956-58 by Arne Gravers and Johan Richter as the result of a design competition in 1953. The one-storey scheme consists of a large rectangular plan with a inner courtyard on which the assembly hall with its large glass wall opens. The opposite wall of the hall is decorated with a great ceramic relief by Asger Jorn, who also did a wall tapestry for the school. A wide, monumental stairway connects the school yard with the main entrance, from which there is a fine view over the city. The pale facades are sided with limestone.

The old, characteristic main building at Askov Folk High School was replaced by a new one in 1956-60, designed by Tyge Arnfred and Viggo Møller-Jensen, who also were responsible for the new student and teachers' housing. The main building is dominated by the triple-aisle dining hall, and the beautiful garden by the principal's curved garden wall, as well as the square tower with a pyramidal belfry based on the same simple scheme as that employed in Jørn Utzon's navigation mark/water tower in Svaneke on Bornholm.

Skive Teacher's College was built in 1957-59 in the form of a Japanese inspired garden courtyard surrounded by the assembly hall, gymnasium, offices, etc as well a long, curved classroom wing in one and two storeys. The adjustment to the rolling site is very successful. The architects were Karen and Ebbe Clemmensen, who later in 1970 were asked to convert the scheme to a high school with additions toward north and west.

Vangebo School in Søllerød was completed in 1960 and based on a winning competition proposal from 1958 by architects Gehrdt Bornebusch, Max Brüel, Henning Larsen and Jørgen Selchau. Here the class room wings are formed as a linked house scheme with small courtyards adjacent to each classroom. The entire scheme is framed by a L-shaped perimeter building housing the special classrooms and other facilities.

282. *Copenhagen Søllerød, Vangeboled. Vangebo school. Plan detail, 1:3000.*

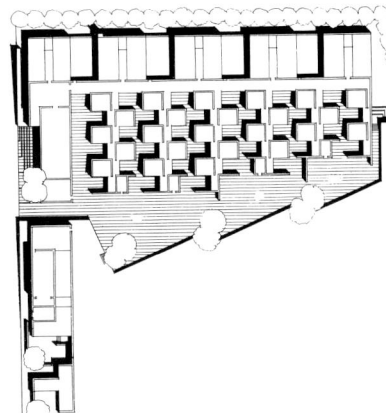

280. *Askov Folk High School near Vejen.*

261

Index of places

Aachen, Karl the Great's sepulchre-chapel p. 51
Aggersborg p. 9, 41/no. 3
Askov folk high school p. 261/no. 280
Bernstorff Slot/country estate p. 22, 130, 131, 133/no. 118
Birkerød Church p. 61/no. 38
Birkholm p. 15
Bjernede Church p. 45, 162/no. 15
Borreby p. 71, 72, 73/no. 52
Christiansfeld p. 134/no. 124
Christianshøj p. 197/no. 199
Christiansø p. 97/no. 83
Clausholm p. 102, 103/no. 90
Dannevirke p. 11, 47
Den Fynske Landsby/open-air museum p. 18, 95/no. 80
Dragsholm p. 14, 65/no. 44
Dragør p. 138/no. 131
Ebeltoft, the old town hall p. 137/no. 128
Egeskov p. 15, 70, 71/no. 50
Eremitageslottet/hunting manor p. 116, 117/no. 107
Esbjerg, Grådyb school p. 146, 147/no. 259
Esbjerg, Skjoldsgade p. 199/no. 202
Fredensborg Palace p. 19, 108, 109/no. 94
Fredensborg, Terrasserne p. 39
Frederiksberg Palace p. 19, 104, 105/no. 91
Frederiksborg Castle, Hillerød p. 16, 28, 80, 81/no. 62
Frederiksdal Slot/country estate p. 115/no. 105
Frederikshavn, the fortress Fladstrand p. 97/no. 84
Frederiksværk p. 21
Frijsenborg p. 27, 161/no. 158
Frilandsmuseet/open-air museum, Lyngby s.18, 23, 95/no. 79
Fyrkat p. 9, 41/no. 2
Fåborg p. 9
Fåborg Museum p. 33, 192, 193/no. 194
Gammel Estrup p. 75/no. 57
Gammel Holtegård p. 120/no. 111
Gisselfeld p. 15, 73/no. 54
Gjorslev p. 14, 66, 67/no. 45
Gl. Skagen, summer cottage in Højen p. 183/no. 187
Gladsaxe town hall p. 237/no. 249
Glorup p. 133/no. 122
Glückstadt p. 17
Gnadau, brethren town p. 134
Gudhjem railway station p. 196, 197/no. 199
Gurre p. 13
Haderslev Cathedral p. 13, 55/no. 26
Hammershus castle ruin p. 13, 14, 62, 63/no. 40
Hellebæk, Jørn Utzon's own house p. 250/no. 265
Helsingør p. 10, 13, 17, 27
Helsingør Cathedral (Skt Olai Church) p. 13, 57/no. 28
Helsingør, carmelite monastery and Skt. Maria Church p. 15, 58,59/no. 32
Helsingør, Kingosvej, Kingohusene p. 39, 254, 255/no. 271
Helsingør, Kronborg Castle p. 78, 79/no. 61
Helsingør, Marienlyst Slot/country manor p. 130, 131/no. 119
Helsingør, Stengade 66 and 72-76 p. 77/no. 58
Hesselagergård p. 15, 68, 69, 71, 73/no. 48
Hillerød, Frederiksborg Castle p. 16, 28, 80, 81/no. 62
Hjerl Hede/open-air museum p. 18, 95/no. 81
Hobro Church p. 157/no. 153
Holbæk, Møllebakken and Bakkekammen p. 194, 195/no. 198
Holsten p. 17
Horne Rundkirke/church p. 45, 162/no. 14
Horsens, Kildegade, The Workers Assembly Building p. 203/no. 207
Horsens Museum p. 193/no. 196
Hover Church p. 42, 43/no. 5
Humlebæk, Louisiana p. 38, 258, 259/no. 278
Hvorslev Church p. 60/no. 35
Hørsholm, Hirschholm Slot p. 20, 119, 151
Hørsholm Church p. 151/no. 146
Hørsholm, Rungstedvej 47 p. 172, 173/no. 175
Hørsholm, Strandvejen 68 p. 251/no. 268
Kalundborg p. 9, 13, 17
Kalundborg, gentry houses p. 17, 90, 91/no. 71
Kalundborg, Vor Frue Kirke/church p. 12, 50, 51, 162/no. 20
Kalø p. 13
Karise, Moltkes Gravkapel/chapel p. 141
Kjeldby Church p. 60/no. 34
Kolding, gentry houses p. 91/no. 72
Korsør p. 9, 13
Korsør. Fortification tower p. 63/no. 41
Kristiania, Norway p. 17
Kristiansstad, Sweden p. 17
Kronborg Castle p. 16, 78, 79/no. 61
Køge, gentry houses p. 17, 90, 91/no. 70
Køge p. 10, 17
Køge, Skt. Nicolai Church p. 13, 57/no. 31
Ledreborg p. 21, 118, 119/no. 108
Ledøje Church p. 51/no. 22
Lejre, archaeological experimental centre p. 9, 41/no. 4
Lerchenborg p. 21, 119/no. 109
Liselund p. 22, 132, 133/no. 121
Louisiana, see Humlebæk
Lund Cathedral, Sweden p. 13
Lyngby, Frilandsmuseet/open-air museum p. 18, 23, 95/no. 79
Lyngby Town hall p. 235/no. 247
Lyngby, Sophienholm p. 144, 145/no. 138
Løgumkloster Church p. 55/no. 25
Margård p. 115/no. 106
Maribo Cathedral p. 13, 59/no. 33
Marienlyst Slot/country manor p. 130, 131/no. 119
Moesgård p. 132, 133/no. 123
Møgeltønder, Slotsgade p. 135/no. 126

Mårup Øde Church p. 42, 43/no. 6
Nakkebølle p. 71
Nyborg p. 9
Nyborg Folkebibliotek/library p. 231/no. 244
Nyborg Castle p. 13, 71/no. 51
Ny Church (Nyker) p. 45/no. 13
Nylars Church p. 45/no. 11
Nysø p. 99/no. 87
Nærumvænge p. 255/no. 273
Næstved p. 13
Næstved, Boderne at Skt. Peders Church/town houses p. 13, 77/no. 59
Næstved, Skt. Peders Church p. 57/no. 30
Odense p. 9, 17, 26
Odense, Den fynske Landsby/open-air museum p. 18, 95/no. 80
Odense, Gerthas Minde p. 189, 190/no. 193
Odense, Nonnebakken p. 41
Odense, Skibhusvej, Fredens Church p. 207/no. 212
Odense, Skt. Knuds Plads, Skt. Knuds Church p. 13, 56, 57/no. 27
Odense Palace p. 111/no. 95
Ols Church p. 45/no. 12
Oringe mental hospital p. 24, 156, 157/no. 151
Overbjerg p. 8
Paris p. 27, 28
Pederstrup p. 149/no. 144
Randers p. 9, 13
Randers, Helligåndshuset/monastery p. 77/no. 60
Randers Statsskole/high school p. 205/no. 209
Ribe p. 9, 17
Ribe, gentry houses p. 17, 88, 89/no. 69
Ribe Cathedral p. 13, 54, 55/no. 24
Ringsted p. 9
Ringsted, Skt. Bendts Church p. 11, 46, 47/no. 17
Rome p. 19
Rome, San Andrea p. 151
Rosenholm p. 75/no. 56
Roskilde p. 9
Roskilde Cathedral p. 13, 48, 49, 141, 162/no. 19
Roskilde, Det gule Palæ/palace p. 110, 111/no. 97
Roskilde Cathedral, The Chapel of Frederik V p. 22, 141/no. 19
Roskilde Cathedral, The Chapel of Hellig Tre Konger p. 162
Bornholm, Round churches p. 12
Rygård p. 14, 69/no. 49
Rønne, Kastellet/fortress p. 97/no. 85
Skagen p. 182, 183/no. 187
Skive Seminarium, now high school p. 261/no. 281
Slagelse p. 9
Slagelse, Skt. Mikkels Church p. 13, 56, 57/no. 29
Slesvig p. 9
Sophienholm p. 144, 145/no. 138
Sorø Akademi/boarding school p. 153/no. 148
Sorø Church p. 11, 47/no. 18
Spøttrup p. 14, 64, 65/no. 43
Stensballegård p. 103
Store Heddinge Church p. 51/no. 21
Sulsted Church p. 61/no. 37
Svaneke p. 139/no. 132
Svaneke, navigation mark/water tower p. 261
Svinninge power station p. 194, 195/no. 197
Sydney Opera House, Australia p. 39
Sæby, Skovallé 20 p. 199/no. 203
Søllerød Park p. 254, 255/no. 272
Søllerød, Vangeboled 9, Vangebo school p. 261/no. 282
Søllerød, Vangebovej (state loan house) p. 251/no. 267
Søllerød, Øverødvej 2, Søllerød Town hall p. 37, 234, 235/no. 246
Sønderho, Captain Brinch's house p. 136, 137/no. 129
Thorsager Church p. 45/no. 16
Turebyholm p. 120/no. 112
Tibirke Bakker p. 200, 201/no. 204
Tjele p. 14, 67/no. 46
Trelleborg s.9, 40,41 / no. 1.
Tveje Merløse Church p. 10, 43/no. 9
Tønder, gentry houses p. 135/no. 125
Tårnby Town hall p. 253/no. 270
Valdemars Slot/farm estate p. 119/no. 110
Vallekilde folk high school p. 172, 173/no. 174
Vallø p. 15, 73/no. 53
Varde, Den Kampmannske Gård and Torvet 5/gentry houses. p. 137/no.130
Venezia p. 15
Venezia, The church of San Zaccaria p. 69
Venge Church p. 43/no. 7
Vestervig Church p. 43/no. 8
Viborg p. 9
Viborg Cathedral p. 13, 29, 162/no. 159
Viborg, the old town hall p. 111/no. 96
Viborg Katedralskole/high school p. 205/no. 210
Viby Church p. 61/no. 39
Voergård p. 15, 74, 75/no. 55
Vordingborg p. 9, 13
Vordingborg, Gåsetårnet/fortification tower p. 63/no. 42
Ærøskøbing, gentry houses p. 136, 137/no. 127
Øresund p. 16
Østerlars Church p. 44, 45/no. 10
Østerlars railway station p. 196, 197/no. 199
Østermarie railway station p. 196, 197/no. 199
Østofte Church p. 60/no. 36
Østrupgård p. 66, 67/no. 47
Ålborg p. 9, 17, 27
Ålborg, Aalborg Manor p. 93/no. 74
Ålborg, Jens Bangs Stenhus p. 18, 92, 93/no. 73
Ålborg, Rihimäkivej/factory p. 257/no. 277
Ålborg, Østerågade 23-25 p. 93/no. 73
Århus p. 27, 31
Århus, The old town in Århus/open-air museum p. 17, 94/no. 78

Århus Cathedral p. 12, 13, 52, 53/no. 23
Århus, J. M. Mørksgade 13/art gallery p. 193/no. 195
Århus Town hall p. 37, 232, 233/no. 245
Århus, Skt. Lukas Church p. 203/no. 206
Århus, Statsbiblioteket/Erhvervsarkivet/library p. 30, 181/no. 186
Århus Statsgymnasium/high school p. 260, 261/no. 279
Århus Theatre p. 30, 180, 181/no. 184
Århus, Toldkammerbygningen/custom house p. 30, 180, 181/no. 185
Århus University p. 36, 230, 231/no. 243

Copenhagen:

Copenhagen p. 9, 17, 27, 32, 33
Abel Cathrines Gade 13, Abel Cathrines Stiftelse/foundation p.173/no. 172
Amagerbro p. 25
Amagertorv 6 p. 18, 93/no. 76
Amaliegade p. 21
Amaliegade 17 p. 123/no. 113
Amaliegade 25 p. 123/no. 113
Amaliegade, the colonnade by Amalienborg p. 142, 143/no. 113
Amalienborg p. 20, 21, 121, 123, 125/no. 113
Amalienborg, A. G. Moltke's Palace p. 125, 145/no. 113
Amalienborg, Brockdorff's Palace p. 125/no. 113
Amalienborg, Levetzau's Palace p. 125/no. 113
Amalienborg, Schack's Palace p. 125/no. 113
Bakkehusene p. 210, 211/no. 214
Banegårdspladsen 2-4, Hotel Astoria p. 222, 223/no. 232
Bellahøj p. 38, 248, 249/no. 263
Bispebjerg, housing p. 36
Bispebjerg, Grundtvigs Church p. 206, 207/no. 211
Bispebjerg Hospital p. 172, 173/no. 173
Bispeparken p. 238, 239/no. 250
Borups Allé 5-23, Hornbækhus p. 212, 213/no. 223
Botanical Garden, Palm House p. 30
Bredgade 28, Odd Fellow Palace p. 123/no. 113
Bredgade 40-42, Bernsdorffs Palace p. 123/no. 113
Bredgade 54, Dehns Palace p. 123/no. 113
Bredgade 62, Surgical Academy p. 140, 141/no. 135
Bredgade 66-72, Frederiks Hospital p. 123/no. 113
Bremerholm-Gammelholm p. 16
Børsen p. 17, 84, 85/no. 64
Charlottenborg, Kongens Nytorv 1 p. 18, 19, 22, 98, 99/no. 86
Christiansborg Palace p. 20, 28
Christiansborg Palace/riding grounds and bridge p. 114, 115/no. 104
Christiansborg Palace Church p. 20, 23, 24, 150, 151/no. 145
Christianshavn p. 17
Classensgade 52-68, Ved Classens Have p. 34, 214, 215/no. 224
Danas Plads p. 177/no. 178
Dantes Plads 32, Glyptoteket p. 28, 170, 171/no. 171
Det Kgl. Bibliotek/library p. 85
Ellebækvej (linked houses) p. 240, 241/no. 253
Fiolstræde 1, Universitetsbiblioteket/library p. 26, 158, 159/no. 154
Fiolstræde 4-6, Metropolitan school p. 153/no. 147
Fiolstræde 18 p. 112, 113/no. 102
Fredericiagade 24, Operabygningen/Østre Landsret p. 107/no. 93
Frederiksberggade 16 p. 189, 191/no. 191
Frederiksholms Kanal 3, Prinsens Palace (The National Museum) s, 20, 115/no. 104
Frederiks Church p. 20, 22
Frederiksstaden p. 20, 121-123, 125/no. 113
Frihavnen p. 29
Frue Plads, University of Copenhagen p. 153/no. 147
Gammel Torv 8 p. 177/no. 180
Gammel Mønt 41 p. 113/no. 100
Gammel Torv 6 p. 222, 223/no. 233
Gammel Vartov Vej 16 p. 186, 187/no. 188
Gammel Vartov Vej 22 p. 187/no. 188
Gothersgade 111, Den reformerte Kirke/church p. 101/no. 89
Grundtvigs Church p. 206, 207/no. 211
Grøndalsvænge p. 198, 199/no. 201
Grønnemose Allé, Atelierhusene/linked houses p. 240, 241/no. 252
Gråbrødretorv 1-9 p. 112, 113/no. 98
Gyldenløvesgade, Søpavillonen p. 165/no. 165
Halmtorvet, Kødbyen/meat market p. 224, 225/no. 237
Hammerichsgade 1-5, SAS Royal Hotel p. 38, 256, 257/no. 274
Hans Tavsensgade/Struenseegade p. 212, 213/no. 222
H. C. Andersens Boulevard 6, Student's Union Building p. 176, 177/no. 179
Holmen p. 21, 126, 127/no. 114
Holmens Kanal 2-4 Erichsen's Palace p. 143/no. 137
Holmens Kanal 7, Grøns Warehouse p. 158/no. 155
Holmens Church p. 16, 23, 85/nr 66
Hovedbanegården/central station p. 178, 179/no. 181
Hovedvagtsgade and Ny Østergade p. 169/no. 168
Hulgaardsvej (row houses) p. 211/no. 216
Conflagration houses p. 19, 112, 113
Kastellet/fortress p. 16, 96, 97/no. 82
Kastrup Airport p. 37
Kastrup, Saltværksvej (row houses) p. 211/no. 220

Kartoffelrækkerne p. 163/no. 161
Kildevældsgade p. 163/no. 162
Kirkevænget, Jesus Church p. 167/no. 166
Kongens Have p. 83/no. 63
Kongens Nytorv 1, see Charlottenborg
Kongens Nytorv 3-5, Harsdorffs House p. 22, 141/no. 133
Kongens Nytorv 9, Det Kgl. Teater/The Royal Theatre p. 28, 164, 165/no. 163
Kongens Nytorv 13, Magasin du Nord p. 28
Krystalgade 25-27, Zoological Museum p. 161/no. 157
Købmagergade, Rundetårn and Trinitatis Church p. 86, 87/no. 67
Langelinie p. 29
Lundevangsvej 11 p. 184, 185/no. 188
Magistervej 4, Grundtvig school p. 239/no. 251
Magstræde 17-19 p. 93
Mariebjergvej, Mariebjerg Krematorium p. 227/no. 241
Marble Church (Frederikskirken) p. 28, 121, 123, 168, 169/no. 167
Ny Carlsberg p. 29
Ny Carlsberg Vej, Carlsberg Brewery p. 25, 166, 167/no. 166
Nyboder p. 16, 87/no. 68
Nybrogade p. 12, 113/no. 99
Nyhavn 9 p. 93/no. 77
Nyropsgade 18 p. 256, 257/no. 275
Nytorv 21-25, Town hall and Courthouse p. 24, 146, 147/no. 142
Nørrebro p. 25
Nørregade, Vor Frue Kirke/cathedral p. 23, 24, 32, 152, 153/no. 147
Otto Mønsteds Gade, Police Headquarters p. 34, 202, 203/no. 205
Overgaden oven Vandet 6, S. C. Stanleys Gård p. 129/no. 117
Pilestræde 34, Berlingske Tidende p. 223/no. 234
Porthusgade 2, Thorvaldsens Museum p. 24, 33, 154, 155/no. 149
Proviantgården and Tøjhuset/Provision yard p. 16, 85/no. 65
Rosenborg Castle p. 16, 82, 83/no. 63
Rosenørns Allé 22, Broadcasting House p. 37, 236, 237/no. 248
Ryvangs Allé 6 p. 185/no. 188
Ryvangsvillaer p. 31, 184, 185/no. 188
Rødbyvej 2, Hansted school p. 246, 247/no. 260
Rådhuspladsen 57, Palads Hotel p. 188, 189/no. 192
Rådhuspladsen, The Town Hall p. 30, 174, 175/no. 176
Sallingvej (row houses) p. 211/no. 215
Samosvej 50, Skolen ved Sundet and Svagebørnsskolen/schools p. 225/no. 239
Sankt Annæ Gade, Vor Frelsers Kirke/church p. 19, 100, 101/no. 88
Skindergade 13 p. 113/no. 101
Skindergade 34, Soldins Stiftelse p. 153/no. 147

Skjoldagervej (linked houses) p. 241/no. 254
Slotsholmsgade 4, Det røde Palæ/palace p. 19, 106, 107/no. 92
Standboulevarden 127, Mother Help building p. 243/no. 256
Sølvgade 48-50, The National Museum of Art p. 171/no. 170
Strandagervej 28 p. 185/no. 188
Strandgade, housing p. 18
Strandgade 1, Christians Church p. 128, 129/no. 115
Strandgade 14, 28, 30 and 32 p. 93/no. 75
Strandgade 25, Asiatisk Kompagni p. 21, 128, 129/no. 116
Strandvejen 54, Tuborgs Administrationsbygning/head office p. 189/no. 189
Svanemøllevej 56 p. 184, 185/no. 188
Sverrigsgade p. 163/no. 160
Søborg Torv, Høje Søborg p. 249/no. 264
Sølvgade 40, Sølvgade Barracks p. 131/no. 120
Søtorvet p. 28, 169/no. 169
Tivoli p. 25
Tivoli, Pantomimeteatret p. 164, 165/no. 164
Toldbodgade 9 p. 113/no. 103
Toldbodgade, Warehouse p. 21, 140, 141/no. 134
Tomsgårdsvej 78-110, Storgården p. 219/no. 230
Vanløse Allé 44, Kathrinedals school p. 224, 225/no. 236
Ved Stranden 14, Gustmeyers Gård p. 142, 143/no. 136
Vejrøgade/Skt. Kjeldsgade, Solgården p. 215/no. 225
Vestagervej 7 p. 184, 185/no. 188
Vester Søgade 44-78, Vestersøhus p. 216, 217/no. 227
Vesterbro p. 25
Vesterbrogade 34 p. 189, 190/no. 190
Vesterbrogade 8, Vesterport p. 223/no. 231
Vesterbros Torv, Elias Church p. 179/no. 183
Vigerslev Allé 77, Head quarters of F. L. Smidths & Co's p. 252, 253/no. 269
Vodroffsvej 2 p. 217/no. 226
Voldparken and Voldparken's School p. 242, 243/no. 255
Øster Farimagsgade 1, Skt. Andreas Church p. 179/no. 182
Øster Farimagsgade 3-7, Kommunehospitalet/municipal hospital p. 25, 160, 161/no. 156
Østerbro p. 25
Østerbrogade 57, Lægeforeningens boliger/housing p. 24, 156, 157/no. 150
Østergade 18 Svaneapoteket p. 223/no. 236
Østergade 27, A . C. Bangs Hus p. 223/no. 235
Åboulevarden 12-18, Åhusene p. 176, 177/no. 177

Copenhagen, Bagsværd:

Søndergårdsparken p. 38, 244, 245/no. 257

Copenhagen, Frederiksberg:

Bülowsvej 13, Landbohøjskolen/agricultural college p. 24, 157/no. 152
Frederiksberg Have. Det kinesiske Hus and Apistemplet/garden pavilions p. 144, 145/no. 140
Frederiksberg Kommunale Funktionærers Boligforening p. 199
Roskildevej 59-61, Søndermarkens Krematorium p. 226, 227/no. 240
Frederiksberg Palace p. 19, 104, 105/no. 91
Fuglebakken (row houses) p. 211/no. 219

Copenhagen, Gentofte:

Bernstorffsvej (row houses) p. 211/no. 218
Gersonsvej 32, Øregård High school p. 204, 205/no. 208
Jægersborg Allé, Bernstorff Slot/country estate p. 130, 131, 133/no. 118
Rygårds Allé, Studiebyen p. 208, 209/no. 213
Skovgårdsvej 56, Skovgårdsskolen/school p. 247/no. 262
Smutvej 14 p. 250/no. 266
Strandvejen 221, Blidah Park p. 218, 219/no. 229
Sundvænget (row houses) p. 211/no. 217
Søholm p. 148,149/no. 143
Vangedevej 178, Munkegårdsskolen/school p. 247/no. 261
Ørehøj Allé 2, Øregård p. 145/no. 139

Copenhagen, Klampenborg:

Strandvejen 413, Bellevuekrogen, Søholm p. 245/no. 258
Sølystvej 5-7 and 9-11 p. 228, 229/no. 242
Strandvejen 419-433 and 449-451 etc., Bella Vista and Bellevue Theatre p. 35, 220, 221/no. 230

Copenhagen, Rødovre:

Damvænget (row houses) p. 211/no. 221
Rødovre Parkvej 150, Rødovre Town Hall p. 38, 257/no. 276

Copenhagen, Springforbi:

Hegels Landsted p. 197/no. 200

Copenhagen, Virum:

Spurveskjul 4 p. 22, 145/no. 141

Index of names

Aalto, Alvar (1898-1976) finnish architect p. 38
Abildgaard, Nicolai A. (1743-1809), painter and arch., prof. p. 125, 145/no. 113, 140, 141
Absalon, bishop p. 47, 49/no. 18, 19
Amberg, H. C. (1837-1919), arch. p. 55/no. 24
Andersen, H. C. p. 25
Anthon, G. D. (1714-81), arch. p. 129/no. 115
Arnfred, Tyge (b. 1919), arch., prof. p. 261/no. 280
Asplund, Gunnar (1885-1940), Swedish arch. p. 223, 233
Asser Rig p. 43/no. 9
Axelsen, Per (b. 1950), arch. p. 149/no. 144
Bauhaus p. 35
Baumann, Povl (1878-1963), arch. p. 186, 213, 215, 219, 223/no. 188, 222, 224, 229, 231
Bedre Byggeskik p. 31, 183, 199, 195/no. 187, 198, 201
Bentsen, Ivar (1876-1943), arch., prof. p. 195, 201, 209, 211, 219, 239/no. 197, 198, 204, 213, 214, 228, 250
Berg, Jørgen U. (1906-83), arch. p. 219/no. 228
Bernstorff, J. H. E., minister p. 131/no. 118
Bie, Curt (1896-1989), arch. p. 225/no. 237
Bindesbøll, M. G. (1800-56), arch., prof. p. 24, 35, 155, 157/no. 149, 150, 151, 152, 153
Bindesbøll, Thorvald (1846-1908), arch. p. 177, 183/no. 178, 179, 180, 187
Bissen, H. W. (1798-1868), sculptor, prof. p. 155/no. 149
Bjørn, Acton (b. 1910), arch. p. 219/no. 228
Blichmann, J. H. (1739-1815), builder p. 138/no. 131
Bo, Jørgen (b. 1919), arch., prof. p. 38, 155, 259/no. 149, 278
Borch, Martin (1852-1937), arch. p. 73, 107, 179/no. 54, 93, 182
Bornebusch, Gehrdt (b. 1925), arch. p. 205, 261/no. 208, 282
Boullée p. 24
Brandenburger, Ernst (d. 1713), arch. p. 103, 105/no. 90, 91
Brandin, Philip, Dutch builder p. 75/no. 55
Brandt, G. N. (1878-1945), landscape arch. p. 213, 227, 237/no. 223, 241, 248
Bretton-Meyer, David (b. 1937), arch. p. 143, 149/no. 136, 143
Brockam, Henrik, Dutch stone cutter p. 101/no. 89
Brockenhuus, Frands p. 71/no. 50, 51
Brüel, Max (b. 1927), arch. p. 261/no. 282
Brummer, Carl (1864-1953), arch. p. 185/no. 188
Brun, Constantin, merchant p. 145/no. 138
Buhl, Ole (1912-1987), arch., prof. p. 249/no. 263
Bøttger, Frederik (1838-1920), arch. p. 163/no. 161, 162
Calmette, Antoine de la p. 133/no. 121
Charlotte Amalie of Hessen-Kassel p. 101/no. 89
Christian IV p. 16, 17, 18, 20, 25, 27, 49, 81, 83, 85, 87/no. 19, 63, 64, 65, 66, 67, 68

Christian V p. 99, 101/no. 86, 89
Christian VI p. 115/no. 104
Christian IX p. 49/no. 19
Clemmensen, Karen (b. 1917) and Ebbe (b. 1917), architects, prof. p. 261/no. 281
Clemmensen, Mogens (1885-1943), arch. p. 65, 71, 73, 201/no. 43, 51, 52, 204
Coucheron, Anton (á 1689) p. 97/no. 83, 84
Dahlerup, Vilhelm (1836-1907), arch. p. 28, 165, 167, 171/no. 163, 164, 165, 166, 170
Dissing + Weitling (Hans D., b. 1926 and Otto W., b. 1930), architects p. 179/no. 181
Dominias Arkitektafdeling p. 249/no. 263
Drosted, Volmar (1890-1956), arch. p. 77/no. 58
Dyggve, Ejnar (1887-1961)and Ingrid Møller D. (1890-1969), architects p. 201/no. 204
Edstrand, Gert (b. 1929), arch. p. 161/no. 157
Eigtved, Niels (1701-54), arch. p. 20, 22, 109, 115, 119, 120, 123, 125, 129, 165/no. 94, 104, 105, 108, 112, 113, 115, 116, 163
Engelhardt, Knud V. (1882-1931), arch. p. 183/no. 187
Engqvist, Hans Henrik (b. 1912), arch. p. 69/no. 48
Erik af Pommern p. 79/no. 61
Erlandsen, Jacob, archbishop p. 63/no. 40
Ernst, Johan Conrad (1666-1750), arch. p. 85, 105, 107/no. 66, 91, 92
Exner, Inger (b. 1926) and Johannes (b. 1926), architects, prof. p. 49/no. 19
Falkentorp, Ole (1886-1948), arch. p. 209, 215, 223/no. 213, 224, 231, 232
Fink, Dan (b. 1908), arch. p. 249/no. 263
Fisker, Kay (1893-1965), arch., prof. p. 35, 197, 209, 213, 217, 231, 243/no. 199, 213, 223, 226, 227, 243, 255, 256
Frederik II p. 16, 77, 79, 81, 85/no. 61, 63, 66
Frederik III p. 97/no. 82
Frederik IV p. 19, 105, 107, 109, 111/no. 91, 92, 94, 95
Frederik V p. 22, 49, 109, 123, 125, 131/no. 19, 94, 113, 120
Frederik VII p. 125/no. 113
Frederik IX p. 49/no. 19
Friis, Johan p. 69, 73/no. 48, 52
Frisendal, Mogens (b. 1925), arch. p. 251/no. 267
Frölén, Hugo F. p. 45/no. 11
Gedde, Christian p. 121
Gisico, bishop p. 57/no. 27
Gottlob, Kai (1887-1976), arch., prof. p. 203, 225/no. 206, 238, 239
Gravers, Arne (1918-82), arch. p. 261/no. 279
Grundtvig, N. F. S. p. 25
Gunnlögsson, Halldor (1918-85), arch., prof. p. 38, 251, 253/no. 268, 270
Gustmeyer, F. L., consul p. 143/no. 136
Gyldenløwe, Ulrik Frederik p. 99/no. 86
Gøssel, Georg (1888-1981), arch. p. 207/no. 211
Hagen, G. B. (1873-1941), arch. p. 205/no. 208
Hansen, C. F. (1756-1845), arch., prof. p. 23, 24, 25, 28, 32, 33, 49, 147, 149, 151, 153/no. 19, 142, 143, 144, 145, 146, 147
Hansen, Christian (1803-83), arch., prof. p. 161/no. 156, 157
Hansen, Hans Christian (1901-78) p. 247/no. 260
Hansen, Hans Munk (b. 1929), arch., prof. p. 141/no. 134
Hansen, Henning (1880-1945), arch. p. 197, 215/no. 200, 225
Hansen, Knud (1898-1954) p. 219, 239/no. 229, 250
Hansen, Konstantin (1804-80), painter p. 153/no. 147
Harboe, Knud Peter (b. 1925), arch., prof. p. 223/no. 234
Harsdorff, C. F. (1735-99), arch., prof. p. 22, 23, 49, 105, 107, 109, 141, 143/no. 19, 91, 93, 94, 113, 133, 134, 137
Häusser, E. D. (1687-1745), arch. p. 20, 115/no. 104
Haven, Lambert van (1630-95), arch. p. 18, 19, 99, 101/no. 86, 88
Heiberg, Edvard (1897-1958), arch. p. 219, 239, 243, 249/no. 228, 250, 255, 263
Helweg-Møller, Bent (1885-1956), arch. p. 223/no. 234, 235, 236
Henningsen, Poul (1894-1967), arch. p. 34, 35
Henningsen, Thorkild (1884-1931), arch. p. 209, 211/no. 213, 214, 215, 216, 217, 218, 219, 220, 221
Herholdt, J. D. (1818-1902), arch. p. 26, 73, 158, 173/no. 54, 154, 155
Hertz, Flemming (b. 1936), arch. p. 141/no. 134
Hetsch, G. F. (1788-1864), arch., prof. p. 67/no. 45
Hilker, C. (1807-75), painter p. 153/no. 147
Hoff, Carsten (b. 1939), arch. p. 201/no. 204
Hoff, Poul Ernst (b. 1903), arch. p. 245, 249/no. 257, 264
Holm, Hans J. (1835-1916), arch., prof. p. 73, 85, 143/no. 53, 65, 136
Holstein, J. L. p. 119/no. 108
Holsøe, Poul (1873-1966), arch. p. 199, 209, 225, 239/no. 201, 213, 237, 251
Høeg-Hansen, A. (1877-1947), arch. p. 193/no. 195
Irming, Mogens (b. 1915), arch. p. 249/no. 263
Iselin, Lisa p. 133/no. 121
Jacobsen, Arne (1902-1971), arch. p. 35, 37, 38, 221, 223, 233, 235, 241, 245, 247, 257/no. 230, 233, 245, 246, 253, 258, 261, 274, 275, 276, 277
Jacobsen, Carl, brewer p. 28, 32, 167, 171/no. 166, 171
Jacobsen, Holger, (1878-1960) arch. p. 203/no. 205
Jacobsen, J. C., brewer p. 25, 28, 81, 167/no. 63, 166
Janssen, Evert (á 1690), Dutch builder, arch. p. 67, 99/no. 45, 86
Jardin, Nicolas-Henri (1720-99), arch., prof. p. 22, 109, 125, 131/no. 94, 113, 118, 119, 120
Jensen, Ferdinand (1837-90), arch. p. 169/no.

267

169
Jensen, Ib Martin (1906-79), arch. p. 235, 247/no. 247, 262
Jensen Klint, P. V. (1853-1930), arch. and engineer p. 207/no. 211, 212
Jensen, Knud W. p. 259/no. 278
Jensen, V. Rørdam (1896-1987), arch. p. 209/no. 213
Jorn, Asger (1914-73), painter p. 261/no. 279
Jørgensen, Valdemar (b. 1893) arch. p. 239/no. 250
Jørgensen, Viggo S. (1902-81), arch. p. 243/no. 255
Kaastrup, Vagn (1903-66) arch. p. 239/no. 250
Kampmann, Christian (1890-1955), arch. p. 205/no. 209, 210
Kampmann, Hack (1856-1920), arch., prof. p. 30, 34, 77, 171, 181, 203, 205/no. 60, 171, 184, 185, 186, 205, 209, 210
Kampmann, Hans Jørgen (1889-1966), arch. p. 203/no. 205
Karl den Store p. 51/no. 21
Kierkegaard, Søren p. 25
Kirkerup, Andreas (1749-1810), arch. p. 133, 145/no. 121, 140
Kjærholm, Poul (1929-80), arch., prof. p. 253/no. 270
Klein, Vilhelm (1835-1913), arch. p. 157/no. 150
Klint, Kaare (1888-1954), arch., prof. p. 193, 207, 239/no. 194, 211, 250
Koch, H. (1873-1922), arch. p. 199
Koch, Jørgen Hansen (1787-1860), arch. p. 105, 111, 125/no. 91, 95, 113
Koch, Peter (1905-80), arch. p. 71/no. 50
Kooperative Arkitekter p. 219, 239/no. 228, 260
Koppel, Eva (b. 1916) and Nils (b. 1914), architects p. 171, 255/no. 157, 170, 272
Krieger, J. C. (1683-1755), arch. p. 109, 111, 112, 113, 119/no. 94, 95, 108
Kristensen, Eske (b. 1905) p. 241, 249/no. 254, 263
Kritisk Revy p. 34
Kühnel, S. F. (1851-1930), arch. p. 94/no. 78
Lange, Jens Iversen, bishop p. 53/no. 23
Lange, Philip de (1704-66) arch. p. 113, 127, 129, 133/no. 99, 114, 116, 122
Langeland-Matthiesen, Aage (1868-1933), arch. p. 177/no. 178, 179
Langkilde, Hans Erling (b. 1906), arch., prof. p. 235, 247/no. 247, 262
Larsen, Henning (b. 1925), arch. p. 261/no. 282
Larsen, Johannes, painter p. 193/no. 194
Larsen, Karl (1892-1969), arch. p. 219, 243, 249/no. 228, 255, 263
Lassen, Flemming (1902-84), arch. p. 231, 235/no. 244, 246
Lassen, Mogens (1901-1987), arch. p. 229/no. 242
Lauritzen, Vilhelm (1894-1984), arch. p. 37, 201, 237/no. 204, 248, 249
Le Clerc, Louis-Augustin (1688-1771), sculptor, prof. p. 115/no. 104
Le Corbusier (1887-1965), French arch. p. 35, 229
Ledoux p. 24
Lodehat, Peder Jensen, bishop p. 67/no. 45
Lund, F. C. (1896-1984), arch. p. 239, 243, 247/no. 251, 255, 260
Lønborg-Jensen, Harald (1871-1948), arch. p. 71/no. 50
Malling, Peder (1781-1865), arch. p. 153/no. 147, 148
Matthiessen, Hugo p. 94/no. 78
Mejborg, Reinhold F. S. (1845-98), prof. p. 73/no. 52
Meldahl, Ferdinand (1827-1908), arch., prof. p. 26, 27, 28, 81, 83, 161, 169/no. 63, 158, 167
Meyn, Peter (1749-1808), arch., prof. p. 141/no. 135
Mies van der Rohe, Ludwig (1886-1969), German-American arch. p. 38, 251
Moltke, A. G. p. 120, 125, 131, 133/no. 112, 113, 119, 122
Morris, William p. 31
Munk, Knud (b. 1936), arch. p. 237/no. 249
Møller, C. F. (1898-1988), arch., prof. p. 133, 181, 217, 231/no. 123, 184, 226, 227, 243
Møller, Georg E. V. (1840-97), arch. p. 171/no. 170
Møller, Erik (b. 1909), arch. p. 231, 233/no. 244, 245
Møller, Helge Boysen (1874-1946), arch. p. 69/no. 48
Møller, Svend (1890-1981), arch. p. 209/no. 213
Møller, Viggo Sten (1897-1990), arch. p. 149/no. 144
Møller-Jensen, Viggo (b. 1907), arch., prof. p. 241, 261/no. 252, 280
Nebelong, N. S. (1806-71), arch. p. 162, 167/no. 159, 166
Nielsen, Harald (1886-1980), arch. p. 199, 201/no. 203, 204
Nielsen, J. Magdahl (1862-1941), arch. p. 79/no. 61
Nielsen, Jørn (b. 1919), arch. p. 253/no. 270
Nielsen, Kai, sculptor p. 193/no. 194
Nielsen, Peer Hougaard (b. 1924), arch. p. 247/no. 259
Nielsen, Peter (1886-1969), arch. p. 209, 215/no. 213, 224
Nielsen, Tage (1914-1991), arch. p. 249/no. 263
Norn, Viggo (1879-1967), arch. p. 193, 203/no. 196, 207
Notke, Bernt p. 53/no. 23
Nyrop, Martin (1849-1921), arch., prof. p. 30, 173, 175, 179/no. 173, 174, 175, 176, 183
Nystrøm, Arne (1900-79), arch. p. 65/no. 43
Nørgaard-Petersen, C. J. (1924-88), arch. p. 247/no. 259
Opbergen, Antonius van (1543-1611), Flemish builder p. 79/no. 61
Oxe, Peder p. 73/no. 54

Paeschen, Hans van, Flemish builder p. 79/no. 61
Pedersen, Marius (1888-1965), arch. p. 195/no. 198
Perret, Auguste (1874-1954), French arch. p. 227
Peters, Harald (1891-1951), arch. p. 199/no. 202
Petersen, Carl (1874-1923), arch., prof. p. 32, 33, 193, 201, 215/no. 194, 204, 224
Petersen, Harald (1890-1954) arch. p. 239, 249/no. 250, 263
Petersen, Ove (1830-92), arch. p. 165/no. 163
Petersen, Vilhelm (1830-1913), arch. p. 169/no. 169
Platen, W. F. von (1667-1732), arch. p. 107/no. 93
Plesner, Ulrik (1861-1933), arch. p. 177, 183/no. 177, 178, 179, 180, 187
Ponsaing, Georg, (1889-1981), arch. p. 209/no. 213
Qvist, J. M. (1755-1818) arch. p. 143/no. 136
Rafn, Aage (1890-1953), arch. p. 34, 187, 197, 203/no. 188, 199, 205
Ramée, Joseph-Jacques (1764-1842), French arch. p. 143, 145/no. 137, 138, 139
Rasmussen, August (1890-1978), arch. s.209/no. 213
Rasmussen, Mads p. 193/no. 194
Reventlow, C. D. F., prime minister p. 103, 149/no. 90, 144
Richter, Johan (b. 1925), arch. p. 261/no. 279
Rosen, Anton (1859-1928), arch., prof. p. 32, 185, 189, 190, 191, 209/no. 188, 189, 190, 191, 192, 193, 213
Rosenberg, G. E. (1739-88), arch. p. 141/no. 134
Rosenberg, J. G. (1709-76), arch. p. 115, 123/no. 106, 113
Rosenkrandtz, Mette p. 73/no. 53
Rosenkrantz, Jørgen p. 75/no. 56
Rue, Tage (1893-1977), arch. p. 225/no. 237
Rüse, Henrik (1624-74), Dutch arch. and engineer p. 97/no. 82
Saly, Jacques-Francois-Joseph (1717-67), sculptor p. 125, 131/no. 113
Schlegel, Frits (1896-1965), arch. p. 227/no. 240, 241
Schou, Charles I. (1884-1973), arch. p. 31, 207/no. 211
Schulin, J. S. p. 115/no. 105
Seest, K. T. (1879-1972), arch. p. 199
Selchau, Jørgen (b. 1923), arch. p. 261/no. 282
Sibbern, H. S. (1826-1901), arch. p. 163/no. 160
Sitte, Camillo (1843-1903), Austrian town planner p. 199
Skeel, Ingeborg p. 75/no. 55
Skjøt-Pedersen, A. (1897-79), arch. p. 219/no. 228
Snare, Esbern p. 51/no. 20
Sonne, Jørgen (1801-90), painter p. 155/no. 149
Stadsarkitektens Direktorat p. 249/no. 263
Stallknecht, Claus (1681-1734), arch. p. 111/no. 96

Stanley, S. C. (1703-61), sculptor, prof. p. 129/no. 117
Steenwinckel d.y., Hans van (1587-1639), arch., sculptor p. 81, 83, 87/no. 63, 67
Stegmann, Poul (1888-1944), arch. p. 231/no. 243
Stephensen, Magnus (1903-86), arch. p. 239/no. 250
Stilling, H. C. (1815-91), arch. p. 85/no. 64
Storck, H. B. (1839-1922), arch., prof. p. 47, 51, 59, 162, 173/no. 17, 22, 32, 159, 172
Strinz, Carl, German engineer and arch. p. 199
Stygge Krumpen p. 75/no. 55
Suenson, Palle (1904-87), arch., prof. p. 253, 255/no. 269, 273
Sunesen, Peder, bishop p. 49/no. 19
Søbødtker, Johannes p. 145/no. 139
Sørensen, C. Th. (1893-1979), landscape arch., prof. p. 103, 231, 243/no. 90, 243, 255
Sørensen, Erik Christian (b. 1922), arch., prof. p. 38, 251/no. 266
Teschl, Leopold (1911-89), arch. p. 205/no. 210
Tessin d.y., Nicodemus (1654-1728), Swedish arch. p. 103/no. 90
Thomsen, Edvard (1884-1980), arch., prof. p. 205, 209, 227/no. 208, 213, 240
Thomsen, Ole Ramsgaard (b. 1937), arch. p. 141/no. 134
Thorball, Knud (1904-80), arch. p. 201, 239/no. 204, 250
Thorvaldsen, Bertel (1770-1844), sculptor p. 25, 153, 155/no. 147, 149
Thurah, Lauritz de (1706-59), arch. p. 20, 73, 87, 101, 105, 109, 111, 115, 117, 119, 120, 123/no. 53, 67, 88, 91, 94, 97, 104, 107, 108, 111, 113
Tietgen, C. F. p. 28, 169/no. 167
Truelsen, Niels F. (b. 1938), arch. p. 193, 197/no. 194, 199
Tschierscke, G. D., arch. p. 119/no. 110
Tuesen, Mogens, mayor p. 77/no. 59
Tvede, Jesper (1879-1934), arch. p. 199, 209/no. 201, 213
Tveskæg, Svend p. 41/no. 1
Urne, Johan p. 69/no. 49
Ussing, Susanne (b. 1940), arch. p. 201/no. 204
Utzon, Jørn (b. 1918), arch. p. 38, 39, 251, 255, 261/no. 265, 271
Valdemar den Store p. 11, 47, 55/no. 17, 21
Varming, Jens Chr. (b. 1932), arch. p. 103/no. 90
Vedsø, Mogens p. 64
Vignola, Giacomo (1507-73), Italian arch. p. 151/no. 145
Vognsen, Peder, bishop p. 53/no. 23
Wagner, Frederik (1880-1946), arch. p. 239/no. 250
Wenck, Heinrich (1851-1936), arch. p. 179/no. 181
Wiedevelt, Johs. (1731-1802), sculptor, prof. p. 109/no. 94
Willumsen, J. F. (1863-1957), painter, sculptor, arch. p. 185/no. 188

Windinge, Bennet (1905-86), arch. p. 245, 249/no. 257, 264
Wohlert, Vilhelm (b. 1920), arch., prof. p. 38, 49, 153, 259/no. 19, 147, 278
Wright, Frank Lloyd (1869-1959), American arch. p. 38, 251

Zettervall, Helgo (1831-1907), Swedish arch. p. 71/no. 50
Zuber, C. J. (1736-1802), arch. p. 133/no. 122, 123
Ørsted, H. C. p. 25

Photos

Aistrup, Inge p. 43ø, 44, 50, 66n, 69, 72n, 74n, 81, 82, 100, 132
Arkitektens Forlag p. 42, 75, 88ø, 95n, 113n, 116, 164n, 211ø og mf, 234, 243n, 248
Arnfred, Tyge p. 261n
Axelsen, Per p. 149
Bernild, Bror p. 246n
Bornebusch, Gehrdt p. 261ø
Clausholm Gods p. 103
Dahl, Thorkel p. 200, 201
Det Arkæologiske Forsøgscenter i Lejre p. 41
Engqvist, Hans Henrik p. 88n, 89ø mf og n tv, 135
Faber, Tobias p. 54, 60, 66ø, 68, 72ø, 78, 94ø, 95ø, 197n, 224n
Finsen, Helge p. 157n
Forsvarets Bygningstjeneste p. 126ø, 127
Hansen, Erik p. 98ø, 242ø, 250ø
Hansen, Hans Munk p. 141ø
Helmer-Petersen, Keld p. 48ø, 131n, 142ø, 148, 161n, 177n, 228mf, 251mf og n, 252, 253, 254ø
Jaeger, Thomas Arvid og Jørgen Hegner Christiansen p. 196, 197ø
Jensen, Aage Lund p. 193mf
Jessen, Jørgen Toft p. 134
Jonals p. 188, 227n, 230n
Kayser, Keld p. 112n
Koch, Mogens S. p. 105n tv
Kristensen, Eske p. 241
Kunstakademiets Bibliotek, Billedsamlingen p. 41n, 45, 48ø, 49mf, 52, 55, 57, 58, 59, 61, 64, 65, 67, 70, 71ø, 73, 74ø, 75, 76, 79n, 80, 83, 85, 86ø tv, 91, 93n tv og th, 97, 98n, 101, 104, 105ø mf og n th, 106 ø, 108ø, 11ø, 114n, 115, 117, 118n, 119, 120ø, 123n, 125ø, 125n th, 126n, 128ø, 129, 130, 132n, 133, 136ø th, 140n, 141n, 144n, 145ø, 147, 150, 151, 153, 154, 155, 156, 157, 159, 161ø, 162, 164ø, 165ø, 167, 170n, 171n, 172, 173, 174n, 175, 176mf, 179tv, 180n, 181, 182ø og mf, 184n

tv og th, 185, 189, 190n, 192, 194, 195, 198, 202, 203n tv og th, 204n, 206, 207, 208, 209, 210, 211n tv, 212, 213, 214, 216, 218, 219, 220, 221, 222n, 223n, 225mf og n, 226, 228ø, 229, 231n, 235n, 236ø, 238, 240, 242n, 243ø, 245ø, 246ø, 247mf, 249, 252ø, 255, 257ø
Københavns Bymuseum p. 84ø
Langkilde, Hans Erling p. 193ø, 199ø og mf, 203ø og mf, 235ø, 247n
Møller, Svend Erik: Enfamiliehuset af i dag, 1952 p. 251ø
Nationalmuseet p. 40, 46, 47, 48n, 49n, 51ø, 51n, 53, 56ø, 56n, 60n tv, 60n th, 61ø, 61mf, 61m, 62, 77, 79ø, 79mf, 84n, 90n, 92ø, 99, 106n, 111, 136ø tv, 137, 138ø, 139m, 143, 145n, 146, 168, 170ø, 174ø
Nordisk Pressefoto p. 121
Pedersen, Poul p. 180ø, 205, 230ø, 231ø, 232, 233
Priskorn, Ole p. 144ø og mf
Rading p. 239
Riis Knudsen Foto p. 94n
Schmidt, Holger p. 109
Skriver, Poul Erik p. 96, 124, 138n, 193n, 211n th, 215n, 244, 260n
Stadsarkitektens Direktorat p. 224ø, 225ø
Strüwing p. 222ø, 236n, 245n, 254ø, 256, 257n, 260ø
Søllerød Kommunes Byhistoriske Arkiv p. 120n
Søndergaard, Steffen M. p. 89n th
T. R. Foto p. 136n
Tegnestuen Kvisten p. 182n, 183n
Tholstrup, Else p. 250n, 254mf
Vilhelm Lauritzens Tegnestue p. 237
Watz, Jørgen p. 108n
Wohlert, Antonio p. 122n, 152
Wohlert, Vilhelm p. 258, 259
All others:
Jørgen Hegner Christiansen

Litterature

Engqvist, Hans Henrik: Dansk stilhistorie. Kbh. 1978 (6. ed.).

Faber, Tobias: Dansk arkitektur. Kbh. 1977 (2. ed.).

Jørgensen, Lisbet Balslev; Skriver, Poul Erik og Dirckinck-Holmfeld, Kim: Guide til moderne dansk arkitektur. Kbh. 1982.

Langberg, Harald: Danmarks bygningskultur bind I-II. En historisk oversigt. Kbh. 1955 (reprint 1978).

Langberg, Harald (red.): Hvem byggede hvad bind I-III. Gamle og nye bygninger i Danmark. Kbh. 1969-1971 (2. ed.).

Lassen, Erik: Huse i Danmark, Kbh. 1942.

Lund, Hakon og Millech, Knud (red): Danmarks bygningskunst. Fra oldtid til nutid. Kbh. 1963.

Lund, Hakon (red.): Danmarks arkitektur bind I-VI.

Millech, Knud og Fisker, Kay: Danske arkitekturstrømninger 1850-1950. En arkitekturhistorisk undersøgelse. Kbh. 1951 (reprint 1977).